MW01295385

Music from the Hilltop

Organs and Organists at Southern Methodist University

Benjamin A. Kolodziej

University of North Texas Press
Denton, Texas

Permissions:
University of North Texas Press
1155 Union Circle #311336
Denton, TX 76203-5017

The paper used in this book meets the minimum requirements of the
American National Standard for Permanence of Paper for Printed Library
Materials, z39.48.1984. Binding materials have been chosen for durability.

Library of Congress Cataloging-in-Publication Data

Names: Kolodziej, Benjamin, author.
Title: Music from the hilltop : organs and organists at Southern Methodist
  University / Benjamin A. Kolodziej.
Description: Denton, Texas : University of North Texas Press, [2023] |
  Includes bibliographical references and index.
Identifiers: LCCN 2023029706 (print) | LCCN 2023029707 (ebook) | ISBN
  9781574419108 (cloth) | ISBN 9781574419214 (ebook)
Subjects: LCSH: Cassidy, Bertha Stevens, 1876-1959. | Barclay, Dora Poteet,
  1903-1961. | Anderson, Robert T. (Robert Theodore), 1934-2009. |
  Southern Methodist University--Organs--History--20th century. | Southern
  Methodist University. School of Music--History. | Organ (Musical
  instrument)--Instruction and study--Texas--Dallas--History--20th
  century. | Organ (Musical instrument)--Performance--Texas--Dallas--
  History--20th century. | Church music--Texas--Methodist Church. | Organ
  teachers--Texas--Dallas--Biography. | Organists--Texas--Dallas--
  Biography. | BISAC: MUSIC / History & Criticism | BIOGRAPHY &
  AUTOBIOGRAPHY / Music | LCGFT: Biographies.
Classification: LCC ML611.8.D35 K65 2023 (print) | LCC ML611.8.D35
  (ebook) | DDC 621.3005--dc24/eng/20230297
LC record available at https://lccn.loc.gov/2023029706
LC ebook record available at https://lccn.loc.gov/2023029707

The electronic edition of this book was made possible by the support of
the Vick Family Foundation.

Typeset by vPrompt eServices.

Dedicated to Robert Theodore Anderson
(1936–2009)

Contents

Contents

Illustrations

Foreword

Alexis de Tocqueville never tired of observing American democracy through the lens of its perduring pragmatism and the chaos of its restive striving after opportunity. Moreover, he insisted the American mind "will habitually prefer the useful to the beautiful and . . . will want the beautiful to be useful."[1] It is fair to wonder what Tocqueville, writing in 1840 within a half decade of Texas's statehood, would have made of the emergence of Southern Methodist University (SMU) to the north of Dallas in 1911. Ten years earlier in 1901, the tapping of the Spindletop oil well near Beaumont supplied one of the hinges on which a profound socioeconomic transformation of the Texas landscape would turn. The unsettled swashbuckling climate of which Tocqueville earlier had written with such fascination clearly ruled the day, as did a blatantly segregationist politics and a rough-hewn frontierism. If this rocky soil on which a new university rose was to nurture something of artistic beauty—particularly the Eurocentric sort of beauty assumed by the period's cultural actors—then it would not be conceived in the abstract but rather hitched directly to something of use.

And so it was to be. In an important sense, this book tells how one of the most vital organ training centers in North America grew from an outpost of the Methodist movement, one conscious of music's integral role in the promotion of piety. This development may seem unlikely on the surface, but its possibilities were inherent in the circumstances and furthered by people of extraordinary commitment. The early symbioses between SMU's theological and musical initiatives yielded a vibrant organ program that would consistently move in sympathy with the priorities of church music education. From the beginning, organ teaching supplied the parishes with excellent organists, even while it began to produce brilliant concert performers and academics who shaped, and continue to shape, the organ culture of the United States and beyond. It can and perhaps should be argued that this robust devotion to the holistic education of organists—on the overlapping fronts of church music, concert performance, and academic accomplishment—has distinguished SMU's program from other important organ centers in North America, especially from those formed from the secular university. Whatever the case, though, this book suggests just how multifaceted the motivations have been and how the corresponding objectives have been pursued over time.

Particularly from our vantage point in the early twenty-first century, the narrative offers other instructive insight, too. It is significant, for example, not merely that the university's organ program was born with the institution itself but also that its first half century was led exclusively by gifted women of resourcefulness, vision, and resolve. (Since Dora Barclay's death in 1961 it has been steered exclusively by men, as has the graduate sacred music program established about the same time.) Likewise of note are the persistent energies that have been directed toward the building of organs at SMU over the entirety of its history—efforts which eventually bled into the larger community and account for the lively organ topography of the Dallas area to this day. In this sense one can draw a striking through line from the 1913 Estey, Opus 1165, in the home music room of Bertha Cassidy to the great Fisk organs, Opuses 100 and 101, of the Meyerson Symphony Center and SMU's Caruth Auditorium, respectively. These instruments, like the repertories and interpretive approaches applied to them over generations, reflect not only the personal leanings of the various teachers but also a century of broad stylistic change in organ culture generally. The history of SMU's love affair with organs and organists reveals how the values of late romanticism gave way to the reactionary neoclassical objectivism of the mid-twentieth century, and this in turn to the tenets of so-called historically informed performance.

Still another fascinating aspect to emerge here is the tension between the stereotypical impulses of rugged Texan individualism on the one hand and, on the other, the apparent propensity of the various movers and shakers to emulate the high culture of the East Coast and beyond. There is a certain extravagant cosplay reflected in the SMU colors of Harvard red and Yale blue—something that has not escaped the Dallas organ scene over its history. Likewise, the inevitable collisions between the stars of the European organ firmament and the area's distinctive culture contribute something more than mere texture to this story. It is difficult to forget episodes like Sigfrid Karg-Elert navigating "cacti in the street," or of Jeannette Dupré on a shopping excursion to the Neiman-Marcus department store, or of the Duruflés on the floor of the Highland Park Cafeteria. There are overtones of *The Far Side* cartoons in such scenes, but even so, one must take seriously the ever-growing stature of a program that made them possible in the first place.

None of this is to say that the colorful personalities who have shaped the organs and organists of SMU have done so unerringly and with optimal effectiveness at all times. People are human, and Benjamin Kolodziej's history makes no effort to cast them as heroes in marble. Tocqueville's democratic chaos has prevailed occasionally, maybe more often than not. One valuable task of a story like this one lies in its power to demythologize the protagonists, to reveal the essential humanity of the undertaking, and (I think) to admonish the current stewards of organ and church music education to think critically about the anxiety-ridden conjuncture at which we now find ourselves, one no less transformative than the circumstances from which the SMU organ programs arose over a century ago. Perhaps the next chapter to be written will reveal as dynamic a story as the one told here.

Christopher Anderson
Dallas, Texas
2023

Acknowledgments

Although I would like to trace this work, a history of organs and organists at Southern Methodist University in Dallas, back to my days as a rather stressed undergraduate organ major at SMU, I am afraid I cannot. In those days I was only concerned about learning organ music and keeping Dr. Robert Anderson pleased with my progress, all while managing to keep up with the usual music and nonmusic classes that so encompass the life of a music major. I do not believe this qualifies me for any special insight into the history of SMU, nor into Dr. Anderson, who in lessons would sometimes regale me with stories of his glamorous past, all while I was furtively thinking ahead to the next complicated measures, wondering whether I had worked them out fully. Mine was the life of a student, not a historian, during those years. I knew it was significant that Dr. Anderson had agreed to stay on as an adjunct after his retirement simply to teach a few remaining students, of which I was his last undergraduate. I knew little about the storied past of the SMU organ program, but I did have the odd sense that I was living through the end of an era. Indeed, such turned out to be the case, the extent of which I was not fully aware until I engaged in research for this project. How many times during the course of this research did I wish I would have truly listened to the history Dr. Anderson imparted to me when I was distracted by the more mundane labors of organ study?

I would like to thank Dr. Christopher Anderson, associate professor of sacred music at SMU, for prevailing upon me to undertake this project in 2016, and for the support he has given to this project through the subsequent years. Carlton "Sam" Young, a legend in Methodist musical circles for reasons too numerous to mention, but whose reputation is solidified by having accomplished the herculean task of editing both the 1966 and 1989 iterations of the Methodist hymnal, offered encouragement and advice in the early years. As a former director of the sacred music program at SMU, his insight was particularly valuable, helping me to navigate and understand the personal and political issues of the time—matters that would have remained unknowable to a researcher limited only to physical documents. Dr. Kenneth Hart, professor emeritus of sacred music at SMU and my former graduate advisor, also lent me significant support, particularly in granting me access to recordings of personal interviews he conducted with Lloyd Pfautsch and Robert Anderson. I regret that his death in December 2022 deprived me of the opportunity to glean his reaction to this study. Joan Gosnell, university archivist at SMU, helped me to traverse the extensive archives related to the music school and the Robert Theodore Anderson Papers (RTAP); without her assistance I would certainly have lost my way in the labyrinthine and dusky corridors of penetrating research. Finally, Dorothy Faller, Robert Anderson's beloved sister, provided encouragement and additional archival material that now resides in the RTAP at SMU.

Space constraints prevent me from thanking all those who consented to interviews and whose only acknowledgment is a footnote or two in the text. I am thankful to the former Dora Poteet Barclay students who, early in my research, so generously shared their remembrances of their teacher. From researchers, musicologists, and former SMU students to academics and performers, so many people from around the world freely shared their memories and expertise; as such, hopefully their contributions prevent this study from congealing into a mere recitation of cold facts and hard data. I hope I have conveyed the essence of the manifold people, with their disparate personalities, who make up the history in this book. I do feel like I have learned to know them in a personal way, and I hope this volume communicates that. Throughout this work I have elected to preserve original spelling and syntax when quoting from letters, articles, and programs, as I believe this reveals much about each writer and the era.

I would additionally like to thank my parents, Annamarie and Eddie Kolodziej, who supported my studies throughout the years, including at SMU. My wife, Carrie, deserves much appreciation for her long-suffering through this project, from my prattling on about stoplists to our visit to Mrs. Cassidy's grave on a wintry afternoon. I owe her a debt of gratitude.

Benjamin Kolodziej, MSM, MTS
Ambleside
Richardson, Texas
Epiphanytide 2023

Chapter 1

Music amid the
Johnson Grass

A bluff overlooking downtown Dallas, six miles from the city by
horse and carriage, seemed an unusual location to inaugurate a
new university with national pretensions. Yet the Methodist Episcopal
Church, South, in establishing Southern Methodist University in 1911,
sought to found a liberal arts university with an emphasis on theological preparation in a region that had more in common with a frontier
town than with any of the cultured cities on the East Coast. In an
audacious move befitting grandiose Texan aspirations, Robert Stewart
Hyer, SMU's first president, appropriated Yale blue and Harvard
crimson for the school colors, setting forth an ambitious vision for
a university that he hoped would eventually rival the revered eastern
schools that had established themselves as academic centers beginning in the seventeenth century.[1] Like its older precursors in Europe
and America, Southern Methodist University was founded by a church
and imbued with spiritual motivation, in this case derived from
Methodism and the theology of John and Charles Wesley. The tension
between intellect and emotion that the Wesleys worked out in John's
preaching and through Charles's hymns likewise characterized this

new university as it sought to undergird rigorous intellectual pursuits with the spirit of Christian faith. The university's Latin motto, *Veritas liberabit vos* (The truth shall set you free), reflected Charles Wesley's yearning to "unite the pair so long disjoined, knowledge and vital piety."[2] The understanding that it was to be a Methodist institution informed its foundation and ensured that a seminary to train clergy would be an integral component of university life. The Reverend Wallace Buttrick, secretary of the national General Education Board, a Rockefeller philanthropy, advised Robert Hyer that Dallas provided many advantages for a new university, and that the city "is the best unoccupied territory in the South. Some day someone will build a university in Dallas and you Methodists are the people who should do it."[3] Musical instruction, both sacred and otherwise, constituted a vital element from the beginning of SMU, reflecting the importance of music within Methodist liturgical piety.

A Church University

Since 1873, the Methodist Episcopal Church, South, had operated Southwestern University, about 170 miles south of Dallas in rustic Georgetown, Texas. Tracing its lineage even further back, to 1840 when the congress of the Republic of Texas issued its first charter, Southwestern was ideally situated in a town away from the moral and academic distractions of the larger cities. By the turn of the century, its buildings and infrastructure were well equipped to handle its growing population of 330 students.[4] In addition to providing science, liberal arts, and ministerial training, the university ran a medical school in Dallas. Nearby, in Fort Worth, was Polytechnic College, the Methodist Church's only other four-year institution in the state.

By the early years of the twentieth century, controversy surrounded the deliberations for the ideal location of a Methodist university in Texas. Robert Hyer had been associated with Southwestern since 1882, serving as its president since 1898, but increasingly had to confront the idea that Methodism's flagship institution in Texas should be located in a large, modern city, both to influence and to be influenced.[5] Seth Ward, the first native-born Texas Methodist bishop and father of eventual organ professor at SMU Annie Byrd Ward Whaling, suggested to Hyer that a new Methodist seminary be established in Dallas to counter the seminary at Vanderbilt, whose theology was becoming less Methodist, according to Ward. Hyer gave tacit approval to this request and the bishop began his efforts, which were brought to a premature halt with his death in 1909.[6]

Ward's death did not bring resolution to the matter with which Methodists were still contentiously wrestling. Hiram Boaz, president of Polytechnic College, suggested that Georgetown was unable, both in terms of its bank assets and the nature of its population, to support a premiere Methodist institution and suggested Southwestern move to the Polytechnic campus, resulting in a merger of the two schools, with Hyer retaining the presidency and Boaz returning to parish ministry.[7] After deliberation, this proposal was rejected by the Southwestern trustees. Shortly thereafter, in 1911, after having met with a receptive city government in Dallas, a commission appointed by the five Texas Methodist annual conferences authorized the formation of an altogether new university in Dallas. Southwestern retained its autonomy and the Fort Worth campus became a women's institution, with other academic functions transferred to Dallas. Boaz moved to Dallas to serve in the new administration, the Southwestern medical and pharmacy school was transferred to SMU, and Hyer was president of the new school. Municipal leaders provided $300,000 and some land while the community zealously supported the endeavor, aware of the cooperation between school and community that manifested itself for several decades and aided the growth of the university,[8] most notably in the collaboration between the school of music and the civic musical establishment in the decade before SMU was able to construct suitable facilities.[9] The undeveloped area north of Dallas where the university settled had few trees and little to recommend it. Kenneth Pope, eventual Methodist bishop and SMU trustee who came to study at the university in 1920, described the primitive conditions extending around the campus as "a sea of Johnson grass. In the spring, chiggers abounded both in the tall grass and on those whose judgment was no better than to walk in it."[10]

The Aspirations of a Frontier Town

Although SMU was founded in 1911, only the medical school inherited from Southwestern University granted diplomas for the next four years. Construction delays prevented classes from commencing until the autumn of 1915, at which time the iconic Dallas Hall—designed by Hyer himself, modeled after Thomas Jefferson's Georgian aesthetic of the University of Virginia, and conceived originally as a memorial to Methodist Bishop Seth Ward—was inaugurated.[11] At first only three schools made up this new university: the College of Liberal Arts, the School of Theology, and the School of Fine Arts. Hyer had cultivated a fine arts school at Southwestern so it was natural that a similar school be included in the foundational framework of SMU.

Between 1900 and 1920 Dallas transformed from a modest town whose major industries consisted of farming and ranching to one that favored goods and services; concomitantly, the population grew from 42,638 in 1900 to a staggering 158,976 in 1920.[12] With this population growth came economic prosperity. Fort Worth's three proposals to attract SMU in 1911, which included cash amounts of $300,000, $400,000, and $500,000, respectively, each with a varying amount of acreage, were rejected in favor of Dallas's less lucrative $300,000 offer, largely because Fort Worth's monetary package was unsecured, with no pledges received and based solely on speculative future land sales. Dallas's offer was based upon actual cash and tangible pledge subscriptions, evidence of a prosperous economy that would warrant the formation of a Federal Reserve bank that same year.[13] That Dallas had only recently been a frontier town was an image its citizenry was keen to forget.

As early as 1895, attempts were made to develop a symphony orchestra,[14] a humble endeavor that by 1897 had added an occasional chorus[15] and that by 1901 had grown into an official symphony

The J. H. & C. S. Odell & Company organ, Opus 287,
at First Baptist, Dallas.

consisting of amateur musicians who concertized regularly.[16] Mrs. Jules Roberts writes in an 1899 column in the *Dallas Morning News*, taking pride in describing the local civic ensembles, "The Frohsinn Singing society is the oldest German musical organization in Dallas. The St. Cecilia Choral club is the oldest English musical organization in Dallas, next in line are the Dallas Quartette club, the Derthick club, History of Music club, the Apollo club, the Schubert club, the Symphony orchestra, Dallas Harmony orchestra, the Oratorio Society, the Philharmonic society, also several excellent bands."[17] Whether these distinguished clubs and organizations with majestic-sounding names evidenced a profound respect for musical masterworks or merely provided an outlet to see and to be seen is mere conjecture, but these efforts were supplemented by the offerings of dozens of churches that had become progressively more elaborate and the focus of which was often the choirs and organs.

These churches tended to purchase pipe organs from established builders, and from about 1895 to 1915, the city's churches included numerous instruments by Hook & Hastings, Pilcher, and Estey. Other firms were represented in First Baptist Church, which housed a J. H. & C. S. Odell & Company, Opus 287, and in the Roman Catholic cathedral's 1871 Reuben Midmer & Son organ relocated from New Jersey and rebuilt by Hook & Hastings in 1902.[18] News accounts of the time are replete with musical soirées rendering the popular classics of the day, from solo instrumentals to chorales to ensembles, not infrequently featuring the organ. In a July 1905 column promoting organist David E. Groves's dedication recital of the Hook & Hastings organ at Trinity Methodist Church in Dallas, the anonymous writer notes, "In line with Dallas' numerous musical advances, it is interesting to note the increased attention paid to good music in the churches, and the different fine organs that are being purchased or planned for. The new instrument at Trinity is of very sweet and pleasing tone, with a good variety of stops, possessing as well great volume and power."[19]

Later that same month another Hook & Hastings instrument, declared by the paper as "one of the best instruments of the kind in the State, having twenty speaking stops and 1,300 pipes," was dedicated at Grace Methodist Church by organist John T. Duncan, who seems to have received second billing to a much-lauded tenor soloist.[20] The dedication of the Pilcher organ at Gaston Avenue Baptist Church

The Hook & Hastings organ at Trinity Methodist
Episcopal Church, South, in Dallas.

that same year drew "over twelve hundred persons" to hear Mrs. James
Harvey Cassidy, future organ professor at SMU, perform Bach and
Guilmant, as well as a number of programmatic pieces with other
musicians.[21]

In 1907, in what must have been a banner year for organ installations, a certain Elmer Sanford Albritton played the dedication recital
at New Tabernacle Methodist Church downtown. A columnist wrote,
"The grand pipe organ, which occupies a conspicuous place, is one
of the largest in the city, and makes a very pleasing appearance.
The diapasons are considered rich and full. The flutes are in variety
with a sparkling melodia; also with a harmonic flute with a smoky
voice. The machinery which supplies the instrument is declared to be
perfectly noiseless."[22] The review of the Pilcher dedication played in
1910 by Albert Dee at St. Mary's Chapel opined, "The chapel organ is
full stopped and wonderfully sweet toned. The reeds are attractively
banked and the natural oak setting harmonizes well with the interior decoration of the college building. There are three banks of keys
and 100 pipes and swells."[23] Clarence Eddy dedicated the Hook &
Hastings organ at the Scottish Rite Temple in 1913, the five-manual,

The interior of the Scottish Rite Cathedral with its fifty-four-rank Hook &
Hastings organ, the largest concert instrument in Dallas for many years.

fifty-four-rank instrument having erroneously been proclaimed "the
largest in the world" by the enthusiastic reviewer. More importantly,
the writer observes that "there are to be three concerts—tonight,
Wednesday night and Thursday night, at eight o'clock. The auditorium seats 900, and the seats for each performance have been going
very rapidly."[24] Full audiences at organ recitals were certainly typical of the time but demonstrate the cultural sophistication Dallasites
had achieved. The desire to purchase organs and to showcase them
required a steady supply of organists that the new Southern Methodist
University supplied in short order.

The First Organ Professor

Dr. Hyer and his deputy, the assiduous and astute Frank Reedy, invited only the most qualified candidates to teach at the new university. Although their aspirations were national, hoping to procure shining lights from throughout academia, there was negligible attraction to uproot careers and reestablish themselves at a new university, so many of the original faculty were local, or at least regional.[25] Among the first thirty-six faculty members was an organ professor. It is likely that Bertha Stevens Cassidy worked with Frank Reedy during their time at Trinity Methodist Episcopal, South, where Mr. Reedy was involved as Sunday school superintendent and sang in the music ministry throughout the same time Cassidy was serving as organist.[26] Although a relative newcomer to the city, Cassidy was rapidly becoming one of the foremost organists in Dallas. Benjamin T. Pettit (1865–1936), the local Estey Organ Company representative, lauded her character in a letter introducing her to the corporate office in Brattleboro in 1913: "She is one of the best women in the world and is liked by everyone who know her except a few amature organists who are jealous of her. She is sought by all committees who come to Dallas looking at organs and is the only organist in this section of the state that does concert or recital work out of Dallas. I know that she is teaching 75% of the organists of Dallas and nearby towns and I could go on and tell you many reasons for her being the most popular woman, musically, in all Texas."[27] Even taking into account the exaggeration this reference undoubtedly represents, Pettit was well-placed to ascertain Cassidy's standing in the local organ world. She did indeed perform throughout Texas, so that by her retirement in 1934 she had played some 250 concerts throughout Texas—no small feat given the distances and travel difficulties involved.[28] Until the mid-1910s, newspapers throughout Texas reported on her many organ concerts, often performed in conjunction with a soloist.[29] She already maintained a large studio with numerous potential university students and was successful enough as a teacher to justify purchasing a home

SMU's first organ professor, Bertha Stevens Cassidy, in 1919.
Rotunda Collection, SMU Archives, DeGolyer Library, SMU.

pipe organ in autumn of 1913.[30] There were other organists in Dallas
from which to choose, but in terms of experience, training, and the
aforementioned intangibles, Cassidy was ideally situated to guide the
formation of SMU's organ department.

Bertha Stevens was born on May 22, 1876, in Cincinnati, Ohio, to the Reverend William and Martha Stevens,[31] Reverend Stevens serving Columbia Baptist Church in Cincinnati until 1899.[32] No doubt hers was a musically and spiritually productive childhood, for she began playing organ and piano by age nine, earned the organist position at Columbia Baptist at fifteen, and later entered the Cincinnati Conservatory of Music, which, before its eventual merger with the College of Music of Cincinnati, also functioned as a finishing school for young society women. Here she studied organ with Lillian Arkell Rixford, receiving the Springer Medal for musical achievement while employed as organist at Walnut Hills Congregational Church of Cincinnati and the First Baptist Church of Dayton, Ohio.[33] She apparently made summer forays to New York City, where she studied organ with Clifford Demarest, one of the founders of the American Guild of Organists (AGO), as well as with Max Spicker, the cantor at Temple Emanu-El on Fifth Avenue.[34] She worked in synagogues throughout most of her career, even having by 1919 "arranged and composed two complete [Jewish] services of sixteen numbers each."[35] In 1900 she married James Harvey Cassidy (1873–1941), whose career in the printing and paper industry took them first to San Antonio, where she became organist and choir director of the Madison Square Presbyterian Church and Temple Beth-El,[36] then to Waco, and finally to Dallas by 1904, where their only child, Viola Adele Cassidy, was born.[37] She is first mentioned in Dallas in 1904, as organist of the First Methodist Church,[38] but from 1907 until June 1913, she was organist at Trinity Methodist Church, where she certainly worked with Frank Reedy.[39] At various times later she was also organist at Temple Emanu-El and the Scottish Rite Cathedral.

Estey, Opus 1165

The Cassidys settled in a neighborhood south of what became Southern Methodist University, from which James Cassidy could commute easily to his office on Ross Avenue and from where Bertha Cassidy could launch her organ teaching enterprise. In early 1913 Bertha

Cassidy telephoned Benjamin Pettit, the Estey representative, inquiring about purchasing a used house organ for teaching.[40] Pettit sensed an opportunity, writing to his superiors in Brattleboro, "No use for me to recite to you the many benefits it would be to us to have an organ in her home for I believe you realize it. It will be the best way of bringing our organ prominently before the very people who are to buy organs, and in a way that will influence them our way."[41] So firm was Pettit's conviction that an organ sold to Cassidy would result in future lucrative contracts that he declined any profit on the proposed job, promising to waive "all commission and install it in her home without charge, [I will] even pay the helpers if you will furnish it at actual cost of construction and pay the freight. You furnish the organ and blower and pay the freight to Dallas and I will do the rest."[42] A little more than a week later came Estey's tepid response, accepting Pettit's offer to sacrifice his commission but counseling that the long-term reward would be minimal: "The chamber organs, and in fact all the smaller instruments, are made at a very small profit. We will throw off the profit entirely and will furnish a specification 3-3-1 with our regular 'A' case, including electric blower, $1250. This price is made with the understanding that we will deliver the organ freight paid to Dallas and that you will care for the expense setting it up."[43]

By May a contract had been signed for a new seven-rank, two-manual, electric-action organ with a radiating, concave pedal-board and a crescendo pedal, to be delivered by October 1, the start of Cassidy's fall teaching term. Pettit was hardly motivated by altruism, for he writes as he returns the Cassidy contract to Estey, "This proves her faith in our organ. She did not even consider another organ and in her quiet, reserved and professional way is talking for the Estey when opertunity presents. She is now working on the Jewish people who will buy, after a while, what they believe to be the best organ of any church in the city. She was organist for these people for several years, in connection with another church, and has more influence with them than any one else."[44]

James Cassidy signed the contract "as principal to the contract as a married woman's signature is not binding to any contract, note or legal document in Texas, unless joined by the husband."[45] Subsequent correspondence through the summer reveals the usual concerns relative to installing a house organ—the matching of wood, electrical upgrades, and even whether they intended to move to a larger home, an idea bandied about earlier in the year.[46] By early September, one can sense concern in Pettit's missive to Brattleboro, no doubt impressed upon him by Cassidy herself: "Mrs. Cassidy is wondering if her organ will be ready for use by October first as per contract. Her fall class opens at that time and many of her pupils are to take their lessons on her organ. Not to have it by that time will be a great inconvenience and loss to her as it will disconcert her plans."[47] A response a few days later assures him of every haste being taken in the completion of the organ, but that it will probably not be shipped until late September,[48] much to Cassidy's irritation, as can be read in Pettit's reply on September 17: "She told me that she will loose six pupils that she knows of for the whole term of nine months. They will take from another teacher who has access to a church organ. That loss of itself amounts to about $60/per month or $720 in all."[49]

If Cassidy was hoping for some sort of rebate for her trouble, the Estey Organ Company entertained no such thought. Neither do the records indicate whether she actually lost those students. The exchange posits a more subtle question: Why did she not have access to her own church's organ? It is possible that the house organ had been precipitated by a change of employment. Although the circumstances as to why she left Trinity Methodist are unclear, in June 1913, in the middle of the house organ process, Cassidy accepted a position at Gaston Avenue Baptist Church.[50] Perhaps there were practical reasons for the change, or perhaps she perceived a certain inelegance about asking a new employer for daily teaching privileges. Regardless, after a sojourn of several years, she seized the opportunity to return to her roots and played in a Baptist Church for the rest of her life.

On October 1, 1913, the Estey shop order for Opus 1165 describes an organ consisting of an Open Diapason 8', Dulciana 8', and Melodia 8' on the Great, with a Salicional 8', Stopped Diapason 8', and Flute Harmonique 4' on the Swell, and a Pedal Bourdon 16', with a tremolo, nine couplers, and Crescendo Pedal. Of particular interest on the shop order is the notation that the voicing be done "very carefully for Organist's use," and, under "special features," the warning, "For organist's residence. Use especial pains throughout."[51] By October 23 the organ was in Dallas, out of the crates, and ready for installation.[52] Either Mr. Pettit overestimated the time required to erect the instrument or his enthusiasm for future sales so motivated him that he had the organ installed by late October. In a letter to Brattleboro on November 1, 1913, he wrote that "Mrs. Cassidy is very much pleased with the organ in every way."[53] Three days later, Cassidy addressed a letter to the Estey corporate offices:

To the Estey Organ Co. Gentlemen,

I wish to express my pleasure and satisfaction with the organ installed in my home this past week. I appreciate the care that has been taken in the voicing to make the tone both pure and well modulated. The key and stop action seem perfect and the bellows and motor noiseless. The beauty of the case is admired by all.

Mr. Cassidy and I are both grateful to you and Mr. Pettit for the interest you have shown in securing us a beautiful little instrument.

Sincerely Yours,
Bertha S. Cassidy[54]

So begins the history of the first organ of Southern Methodist University, one that it did not officially own but that would be used to the university's advantage.

Teaching Studio of Bertha Stevens Cassidy
3209 Fairmount St., Dallas, TX
Estey Organ Company, Opus 1165 (1913)[55]

GREAT (enclosed)
  8 Open Diapason (10 pipes in case)
  8 Dulciana
  4 Melodia

PEDAL
 16 Bourdon (30 pipes)

MECHANICALS
Crescendo Pedal
Swell expression pedal
There were no other playing assists.

SWELL (enclosed)
  8 Salicional
  8 Stopped Diapason
  4 Flute Harmonique
     Tremolo

COUPLERS
Great to Pedal
Swell to Pedal
Great Unison Separation
Swell to Great 16, 8, 4
Swell to Swell 16, Unison
Separation, 4

Bertha Cassidy's home teaching studio organ.

Establishing an Organ Department

When it came to appointing music faculty for the new university that frustratingly still had not opened by 1914, Dr. Hyer's role is unclear. On the one hand, he does not seem to have had as many opinions as he had about other departments, although his daughter claimed he "gave a great deal of time and thought to the music department. While not being particularly musical himself, he appreciated the fact that a music department is an integral part of a co-educational college, and he wanted to obtain the best teachers available. To do this, he consulted many outstanding musicians, the result being that for the first few years there were at Southern Methodist University many of the best music teachers to be found anywhere in the Southwest."[56] He maintained a little book in which he and his secretary, Dorothy Amman, kept track of potential faculty hires, along with their qualifications and any interactions he had had with them. Yet the entire roster of music faculty employed by the university when it opened in 1915 is conspicuously absent from this well-organized book.[57] For reasons that will be explored later, the School of Music was arranged differently from the other schools at SMU, with teachers being paid wages instead of a salary, so this may be part of the reason. But it also may be that such hires were left to the influential bursar, Frank Reedy.

A distinctive man with a handlebar mustache enhancing his commanding presence, the officially uneducated Reedy came to the attention of Hyer when Reedy tried to register as a student at Southwestern University in 1909.[58] Hyer instead appointed him as the "Bursar, Registrar, Business Manager, Advertising Agent, Secretary, Collecting Agent, Promotion Director, Bookkeeper, etc., etc.," doing "anything that might have a bearing upon enlargement of Southwestern, endowment, equipment, prestige, and student body."[59] Hyer and Reedy maintained their relationship when they started the new school in Dallas, and early university records are replete with Reedy's directives, always signed with the unassuming sobriquet "Bursar." Always involved in music matters, it was

Reedy who was "responsible for the first attempt in the way of an orchestra at S.M.U., and through his fostering and sponsorship has been developed the present orchestra, of which the university is justly proud."[60] Reedy himself may very well have been the intelligence in assembling the music faculty. This is at least obliquely suggested by Mrs. Cassidy's own account of her hiring, which she recounted in the third person:

> In June of 1915, while Mrs. J. H. Cassidy, the present head of the Organ Department, was studying in New York, she received a letter from Mr. Frank Reedy, then Bursar of S.M.U. This letter stated that the new University had received applications for courses in organ study and that the President wished to meet every need in the new school of Music. Mr. Reedy and Dr. Hyer asked if Mrs. Cassidy would consider joining the Faculty and permitting the University to use her studio organ on Fairmount Street until such time as organs might be installed at the school. They expressed the hope that they might be able to have studio organs within two years.
>
> Mrs. Cassidy accepted the proposition and was made the first woman professor of S.M.U. and until 1926, the only woman to hold the rank of professor on the entire faculty.[61]

So begins Mrs. Cassidy's almost twenty-year tenure at SMU, overseeing a conservatory-style education at a liberal arts institution.

The first several years of the university were inauspicious. Harvie Branscomb, a later member of the faculty at SMU and eventual chancellor at Vanderbilt University elucidated some significant challenges:

> As one came to know the faculty, however, a number of them, one could see, were first-rate in ability, though the older ones had been drawn mostly from Texas schools and colleges and were provincial in outlook. Alongside the academic elders were a number of would-be scholars picked up in various places. The faculty was not an accomplished one, but it had the virtues of integrity and simplicity. . . . The instruction we gave was not profound—the academic elders had codified knowledge in their

respective fields at an early date . . . and we younger ones only
knew enough to keep one day ahead of the class.[62]

To clarify, the first faculty members were rather young, with an
average age of 35, while Cassidy was one of the elders, beginning
her career at SMU at age 39.[63] Harold von Mickwitz, from the Bush
Conservatory in Chicago, served as the first dean of the School of
Music, Kirk Townes as professor of voice, and Harold Hart Todd,
composer of the school song, as professor of piano and theory.
His wife, Anna Lisbeth Todd, a descendant of Austrian composer
Franz Gruber of "Silent Night" fame, taught piano until 1957.[64]
C. Boris Grant, a piano pupil of von Mickwitz from Chicago, was
appointed professor of piano and Walter Fried as professor of violin,
and finally there was Bertha Cassidy, who in the earliest records
is referred to as "Head of the Department of Organ," a title that
suggests a role as much a coordinator as a teacher, possibly in antic-
ipation of hiring additional organ faculty. The majestic building on
campus, Dallas Hall, belied the modest character of the faculty but
housed a majority of the university's classes the first several years.
In the first year, there were ninety students in the School of Music
sharing two Steinway grand pianos, two Mason & Hamlin grands,
and ten uprights. Most of the studios were located in the basement
of the women's dormitory, except for Mr. Todd's studio, which
was located in Dallas Hall based on his teaching of the "theoretical
branches."[65]

Unlike the theology or liberal arts schools, whose faculty held
academic degrees and were paid a salary, teachers in the School of
Music were largely conservatory trained and lacked academic degrees,
and instead of a salary were paid a wage based on the number of private
lessons taught. SMU was not unique in this arrangement.[66] Underscoring this disparity, between 1915 and 1918, faculty meetings, in which
decisions pertaining to the entire university were made, consisted only
of the theology and liberal arts faculty; the music faculty was not fully
integrated into the more academic realms. The first *Bulletin of Southern*

Methodist University, 1915–1916 described precisely the expectations for music students, and by extension, the music faculty:

> Fees must be paid strictly in advance for the term. Lessons cannot be made up nor tuition refunded except in cases of protracted illness, and then only when notice has been given the instructor in advance. Charges for tuition by the various instructors will be furnished upon application to the Bursar of the University.
>
> A student must register before any lessons may be taken. Students will not be received for less than one term or the unexpired portion of it.
>
> Students taking the course leading to the degree of Bachelor of Music are required to take two lessons a week in practical subjects. Students who do not intend to graduate may be permitted to take one lesson per week.[67]

Not only were instructors paid per lesson, but students could study without pursuing a degree, a program known as following a "music special." Mary Thomas claims that "the School of Music appealed to a new university because it attracted women students and had the advantage of paying its own way."[68]

That the School of Music appealed primarily to females is borne out in early editions of the *Rotunda*, the official yearbook. In the 1917 edition, faculty pianist C. Boris Grant was proprietor and director of an eponymous music club, presiding over 16 student members—all female.[69] The Euterpean Club, consisting of students of Mr. and Mrs. Todd, likewise boasted 42 members—all female—by 1919.[70] The 1917 edition also lists the members of Bertha Cassidy's "First Certificate Class from the Organ Department of School of Music at Southern Methodist University," all five of whom were female.[71] As late as 1924, 19 of the 20 members of the newly organized Bach Organ Club, overseen by Mrs. Cassidy, were female.[72] The 1916 course catalog enumerates 142 students in the "Department of Fine Arts and Household Arts and Sciences," of whom 137 were female.[73] By 1919, after the School of Music had become a fully independent entity, 68 of the 72 music students were women.[74]

There were certainly male musicians among the ensembles
from the earlier years, particularly in the all-male glee club and the
orchestra. Although societal expectations of the era were congenial to women's study of music, SMU's theology school no doubt
benefited from the wives of its ministerial students studying organ
and church music. Such study would be immediately useful to its
graduates when assigned to a parish. This may partly account for the
dearth of actual degrees in music and organ awarded to the women
organ students, who generally partook in the condensed organ certification program, allowing more flexibility to depart when their
husbands received parish assignments. Church participation was a
hallmark of the early days, a university chapel having been organized, with "attendance at one Sunday church service, either at the
University or in the city . . . required of all resident students."[75] Since
Bertha Cassidy maintained her own hectic schedule at one of her
churches, the Scottish Rite Cathedral, and the Jewish temple, it is
likely that these university services allowed the organ students to
garner service-playing experience.

The 1925 Bach Organ Club at SMU. Rotunda Collection,
SMU Archives, DeGolyer Library, SMU.

The Organ Course of Study

In practice the School of Music may have taken on the character of a girl's finishing school, familiar to Bertha Cassidy from her experience at the Cincinnati Conservatory of Music. One nonmusic student, Flora Lowrey, depicts a campus characterized as much by free and comfortable personal interactions as it was by academic standards: "There was a rapport between the first faculty and the first student body, and relationship was informal. There were no snack bars, no place to drink a cup of coffee together, but we walked together through paths (there were no walks), talked together in the parlor, discussed issues in the classrooms and offices. We all had the same goals. We were establishing a university, setting precedents, and laying a foundation. The spirit of endeavor was high, and we worked together in perfect accord."[76] Such a description, although here not applied specifically to the Music Department, certainly could have been applied to the Organ department in those formative years, where collegiality proceeded from familiarity. That Bertha Cassidy taught organ lessons at her house instead of at the university likely promulgated an attitude of informality, despite Mrs. Cassidy's personal penchant for conventional propriety. A notice in an issue of the *Semi-Weekly Campus* in April 1923 speaks to this camaraderie in the music school in reference to a studio concert at the Cassidy home performed by her studio as well as Mrs. Roscoe Golden's vocal studio. Five organists (all female) played standard period pieces by the forgotten composers Kinder, Friml, Johnson, and Johnston, along with a Bach prelude and fugue. The article notes that "a social time followed the program when games were played and refreshments served to forty guests."[77]

The university's first annual catalog from 1915 outlines the basic course of study for a certificate in organ performance that remained little changed throughout Cassidy's tenure:

First year: Pupils must have some knowledge of piano before beginning the organ. Whiting Nos. 1 and 2. Dudley Buck's Pedal Phrasing, Rink's books, 3, 4 and 5, hymn playing and easy accompaniments. Bach's easy preludes and fugues, first year organ compositions for church repertoire.

Second year: Pedal scale work; Bach's trio sonatas and concertos; shorter compositions of American, French, English and German composers; modern sonatas and study in registration.

Third Year. Bach Fourth Volume, and great G Minor fugue, sonatas by Mendelssohn; concertos by Handel, sonatas by Merkel, Rheinberger, Guilmant, concert repertoire, oratorios, accompaniment and choir direction; transcriptions and orchestrations.[78]

The Whiting volume refers to George Elbridge Whiting's (1840–1923) *First Studies for the Organ: 24 Pieces*, published in two volumes in 1879.[79] Whiting, who had been professor of organ in the College of Music of Cincinnati, later became one of the founders of the AGO. Another founder of the AGO, Dudley Buck, is represented in the 1868 *Eighteen Studies in Pedal Phrasing*, containing pieces that, while all utilizing hands as well as pedal, concentrate on establishing a subtle pedal technique.[80] The "Rink's books" certainly refers to Christian Heinrich Rinck's (1770–1846) *Praktische Orgelschule*, Opus 55, whose six volumes were published by W. T. Best circa 1858, containing graded pieces, pedal exercises, and practical service music for the beginner.[81] Most likely the "Bach Fourth Volume" referred to the fourth volume of the Widor-Schweitzer Bach editions, which had only recently been published (1912–1914). The fourth volume contains a number of masterworks, including the "Great" Fantasia and Fugue in G minor, BWV 542, presumably the piece to which she is referring, although curiously without its attached Fantasia. Surprising, perhaps, is the inclusion of Bach's trio sonatas in the second year. Had she had past success introducing such complex works to students in their second year of organ study? Perusing organ studio and degree recitals from the first decade reveals no trio sonatas being performed, although other Bach works, mostly preludes and fugues, make an increasing appearance.

The syllabus remained unchanged during the first nine years of SMU's organ program during which it was based out of the Cassidy home, which by 1919 had moved to Lindenwood Avenue, a short walk from campus.[82] Only in the 1924–25 catalog did she add to the first year's program of study Clarence Dickinson's *Art and Technique of Organ Playing*, recently published in 1922,[83] and Edward Shippen Barnes's *School of Organ Playing*, published in 1921.[84] Her growth as a teacher is evident in her shift away from the organ methods with which she was familiar from her own youth to more recent studies that she would have known as a trained professional.

For those not able to pursue a bachelor's degree, there was an alternate route of study that she outlined in the first annual catalog: "A special course for the simpler church playing may be had upon application, but such courses will not entitle the student to certificate and recognition, beyond a note of commendation. Lessons and practice will be upon a complete modern organ of two manuals with electric power, and in the special course, above offered, registration will be adapted to the particular church organ to be played by the organist."[85] This course of study was probably little more than the private lessons that she had always given at her home. From a financial perspective, it was to her advantage to keep as many students as possible, particularly those who had no interest in pursuing an official course of study. Interestingly, she specifies that "lessons and practice" will both be upon her home instrument—an act of professorial dedication, certainly, considering how busy her household must have been. However, it is doubtful Mrs. Cassidy intended the arrangement to last over a decade, her initial employment inquiry with Mr. Reedy having suggested that SMU be able to supply adequate organ facilities "within two years."[86]

Indeed, by the beginning of the next school year, in 1916, Mrs. Cassidy requested Frank Reedy to secure local churches for her students' practice, a request with which he complied, imploring one local pastor to accord organ practice privileges at ten cents per hour for SMU students, a need precipitated by the fact that Mrs. Cassidy "has so many students for the pipe organ that every hour of the day is reserved on the organ in her home on Fairmount."[87] One can imagine Mrs. Cassidy (or perhaps Mr. Cassidy) utilizing all her political capital with the local ministerial authorities to obtain use of their churches for practice.

Lucille Price of Honey Grove, Texas—the first organ student to receive
a bachelor of music degree. Rotunda Collection, SMU Archives,
DeGolyer Library, SMU.

The three-year program must have taken time to implement or
was variable based on the accomplishment of the student. A description, probably written by Bertha Cassidy herself, addresses the
circumstances of the first graduates:

> The Organ Department first offered a two year church playing
> course, entitling the student to a certificate at the end of two

years. Five students received this certificate at the end of two years. They were Virginia Winfrey, Mrs. Zella Stanyer of Dallas, Rosabel Hearndon, Julia Mae Ward of Waxahachie, and Mary Orr of Boston, Massachusetts. Mrs. Stanyer returned to the University later for an artist diploma. Rosabel Hearndon, Julia Mae Ward of Waxahachie, and Mary Orr are holding organ positions.

Lucille Price of Honey Grove was the first organ student to receive the B.M. degree. She is at present organist of Westminster Presbyterian Church in Dallas.[88]

As the Organ department rapidly grew, organs of many Dallas churches were used for student practice and more degrees and certificates were conferred.

Establishing a Public Persona

The School of Music quickly became the public representation of the new university to the city of Dallas. On October 29, 1915, the music faculty presented itself for the first time to the public at a performance at Dallas's Scottish Rite Cathedral, site of the aforementioned sizable Hook & Hastings organ. The concert featured all the faculty but showcased Kirk Townes, professor of voice, and C. Boris Grant, professor of piano. Shuttle cars ran along the five-mile route between the cathedral and the university, allowing students to attend and ensuring all nine hundred seats were filled. A news release the month before provides background to the event:

> It will be an effort to show the people of Dallas the musical temper which the university faculty has to present. No single artist will be featured over another and no attempt will be made to attract attention to any one of the artists. This was a consideration upon which the Scottish Rite Masons offered the cathedral and organ. Another consideration was that no charge be made. . . .
>
> Dr. Hyer readily accepted the proffer and began immediately to make arrangements for the affair. Frank Reedy, bursar, was

instructed by President Hyer to leave nothing undone that might interfere with the giving of the concert.

"It is a splendid opportunity to show the people of Dallas just what we have to offer them through our fine arts department," Mr. Reedy said in speaking of the concert. . . . "We want Dallas people to know what the school has to offer and when Dallas people become convinced the rest is easy."[89]

Bertha Cassidy performed Bach's Prelude and Fugue in A minor (BWV 543 or the shorter, far less technically challenging BWV 559?), "Sunset" from Clifford Demarest's *Pastoral Suite*, and Harry Crackel's Caprice in G Minor. A writer in the SMU paper gave the following account: "The program was opened by Mrs. J. H. Cassidy, who is cathedral organist as well as a member of the musical faculty of the University. She appeared in a group of numbers admirably chosen for displaying the wide range of powers of the organ and of her own command of the instrument. Her interpretation of the Demarest and Crackel numbers, which, with their soft echo effects, contrasted with the brighter tones of the flute and clarionet stops, were perfectly delightful. There her real power as an artist was shown in her rendition of the Bach Prelude and Fugue."[90]

Because SMU lacked a suitable performance venue on campus, this began a decade of successful concerts, both organ and otherwise, at local churches, nurturing a symbiotic relationship with the university and the city. Bertha Cassidy never hesitated to utilize her places of employment as performance venues for her students; she was associated with the cathedral since her husband was a member there, first mentioned in 1909, and likely they both were instrumental in initiating this first concert.[91] In the subsequent decade, Temple Emanu-El[92] and Gaston Avenue Baptist Church[93] hosted SMU faculty or student organ concerts, in addition to frequent concerts at the Cassidy home. In 1919 Cassidy succeeded Will Watkin as organist at First Baptist Church in Dallas, which housed "an old Odell of 28 registers being rebuilt and enlarged to 44 registers, with 6 new strings and an Echo

The Hook & Hastings console at the Scottish Rite Cathedral.

of 6 voices. . . . The congregations average about 4,000 each service," and student recitals were given soon after.[94]

These concerts allow a glimpse into Mrs. Cassidy's status as a performer and her preferred repertoire, good indicators of the music the organ studio learned. The February 28, 1923, edition of SMU's

Semi-Weekly Campus gives notice of an organ studio recital held in conjunction with the vocal studio and performed at the Cassidy house. By this time Bertha Cassidy's daughter, Viola, was an organ major, performing Lemmens's *Fanfare*. Charles Morgan performed Dawes's *Melody*; Mary Richardson, Westeront's *Rondo*; Alverne Davise, Roland Diggle's *Meditation*; Mrs. Dawson Bryan, Lemaigre's *Pastorale*; Louise Weaver, Dickinson's *Berceuse*; and Jeanne Toomer, Guilmant's Caprice in B Flat.[95] One can surmise that these were second- or third-year students, given that this repertoire fits the basic schema outlined for those years. The campus paper in May of that same year reports on the recital of Mrs. Waltarene Barnes Lane, "candidate for a bachelor of music degree at SMU," who, assisted in the program by two vocalists, performed at Oak Lawn Methodist Church:

Allegro from *Sonata in E Minor*	Rogers
In Autumn	Brewer
Madrigal	Rogers
In the Morning (*Peer Gynt*)	Grieg
Aria "O Star of Eve" (*Tannhäuser*)	Wagner
Invictus	Huhn
Uncle Rome	Homer
Prelude and Fugue in C Minor	Bach
Twilight Dreams	Sibella
A Love Note	Rogers
My Laddie	Thayer
Finale from *First Sonata*	Mendelssohn[96]

The Bach and Mendelssohn pieces certainly fit within the purview of the organ masterwork tradition, but the preponderance of period pieces demonstrates an interpretation of the second-year course of study that specifies only the study of "American, French and German composers."[97] That this concert was performed on an organ other than Cassidy's home organ probably indicates that the studio had already outgrown the modest tonal resources offered by the Estey.

A *Semi-Weekly Campus* article from February 1924 covers a recital "made up entirely of organ music" at First Methodist Church:

Toccata	Nevin
Miss Mary Ella Lowry	
Grand Aria	Clifford Demarest
Misses Viola Cassidy and Dora Poteet	
Organ and Piano	
Concert Overture in C Minor	Hollins
Miss Kit Carson	
Song of the Basket Weaver	Russell
Miss Florence Wood	
Toccata from Sixth Symphony	Widor[98]
Miss Dora Poteet	

This two-manual, 1894 Hook & Hastings would have been slightly more artistically suitable for the larger concert pieces this recital required.[99] Dora Poteet, Cassidy's protégé, here appears in a duet with Viola Cassidy and concludes the program with the Toccata from what was certainly Widor's Fifth Symphony. The contrast between the Widor and Alexander Russell's "Song of the Basket Weaver" from his 1921 *St. Lawrence Sketches* represents the disparity between early twentieth-century musical taste and the repertoire that predominated shortly.

Bertha Cassidy as Performer

Even given the propensity for audiences to attend organ concerts in droves during that era, and also considering the tendency for news-paper accounts to present such events in the most obsequious of terms, Mrs. Cassidy's recital at the Scottish Rite Cathedral in February 1918 was clearly a popular civic event:

Long before the time for beginning the program for the organ recital by Mrs. J. H. Cassidy at the Scottish Rite Cathedral yesterday afternoon every available seat in the large auditorium and the balcony as well was filled. Practically all standing room was taken up by those who came late, and others, numbering over five hundred, were turned away for want of seats.

The large audience gave evidence of its appreciation of the organist's ability by the liberal applause of each number. If there was a single organ number that drew greater applause than another it was hard to detect. . . .

The last number, "The Minster Bells," was especially pleasing. . . . The electrical effects were used on the stage showing the woodland scenes. This number was merged into the "Star-Spangled Banner."[100]

Cassidy rounded out the program with the "Overture to *Ruy Blas*" by Mendelssohn; "From the South," by Gillette; "Valerie," by Federlein, "Adagio Pathetique" for violin and harp, by Godard; "A Heart That Loves Thee," by Gounod, in which she was joined by singers; and concluded with "Scherzo" from Guilmant's *Fifth Sonata*. If this concert strained the reviewer's ability to curb his or her enthusiasm, the next month's program warranted an even fuller description in the most approbatory manner:

The monthly concerts at the cathedral . . . have become so popu-lar that the auditorium is too small to accommodate the people who turn out to hear them. The hall has room for 1,100 persons, but it was estimated than more than a thousand were turned away after the seats were all taken. . . .

Mrs. Cassidy, who began the recital twenty minutes before the appointed time, because the hall was then more than crowded and there was no use in making the people wait any longer, opened with the "Pilgrim's Chorus" from "Tannhauser," in which all the orchestral effects of the organ were brought out. "The Angelus," founded on a sixteenth century hymn, by Tomlinson, was intro-duced by the ringing of the chimes, followed by the Arcadian hymn on the vox humani of the echo organ, the whole effect of which was pastoral serenity, innocence and triumphant faith. In the last of the first group the "Military March," by Clarke, all the trumpets and tubas of the pedal and solo organs were used with the solo tuba clarion, with grand effect.

But the big number of the program was "The Alpine Fantasia," (the storm in the mountains), by Flagler, which is a wonderful essay in descriptive music. This number Mrs. Cassidy made popular in her Ocean Grove concerts during the convention of the National Organists' Association there. The fantasia starts with a passage involving the shepherds' pipes, the music of which echoes and reechoes over the mountains, giving the tones of the oboes. Then the thunder rolls and gathers for tremendous crashes, making an uproar that closely imitates the real thing. As the storm abates and passes, the shepherd pipes are again heard in the distance, succeeded by the vesper hymn on the vox humani, accompanied by the chimes and the convent bell.

By request, Mrs. Cassidy included among her selections her own organ arrangement of "Annie Laurie," in which the clarinet is used for the solo and the flutes for the accompaniment. The homely old melody, thus dressed up, has become a great favorite with the Dallas people. "The Rosary," the Barcarolle," from "The Tales of Hoffman," and Flagler's "March in D" were also effective numbers:

The recital was a musical treat, showing that what the Scottish Rite Masons are attempting to do in the way of furnishing the people with high entertainment and of elevating the musical taste of the community is meeting with appreciation and success.[101]

This reviewer was fairly conversant in organ terminology, and seemed to know Cassidy personally or at least to have spoken with her, given his or her particular knowledge of her National Organists' Association performances in Ocean Grove. This is a hint at Cassidy's national reputation. The concert might have presented the standard fare for recitals at the time, with an emphasis on programmatic pieces, but it was for popular music and transcriptions that the large Hook & Hastings organ at the cathedral was built. Storm pieces, such as that by Flagler, had been fashionable throughout the nineteenth century, and Strauss's *Alpine Symphony*, a similar venture, had been premiered rather recently, in 1915. That Cassidy performed her own arrangement of a folk song reveals her own latent interest in composition.

Bertha Cassidy had organized the Dallas Organist Association sometime prior to 1918, in an effort to foster "greater unity among the church organists," but her connections with the New York organ culture, in particular having studied with Clifford Demarest and having earned the associate certification of the AGO (AAGO) in 1917, no doubt spurred within her the idea of forming an AGO chapter in Dallas.[102] This was the era in which membership had to be earned, not merely dues paid, so to launch a chapter presupposed enough qualified organists who could support it.

In May 1918 Clifford Demarest, traveling around the United States in an effort to foster growth in the AGO, stopped in Dallas to launch what became the Texas chapter. A meeting at the Adolphus Hotel drew sixty people, of which thirty-five joined the AGO, with eighteen taking the associateship examination. Demarest praised the chapter, saying, "If other chapters would emulate this splendid example our academic membership would soon be of a better proportion than it is at the present time and one of the main objects of the Guild become a reality."[103] Part of the SMU organ curriculum included preparation for AGO examinations, which Cassidy clearly articulates in the curriculum descriptions found in the earliest university catalogs: "The three-year course of organ and theory of music conforms to the standards and work required for associateship in the American Guild of Organists. Students passing the examinations in all branches receive the degree of Bachelor of Music and recommendations for entrance to the Guild of Organists of America and Canada."[104] Perhaps passing the AGO examination motivated Cassidy to form the Bach Organ Club in 1924, whose "charter members will include twenty organists, each having passed the test, which is satisfactory playing of a Bach prelude and fugue."[105]

The First Decade Concludes

As the first decade of Southern Methodist University's organ program drew to a close with hopes for an optimistic future, at least one part of the realm seemed beset by simmering strife. Mr. Benjamin

Thomas Pettit, the enthusiastic Dallas Estey representative who had so painstakingly installed the university's first teaching instrument—Estey, Opus 1165—in the Cassidy home in 1913 had grown increasingly vexed in his perception that Cassidy had abandoned any loyalty to Estey in favor of other builders, namely Hillgreen, Lane & Company.[106] Although there is no historical evidence to support a contention that Cassidy was either employed by or received commissions from Hillgreen, Lane for her positive recommendations, given the number of Hillgreen, Lane organs that she apparently recommended (based on the increasing number of dedication recitals she played throughout Texas during the twenties), the circumstantial evidence certainly intimates a close connection to that company. Did she style herself as an objective consultant to the many committees that sought her advice, all while being financially beholden to Hillgreen, Lane? There can be no doubt that she favored and recommended Hillgreen, Lane; two Hillgreen, Lane organs were about to be installed in McFarlin Auditorium, no doubt with her approbation. Yet as her reputation as a public recitalist continued to grow, largely assisted by her dedication concerts on Hillgreen, Lanes, one wonders whether these committees were actually expecting an objective consultant. Her concerts were well covered in the local papers, and certainly these committees would have known about or could have surmised her close connection to the company. It may be that her music presented Hillgreen, Lane instruments as winsomely and musically as possible—perhaps allowing them to appear as better instruments than in many cases history has deemed them to be. If this speculation is true, it is a testament to her professionalism and musicality.

Cassidy had always maintained friendly relations with Estey, as is suggested in a letter of October 6, 1924, in which she writes to Pettit:

In noticing the Estey advertisement in the American Organist of studio organs, I want to add my word of praise.

Dallas Estey Organ Company representative Benjamin Thomas Pettit
with his wife, Anna. Courtesy of Helen Baker Vogelsang.

The Estey studio organ in my home now reaching its elevents
year of service has prooved a remarkable instrument. The tone
well balanced and pleasing, the mechanism standing up to many
hours of use each day and the motor supplied is a gem. Wish all
teachers might have as satisfactory instrument,

Sincerely,
Mrs. J. H. Cassidy[107]

This rather innocuous letter must have provoked raw emotions in Mr. Pettit, who believed that Cassidy's words rang hollow, as he believed her surreptitiously to have turned her favor to a competitor. He forwards her letter to Brattleboro while attaching his own comments addressed to his superiors:

> I have informed the factory from time to time about Mrs. Cassidy's unfavorable attitude toward our organ, especially our larger organs. She had advised in favor of other organs in every instance for the past several years. It was her that decided in favor of the Hillgreen & Lane for the Norman, Oklahoma church last spring when a $17,000 organ was bought and now I understand that she is to advise in the selection of an organ for the new McFarlan Hall at Southern Methodist University, Dallas and it is rumored that she will advise as in the case of Norman. The same family that paid for the Norman organ will pay for the S.M.U. organ, so she could hardly afford to advise differently. There being considerable talk afloat about her getting pay for her advice and her desire to have me think differently (This is surmise) she wrote me a letter concerning her organ, copy of which is enclosed.
>
> I thought the factory would be interested in knowing how tactfully she is trying to keep us blinded. All she says about her organ is true but she tells others that while we make a good small organ, there we stop, for she does not like our larger organs. I am not offering her a commission.[108]

The surviving correspondence between Cassidy and Pettit concludes with Pettit's response on October 30, 1924, in which he thanks her for her kind words, but then subtly admonishes her: "As you used to say to purchasing committees when opening their new Estey Organ, that the one thing you had noticed in Estey Organs was that the quality run regular. That is they were all of the same high quality and not an occasional poor one. We rember these remarks quite well and appreciate them as coming from a competent judge. Since you have not had the opportunity of keeping up with our modern construction and quality, let us assure you that the Estey Organ is still supreme."[109]

If there was a response to this, Pettit chose not to share it with
Estey corporate. By this time Cassidy was firmly entrenched with
Hillgreen, Lane. The little Estey that had served so capably as the
first instrument of SMU's organ department found itself relegated
to the status of a simple home instrument. Later evidence suggests
it was still used as a practice instrument for many years, but was
no longer the focal instrument of the department. The subsequent
building of McFarlin Memorial Auditorium signified unprecedented
growth in the School of Music.

Chapter 2

A Center of Artistic Performance

F ollowing the Great War, Southern Methodist University experienced taxing growth on its limited infrastructure, consisting as it did of only two principal buildings. At the end of the 1918 academic term, SMU counted 1,012 students enrolled, including 233 summer and "normal" school students;[1] however, by the 1925–1926 school year, 2,913 students were registered.[2] Although the School of Music maintained a fairly consistent enrollment, the unprecedented growth of the university as a whole created crowded conditions. The School of Music was relegated to the third floor of Dallas Hall and to the basement of the Women's Building, occupying territory that the academic departments coveted. Herbert Gambrell, chairman emeritus of the history department at SMU, wrote in positive terms of these challenges, "It all seemed pretty grand, that university under a single roof. Of course, fumes from the chemistry laboratory and hamburger grill in the basement had a way of rising and penetrating; and the sounds of piano's lungs and brass instruments at work on the third floor floated downward."[3] The organ department still met at Cassidy's home, although recitals were increasingly held elsewhere, employing organs with a wider tonal palette. The next new building not only relieved congestion but also provided a suitable home for the School of Music, allowing dedicated music practice rooms, two performance halls, classrooms, and offices for faculty. Thus was McFarlin Auditorium inaugurated with great fanfare in March 1926.

McFarlin Auditorium

Robert McFarlin, a wealthy oilman and philanthropist with deep roots in Texas and even deeper connections to Oklahoma, and his wife, Ida Barnard, paid for the building, after which it was deeded to SMU. An announcement in the *Dallas Morning News* in February 1924 enumerated this donation to the university: "The largest single gift ever received by Southern Methodist University . . . was announced Wednesday by Bishop John M. Moore of the Methodist Episcopal Church, South, on his return from San Antonio, where he received word from Mr. and Mrs. R. M. McFarlin of that place that the gift would be made. The money will be used for the construction of a great auditorium on the campus of the university. It will have a seating capacity of 3,500 persons. A pipe organ to cost approximately $25,000 is included in the gift."[4]

The McFarlin's philanthropy favored churches and universities, having recently underwritten McFarlin Memorial Methodist Church in Norman, Oklahoma, complete with its Hillgreen, Lane organ on which Bertha Cassidy played the dedication concert in December 1924.[5] In a congenial gesture of cooperation between university administration and the organ department, school officials had involved her in the organ selection process from the early planning stages, as the article continues: "Bishop Moore, Mrs. James Harvey Cassidy and Mrs. Homer Chapman were in San Antonio Tuesday in consultation with Mr. and Mrs. McFarlin and the architect, Mr. Hunt. Tentative plans were completed for the furnishings and the organ."[6] The university intended the building to be grand in conception and luxurious in appointment, sparing no expense in presenting the auditorium to the public. Incorporation of a heating and refrigerated air cooling system was a novelty at the time, inspiring the general contractor to proclaim shortly before the opening, "Only two auditoriums in the United States compare favorably with this one in dimensions, quality of acoustics and interior beauty."[7] Along with other sumptuous appointments, such as a $3,750 chandelier, the auditorium's four-manual Hillgreen, Lane & Company pipe organ was ready for the inaugural fete: "The seven-unit organ cost, fully installed, $55,000. It provides a great organ, a swell organ, an echo organ, a solo organ, a choral organ and two practice organs for students in the new pipe organ school to be inaugurated at the university this spring."[8] Although (1) the cost total is erroneous, (2) there was only one additional organ to be installed, so one cannot be sure what is meant by seven "units" (there are six divisions on the organ), and (3) the only thing new about the "pipe organ school" was that it finally had permanent quarters, the organ was indeed "fully installed" and playable by the opening exercises.

The dedication of the building spanned five days, beginning Wednesday, March 24, 1926. At least two days featured the organ prominently. The dedication service opened with an organ prelude performed by Bertha Cassidy.[9] On Thursday, March 24, W. B. Bizzell, president of the University of Oklahoma, expounded on the purposes for which the auditorium would be utilized: "I can readily conceive that in future years this will be the center of public discussion and artistic and literary performance."[10] Later that day, Charles Courboin played the first dedication recital, followed by a second recital Friday afternoon. The final event was an evening performance of Handel's *Messiah*, with Dean Paul van Katwijk conducting the 150-voice choir, and Cassidy, serving as orchestra, accompanying the chorus.

Belgian-born concert organist Charles Courboin had begun his association with the Wanamaker organ, playing popular recitals at the behest of Alexander Russell, the longtime titular organist at the famous Philadelphia department store. The campus paper extolled Courboin, the "well-known organist, who has dedicated more organs than anyone in the country," also noting that "Mr. Courboin was the guest soloist of the world's largest and most beautiful organ, that in

Charles Courboin seated at the console of the McFarlin Auditorium Hillgreen,
Lane & Company organ. Meadows School of the Arts Records,
SMU Archives, DeGolyer Library, SMU.

the grand court of the Wannamaker's great department store, in 1919.
At that time Mr. Courboin played something like 275 compositions
in twenty seven recitals to about 130,000 people. He also was guest
soloist for the organ of the Detroit Symphony Orchestra, which rates
as probably the best orchestra of its kind in America."[11] His program
at SMU, which included notes printed in the campus paper the day
preceding the concert, follows:

Passacaglia	Johann Sebastian Bach
Aria	Antonio Lotti
Allegretto	Auguste de Boeck
Third Chorale in A Minor	César Franck
The Bells of Ste. Anne De Beaupre, from *St Lawrence Sketches*	Alexander Russell

Sketch No. 3	Robert Schumann
Afternoon of a Faun	Claude Achilles Debussy
Primitive Organ	Pietro Yon
March héroïque	Camille Saint-Saëns[12]

A review in the *Dallas Morning News* the next day describes the energy of the performance and alludes to the higher cultural status to which the new auditorium entitled the university:

An audience conspicuous by its brilliance in the artistic, social and religious life of Dallas and which filled the vast hall to standing room only heard the dedicatory recital on the new $25,000 Hillgreen, Lane pipe organ Tuesday night in the McFarlin Memorial Auditorium at Southern Methodist University.

Charles M. Courboin, formerly organist of the Antwerp Cathedral and now in this country, was the artist of the evening, offering a program of organ music that ranged from the lightest musical fantasy to the Bach Passacaglia and which revealed the instrument in every phase.

At the conclusion of the set program the crowd refused to leave and insisted on encore after encore. As a final number Mr. Courboin played the "Ave Maria" while the lights of the vast interior were trimmed down to give a cathedral like hush and hue.

Musicians of the city and the music faculty of Southern Methodist University held an informal reception for the distinguished organist afterward. Many members of the Dallas Chapter of American Guild of Organists were present.[13]

The review of the concert must be tempered with an awareness of the tendency for journalists of the time to embellish their accounts. Such a large auditorium certainly deserved a large organ, which the local paper had quantified as "larger than any two [organs] now in Dallas combined," which is of course false, given the large Hook & Hastings at the Scottish Rite Cathedral.[14] That the organ was a modest instrument was obfuscated by the fact that "no organ pipes are visible but the tones speak through delicate ornamental grille tracery behind which the heavy shutters of the organ are located. This organ grille extends entirely around the proscenium and arched panels are at either side behind which silk curtains are carefully drawn."[15] As was typical with most auditorium installations at the time, the pipework was buried within chambers, with dense drapery hindering sound egress even further. So muted must the organ have been that by 1929, two microphones had been installed "to pick up the music from the Hillgreen, Lane organ to better advantage. . . . Listeners report the organ program coming through better than ever with low as well as high notes unusually distinct."[16] Although numerous deficiencies inhibited a prolonged lifetime for the organ, a few factors recommended Hillgreen, Lane as a prudent selection. Founded in 1898, the company was old enough to have earned a reputation yet still young enough not to have achieved its full potential, possibly appealing to a university in similar circumstances. The Juilliard School in New York City had installed two Hillgreen, Lanes in 1924, and Carnegie Hall's Roosevelt organ was rebuilt by Hillgreen, Lane in 1916.[17] Rollin Smith asserts that Hillgreen, Lane strove neither to be the "largest" nor the most "artistic," producing rather "undistinguished" instruments, as indeed they turned out to be at SMU.[18] Cassidy may have become familiar with the Alliance, Ohio, firm while on return visits home. Although Cassidy had graduated and moved to Texas by then, Sidney Durst, organ teacher at the Cincinnati Conservatory of Music and founding member of the Cincinnati Chapter of the AGO, had installed a Hillgreen, Lane in his home in 1909.[19]

Hillgreen, Lane & Company

In 1919 Bertha Cassidy left Gaston Avenue Baptist Church for First Baptist Church downtown, replacing organist Will A. Watkin, who happened to be proprietor of Watkin Music Company,[20] the regional representatives for Chickering Pianos and Hillgreen, Lane pipe organs. As regional representative for Hillgreen, Lane, Watkin would have known Cassidy. Some of her numerous dedication concerts around Texas may have been under his auspices,[21] and Watkin Music eventually sponsored Charles Courboin's dedication concert at McFarlin.[22] How SMU authorities selected Hillgreen, Lane to build the auditorium organ is unclear. It is likely that Bertha Cassidy was delegated license for such a decision, which, if a correct assessment, speaks favorably of the esteem with which she was held within the university community. Certainly she worked out details with the McFarlins on her visit in 1924. She already knew the McFarlins and had probably worked with them in the selection of Hillgreen, Lane, Opus 757, at McFarlin Memorial Methodist in Norman. She played the dedication recital there. Records from First United Methodist Church in Paris, Texas, for which she played the dedication of the Hillgreen, Lane organ on April 13, 1924, ambiguously refer to her as an "employee of Hillgreen, Lane."[23] It is less likely that she would have been employed by Hillgreen, Lane than that she would have been hired by Watkin. A subcontractor himself for the larger firm, it would have been Watkin's responsibility to tend to the details for each job, whether that entailed engaging a trusted consultant at the request of an organ committee or booking a local recitalist for the dedication concert.[24] Given Cassidy's standing in the musical community, her cooperation would have been an asset for any organ company or their local installer. A 1938 article stated that she "has planned specifications for more than 200 organs in Texas," implying that she played an important role in the purchase and design of new organs in addition to simply playing their dedications. Between 1915 and 1930, Hillgreen, Lane installed about one hundred organs throughout Texas. Even assuming she was involved with all of them, this implies that she also designed instruments by other firms.[25]

On May 4, 1925, representatives for Hillgreen, Lane, under the auspices of Will A. Watkin Company, and representatives for Robert McFarlin drew up a contract to build a four-manual, forty-four-rank organ for the auditorium and a three-manual, six-rank "studio" organ for a small recital hall within the building, for a combined sum of $25,000, although university and local papers routinely and inaccurately quoted that amount as the value of the main organ alone.[26] The instrument installed in the organ studio, a large room on the second floor, had three manuals and sixteen stops, and was almost a copy of Cassidy's home organ. An 8′ Bourdon, 8′ Dulciana, and 8′ Flute comprised the Great, and an 8′ Salicional, 8′ Stopped Flute, and 4′ Flute made up the Swell, with the ubiquitous 16′ Bourdon in the Pedal. Both organs were equipped with swell pedals for every division, suggesting that even the larger organ was mostly, if not completely, expressive.[27]

By mid-April 1926, the School of Music had occupied its new building, having vacated the cramped quarters in the basement of the Women's Building and the third floor of Dallas Hall. A notice in the *Semi-Weekly Campus* suggests that the second Hillgreen, Lane organ had not been completed by the building dedication: "The three-manual Hillgreen, Lane & Company, practice pipe organ on the second floor, installed by the Will A. Watkin Company, has been completed and is ready for use. C. H. Brick, organ tuner, connected with the firm, tuned both organs last week. According to Mr. Brick, the organs have to be tuned every week or two weeks, and the Will A. Watkin Company will keep Mr. Brick here until a regular tuner is employed by the university."[28]

The organ rehearsal studio in McFarlin Auditorium. Meadows School of the Arts Records, SMU Archives, DeGolyer Library, SMU.

Studio Organ
McFarlin Memorial Auditorium
Southern Methodist University, Dallas
Hillgreen, Lane & Co., Opus 823 (1926)[29]

I. CHOIR (duplexed from Great)

8 Dulciana (Gt.)

8 Flute (Gt.)

4 Flute (Gt.)

2 Flute (Gt.)

III. SWELL (enclosed)

8 Salicional

8 Stopped Flute

4 Flute (ext. 8')

PEDAL

16 Bourdon (ext. Gt. Flute)

8 Open Flute (Gt.)

ACCESSORIES

Three combination pistons were available for each division.

Great to Pedal reversible

Crescendo Pedal

II. GREAT (enclosed)

8 Open Diapason

8 Dulciana

8 Flute

4 Flute (ext. 8')

2⅔ Twelfth (ext. 8')

2 Piccolo (ext. 8')

COUPLERS

Swell to Swell 16, 4

Swell to Great 16, 8, 4

Choir to Great 16, 8, 4

Swell to Choir 16, 8, 4

Great to Great 4

Great to Pedal 8

Swell to Pedal 8

Swell Quint to Pedal

Choir to Pedal 8

McFarlin Memorial Auditorium
Southern Methodist University
Hillgreen, Lane & Co., Opus 822 (1926)[30]

GREAT (enclosed)
  16 Open Diapason
   8 First Diapason
   8 Second Diapason
   8 Third Diapason (ext. 16')
   8 Melodia
   8 Gamba
   8 Doppel Flute
   8 Gemshorn
   4 Octave
     Mixture III (synthetic)
   4 Flute d'Amour
   2 Fifteenth
  16 Trombone
   8 Tuba (ext. 16')
   4 Clarion (ext. 16')
     Harp Marimba

SWELL (enclosed)
  16 Bourdon
   8 Diapason
   8 Viole d'Orchestre
   8 Salicional
   8 Vox Celeste (t.c.)
   8 Gedeckt (ext. 16')
   8 Hohl Flute
   4 Flute harmonique (ext. 16')
   4 Violina
   2 Piccolo (ext. 16')
     Dolce Cornet III

ECHO (enclosed; playable from
  Solo or Great)
   8 Echo Salicional
   8 Vox Angelica
   8 Echo Flute
   4 Rohr Flute
   8 Vox Humana
     Cathedral Chimes

PEDAL
  32 Resultant
  16 Double Diapason Major
  16 Double Diapason Minor (Gt.)
  16 Bourdon
  16 Violine
  16 Lieblich Gedeckt (Sw.)
   8 Flute (ext. 16')
   8 Dolce (ext. Sw. 16')
   8 Cello (ext. Violone)
   4 Violone (ext. 16')
  16 Trombone (ext. Solo)
   8 Tuba (Gt)
   4 Tuba Clarion (Gt)

COUPLERS
Swell to Pedal
Swell Quint to Pedal
Great to Pedal
Choir to Pedal
Solo to Pedal 8, 4

8 Cornopean

8 Oboe

8 Vox Humana

CHOIR (enclosed)

8 Violin Diapason

8 Dulciana

8 Unda Maris (t.c.)

8 Quintadena

8 Concert Flute

4 Forest Flute

8 Clarinet

SOLO (enclosed)

8 Stentorphone

8 Gross Gamba

8 Gamba Celeste (t.c.)

8 Tibia Clausa

4 Flute

16 Ophicleide

8 Tuba Marabilis

(ext. Ophicleide)

8 French Horn

4 Tuba Clarion

(ext. Ophicleide)

Echo to Pedal

Swell to Great 16, 8, 4

Swell to Swell 16, Unison Off, 4

Swell to Choir 16, 8, 4

Choir to Great 16, 8, 4

Choir to Choir 16, Unison Off, 4

Solo to Great 16, 8, 4

Solo to Solo 16, 4

Great to Solo 8

Solo to Choir 8

Great to Great 16, Unison Off, 4

COMBINATION PISTONS

Great and Pedal: 5

Swell and Pedal: 6

Choir and Pedal: 5

Solo and Echo: 5

Master Pistons: 5

MECHANICALS

Balanced Great, Swell, Choir,
    Solo and Echo pedals.

Balanced Crescendo pedal

REVERSIBLES

Great-Pedal

Sforzando

ACCESSORIES

Separate Great, Choir, Echo,
    Solo tremolos

Wind and Crescendo indicators

The main organ was located in chambers on either side of the stage, playable from a moveable theater-style console.

Surely these quarters, providing sufficient practice, teaching, and performance spaces, would have seemed refreshingly luxurious to organ professor and students alike, with the new building gradually assuming the role of an artistic hub for the greater community.

Newspaper accounts provide an indication not only of how frequently the organ was played during these early years but also of the literature the faculty and students performed. Bertha Cassidy initiated weekly Wednesday afternoon "organ hours" in February 1927, at which she demonstrated "perfect control over the mighty McFarlin Organ." For the first program she performed Buck's "Descriptive Piece—On the Coast," the March from Widor's Second Symphony, MacMasters's *Pastorale*, the Fire Magic from Wagner's *Die Walküre*, and Schumann's *Sketch in F Minor*.[31] By 1928 the weekly recitals had migrated to Sunday afternoons at 5:00 p.m. In one such performance in April, Mrs. Homer Chapman, "a senior student at the university," played the Recit and Finale from Mendelssohn's First Sonata, Federlein's *Serenata*, Coerne's *Nocturne*, Tchaikovsky's *Humoresque*, the "Volga Boat Song" and Franck's Choral in A minor. Mrs. Chapman had accompanied Bertha Cassidy on her visit to the McFarlins in 1924.[32] The *Dallas Morning News* published reviews of some of these concerts that sometimes counted only eight people in the audience, although, "notwithstanding the pathetic size of the audience, Mrs. Homer Chapman pluckily went through her program on the Noble McFarlin Auditorium organ and played beautifully, as if inspired by the sea of dun-colored chair backs."[33] The dun-colored chair backs apparently inspired numerous student and faculty recitals that were broadcast each week over WFAA radio.[34] Regular organ recitals included guest performers on occasion, including Henry Valentine Stearns, organist at Washburn College in Topeka, who played a recital in March 1927, the first event of a three-day celebration commemorating the first anniversary of McFarlin Auditorium. The one thousand people in the audience, of which five hundred were SMU students, heard music of Bach, Karg-Elert, Debussy, Rheinberger, Foote, Yon, and Bonnet, among others.[35] Only a month earlier, Palmer Christian, head of the Organ department at the University of Michigan, performed a recital of Bach, Karg-Elert, Hollins, Vivaldi, Corelli, Wagner, Dickinson, Russell, and Saint-Saëns, with assistance from various local musicians.[36]

New Growth, New Faculty

Already by the 1925–1926 academic term, growth within the organ department had necessitated hiring two additional organ instructors, Mrs. Annie Byrd Ward Whaling and Miss Dora Poteet. Born in Houston in 1891 to Methodist Bishop Seth Ward and Margaret Elizabeth South Ward, Annie Whaling's Texas roots were extensive and deep and exemplified the faculty's regional nature in those first decades. Bishop Ward, born in 1858, was the first Texan to be appointed a Methodist bishop and fostered interest in Methodist universities throughout his career. Ward himself had urged Robert Stewart Hyer to consider founding a Methodist university in Dallas, and his death in 1909 had motivated Hyer's design for a Pantheon-like, "memorial" building on Southwestern University's campus to honor the bishop.[37] Although never rendered on that university's campus, the memorial building to Bishop Ward eventually materialized as Dallas Hall on the SMU campus. The Methodist Church established the short-lived Seth Ward College (1910–1916) near Plainview, Texas, resulting in the founding of the eponymous town of Seth Ward.[38]

Annie Byrd Ward studied organ with Hu T. Huffmaster at St. Paul's Methodist Church in Houston, and by the age of 17 was appointed organist of Central Christian Church in Houston.[39] By the next year she was listed as assistant organist at St. Paul's Methodist, assisting her teacher.[40] In 1911 she married the Reverend Horace Moreland Whaling,[41] who joined the theology faculty at the new university in Dallas, eventually becoming a vice president of SMU and minister at the newly founded Highland Park Methodist Church on campus.[42]

On moving to Dallas, First Methodist Church hired Annie Whaling as organist, a position that had been held by Bertha Cassidy from 1904 to 1907. For reasons that are unclear, she resigned in 1922 to be succeeded by 16-year-old Dora Poteet, characterized by the *Dallas Morning News* as possibly "the youngest musician in the State holding as responsible a position as the charge she now has."[43] Poteet and Whaling worked together from the 1925–1926 school year until the Whalings' retirement to Austin in 1937—several years after Cassidy's official retirement. Nothing in the records indicates acrimony between the two; rather, the newspaper account states that Poteet had worked for six months as assistant organist, presumably under Whaling, before taking over her organist duties. Perhaps Annie Whaling had taught the younger organist to thrive in one of Dallas's prominent church positions, launching a career that, at that time, was more dependent upon holding prestigious posts than collecting academic or conservatory degrees. The two women eventually ended up guiding the organ program beyond Bertha Cassidy's retirement through the arduous years of the Great Depression.

The three women must have collaborated well, as all three shared the same positions at First Methodist, the Scottish Rite Cathedral, and Temple Emanu-El, often assisting one another. Annie Whaling is first mentioned in 1923 as playing at the Scottish Rite Cathedral,[44] the year after her resignation from First Methodist Church. By 1930 Whaling is mentioned playing officially at Temple Emanu-El.[45] Dora Poteet played at the Scottish Rite Cathedral and even occasionally at the temple in subsequent years.

By the mid-1920s, Bertha Cassidy was managing a busy concert career that required frequent travel across the state, and she was organist at First Baptist, the Scottish Rite Cathedral, and Temple Emanu-El, in addition to her teaching duties at SMU, which, before the completion of McFarlin Auditorium, required her to supervise lessons and practice in her home. In late 1927 Cassidy also began teaching at Southwestern Baptist Theological Seminary in Fort Worth, an institution that also possessed a Hillgreen, Lane organ.[46] Although her years as founding dean of the Texas Chapter of the AGO (now the Dallas Chapter) had passed, she remained active in that organization. Even a cursory glimpse at the archival records reveals a woman whose accomplishment, energy, and devotion to her craft led to a career that could result in exhaustion.[47] Thus, when her protégé, Dora Poteet, graduated in 1925, Cassidy hired Poteet as instructor of organ.[48] Hiring Annie Whaling as associate professor of organ was likely also a matter of opportunity. She had been associated with the university through her husband for almost a decade. Both of these hires would have reduced Cassidy's workload.

That the organ department was growing is evidenced by a 1926 archival document that details the "collections" of each department within the School of Music. This is not necessarily reflective of personal pay, although it is broken down per faculty member. At $25,579, the four faculty of the piano department brought in the most earnings, with the two vocal faculty listed as bringing in $6,451 in total revenue, followed by Bertha Cassidy as the sole faculty member of the organ department earning $3,105. Walter Fried, the violin professor, brought in $2,556 the same year.[49] But with the School of Music having grown to 202 students by 1928, all three organ instructors had to summon the energy to teach an organ studio that A. H. Henning claimed was "one of the largest in the South."[50] The growing organ department taxed the two new instruments, and in the summer of 1928 a third organ was installed in the School of Music facilities:

> Because of the increasing number of organ pupils in the music school a new organ was bought and established in McFarlin Memorial auditorium this summer, it was learned Tuesday. This instrument, a two-manual Estey organ, was installed in the closed space between the organ room and the studio of Mrs. J. Roscoe Golden, on the second floor——of the auditorium. It is a reed organ and is in a box resembling an electric piano. The Estey organ makes the third installed in the building. . . . The increase in organ classes made necessary the purchase of the new instrument. Senior organ recitals are given on the large organ

in the auditorium; student recitals are given in the organ room. The new organ will be used as a practice instrument for the pupils of all three organ teachers in the department.[51]

This brief notice clarifies the distinctive purposes for each instrument: all students practiced on the Estey, junior and studio recitals were given on the small Hillgreen, Lane, and senior recitals were performed on the large instrument.

Curriculum and Repertoire

The addition of two organ teachers had no bearing on repertoire requirements found in the course catalogs of the late 1920s. A studio recital advertised in the *Dallas Morning News* in December 1928 details the repertoire played by all three of the professors' students on the diminutive Hillgreen, Lane organ in the recital hall.[52] Lemmens's *Chorus of Shepherds* and Cherpachov's *The Shepherd's Pipes* establish the theme of the program that continues with Hamblen's "O Babe Divine," and two pieces entitled "Christmas" by d'Antalffy and Gaul, followed by George Elmore's *Birthday of a King* and Dudley Buck's *The Holy Night. Cantique de Noël* by Adam and *Fantasia on "Joy to the World"* by Lemare concluded the recital. A 1932 solo recital performed by Annie Whaling on the main organ at McFarlin Auditorium included *Heroic Piece* by Rossiter Cole, *Chanson* of Candlyn, Bingham's *Twilight*, the *Scherzo* by Meale, Wagner's "Dreams," and *Fiat Lux* of Théodore Dubois.[53] In another recital from 1932, under the enticing headline of "Nevin's *Sketches* on S.M.U. Organ Program," Annie Whaling performed a Bach cantata movement transcription, Russell's "Up the Saguenay," "Scherzo" from James H. Rogers's *Sacred Suite*, and *I Am the Resurrection and the Life* by de la Tombelle, in addition to Nevin's *Sketches*.[54] Dora Poteet, whose repertoire eventually earned her acclaim throughout the United States, in 1928 was still playing many character pieces. The organ department during this era sought not to create concert performers but to nurture competent church players who could render music creditably in Protestant churches largely within Texas. Whether these ambitions could be considered modest or simply pragmatic reflects the cultural shift that ensued during subsequent decades in which music for its own sake, and consequently performance at its highest standard, gained precedence over more utilitarian liturgical music.

This concern for the utility and ultimate employability of all School of Music graduates prompted the development of a curriculum in Practical Church Music, first noted in the 1925 course catalog, directed by choral and vocal professor J. Abner Sage. Coursework, developed as a collaborative venture between the theology and music schools, included instruction in voice, piano, music appreciation, ear training, hymnology, organ, orchestration, conducting, music history, music theory, and the "interpretation of song," leading to a certificate in practical church music after two years.[55] In 1927 the School of Theology lists a course dedicated to church music, specifically intended for ministerial students, but discerningly prescient in its realization that ministers would have to converse cogently about musical matters, just as the church music courses for musicians acknowledged the most likely venue for their music making. This course, also taught by Professor Sage, was intended as "a study of the use of music in public worship; a practical application of the hymn book in the minister's work; elements of voice training; leadership of congregational singing. The *Methodist Hymnal* forms the basis for the course. Various works on hymnology are used as guides in the study of the subject. It is required that both words and music of many standard hymns be memorized."[56] This rigorous course portends the eventual formation of the master of sacred music (MSM) program in the late 1950s, both being borne out of the realization that ministers and musicians needed to possess basic competencies in each other's fields.

The Cassidys' European Sojourn

During the summer of 1927, Bertha Cassidy and her daughter, Viola, who by this time had graduated with an organ performance degree from her mother's studio, journeyed to England and Germany on a brief study tour. This piqued the interest of the Dallas press, probably because of a combination of the rarity and difficulty of European travel coupled with Cassidy's semi-celebrity status in the local music world. A press announcement in May 1927 proclaimed that the "Cassidys will coach abroad this summer . . . [they] will sail for Europe June 11. They will study organ and oratorio interpretation with Dr. Cyril B. Rootham in St. John's College, Cambridge University, England, and organ with Dr. Seigfried Karg Elert at the Leipsic Conservatory. They plan also to attend the International Festival of New Music to be held at Frankfort am Main, Germany."[57] Such was the interest in her travels that the *Dallas Morning News* published her own accounts of her trip, the first of which was written from Cambridge on June 26:

> Organs and organists of England were the chief interests of two Dallas musicians who landed just the other day at Liverpool. We went straight to the Liverpool Cathedral to hear England's greatest organ played by Henry Goss Custard, a noted virtuoso, who has been booked for American recitals next season.
>
> The Liverpool Cathedral organ is truly a fine modern instrument and responded wonderfully to Bach's St. Ann Fugue and Dvorak's Largo. The choir voices were pure and full-toned with an excellent tenor solo done by Welsh Evans. The teamwork, however, between choir and organist was not quite so good. This state of affairs is found in almost all large European cathedrals.
>
> Next we made on to marvelous Cambridge. . . . At St. John we found Dr. Rootham as permanent organist and director of all Cambridge's music. He is a thorough scholar, which fact does not mitigate his charming personality. . . .
>
> Dr. Rootham has a rare and incessant enthusiasm for Bach and Handel, whose works are the devotion of a lifetime.
>
> He is a busy man with his artistic and executive duties, but he found much time to show many courtesies to us Texans. He is alert and objective and became strangely interested in such a community as Dallas. He listened with keen attention to what we had to tell him about music in our home city. He was aghast at the opera season, the symphony orchestra, and the oratorio work that features Dallas' annual activities and could not conceive of

such things in what he believes is the wild and woolly North American West. . . .

The quaint old organs in the college chapels with their odd ornamentations resemble nothing so much as Chinese houses lifted aloft in the center of rooms. The tonal quality of these instruments is clear and pure, but there are no sympathetic string stops and their broad effect is one of cold monotony.

The organ in St. John, which is Dr. Rootham's, has been rebuilt recently. In listening to it we found it most satisfactory in the Bach chorales.[58]

As Cassidy intimates, Cyril Bradley Rootham (1881–1938), conductor of the Cambridge University Musical Society, a fellow of St. John's College, and composer in his own right, championed early music in his role as a member of the Purcell Society Committee.[59] Counting Arthur Bliss among his students, Dr. Rootham likewise advocated modern music, staging the first English performance of Honegger's *King David*, and was elected a Fellow of the Royal College of Music in 1933.[60] Presumably, Viola and Bertha Cassidy would have availed themselves of Rootham's expertise in oratorio conducting, but whether they coached with him or merely observed, the elder Cassidy does not state.

Their sojourn to England must have been brief, as her next missive is written from Leipzig on July 8:

The traveling Dallasites are now in Leipzig, where we gratified an ambition to see and hear Siegfried Karg-Elert, proclaimed in one of the latest musical books as the foremost living composer for the organ. This opinion is shared by most American and English organists. His German colleagues are inclined to be jealous and withhold supreme indorsement. His greatness, however, is undeniable. . . .

We had no trouble gaining an audience with him or in remaining in his good graces. This was accomplished by showing him programs of Dallas organ recitals in which his programs were used. He was grateful for this sign of appreciation in a spot so far away. He also expressed approval of the class of organ music presented in Dallas.

We spent a day with him in his conservatory. We found him running to and fro among his students wearing a Swiss costume . . . We thought he resembled a jolly Schubert. He is a stout little fellow.[61]

Bertha Cassidy further described his pedagogical style as "eccentric": "He alternately joshes and rails at his students. . . . One very talented German boy played a number for us. During the performance Dr. Karg-Elert made grimaces behind his back. At the conclusion he praised the lad to his face. As the boy left Dr. Karg-Elert turned to us and remarked, 'Some day he will learn emotion is of the heart and not of the body.'" The Cassidys later met Frau Karg-Elert and their daughter, Katherina, at his home, where "he played on the harmonium for us for two solid hours and evoked complete orchestral effects from the instrument." Marveling at his "enormous creative activity," which Karg-Elert himself attributed to smoking 120 cigarettes a day and sleeping only three hours a night, Mrs. Cassidy concludes her report noting that "American-built instruments are more adequate for his compositions than the English."[62] The Cassidys' contact with the noted composer entailed organ lessons as well, as the elder Cassidy, in her subsequent performing career, always included mention of her study with Karg-Elert when writing her biographical particulars.

Karg-Elert himself writes in a letter to Godfrey Sceats on July 15, 1927, that "I seriously intend to take English lessons on my return, actually from an interpreter from whom I have already worked. In the few lessons I gave Mrs. and Miss Cassidy from Texas, it was he who translated our conversation (did you ever!? The ladies paid him $50 per hour!!! [Perhaps he meant per lesson?] Yes, yes—America, the land of dollars)."[63] To Karg-Elert at this point in his career, and to most people suffering through the inflation of the Weimar Republic, $50, or about 210 German marks, would have seemed an exorbitant sum, and it is possible something may have been lost in translation. Adjusted for inflation, $50 in 1927 is about $775 in 2021 dollars.[64] Whether the translator was paid $50 per lesson, or, more likely, $50 for his entire service over a series of lessons, Karg-Elert implies a brief duration of study, comprising only a "few lessons." Mrs. Cassidy's letter was written on July 8, with Karg-Elert's written only nineteen days later and after the Cassidys' departure. Even allowing the possibility that the Cassidys had been in Leipzig for several days by July 8, their entire course of study with Karg-Elert must have been brief, as the Cassidys were in Frankfurt am Main by July 15, the date of another letter back home from the observant organ professor.[65] Although Karg-Elert discreetly failed to note his price for lessons, it is not unreasonable to assume he was paid at least as much per lesson as the translator, given the primary purpose of their trip to Europe was to study with him and Dr. Rootham. The Cassidys concluded their European sojourn with a visit to the Bayreuth Festival in August.[66]

Organ study with Sigfrid Karg-Elert must have been a highlight of Bertha Cassidy's career. Whether her experience with Dr. Rootham was less productive or the nature of her study with him was more as an observer than a student, any professional connections with him would fail to bear the same fruit as did her personal connection with Karg-Elert. She did not include study with Rootham in her future professional biographical descriptions. If Karg-Elert's music had appeared on Dallas programs only sporadically prior to 1927, it now received singular attention and become a staple of Dallas organists' repertoire, due to the tireless championing of the Cassidys. On the dedication recital of the Hillgreen, Lane, Opus 905, at First Baptist Church in Bryan, Texas, in May 1928, Bertha performed Karg-Elert's *Canzona*,[67] which she repeated at Highland Park Methodist Church in Dallas for the convention of the Texas Chapter of the AGO.[68] In November 1928, in the church music weekly details as published in the paper, she is listed as performing Karg-Elert's *Chorale* for Friday services at Temple Emanu-El.[69]

Viola Cassidy, often overshadowed by her mother's professional accomplishments, seems also to have been inspired by her lessons

Viola Cassidy. Rotunda Collection, SMU Archives, DeGolyer Library, SMU.

with Karg-Elert, holding a Mu Phi Epsilon chapter meeting at her home on Lindenwood Avenue in February 1929, which, although led by Dora Poteet, featured a lecture by the young "Miss Cassidy, who traveled in Europe two years ago . . . [and] will talk on Leipsig as a music center." In what certainly represents a departure from the picturesque show pieces of earlier years, the four performers (among whom were neither Poteet nor Cassidy) played a *Minuet* by C. P. E. Bach, Rheinberger's *Phantasia*, Mendelssohn's Second Sonata, and Karg-Elert's *Canzona*.[70] In April 1930 Evelyn Foreman, a "senior organ pupil" of Cassidy, performed for her senior recital Karg-Elert's *Legend of the Mountain*, in addition to all three movements of Bach's Concerto in G Major and Sowerby's *In Autumn*.[71] Ever vigilant for opportunities to spread word of his music to other organists, at the May 1931 meeting of the Texas Chapter of the AGO in Fort Worth, Mrs. Cassidy lectured on "Karg-Elert and Modern Music."[72] Karg-Elert's music became a staple of organ recitals at SMU and by local organists during the initial years of the Great Depression.

Sigfrid Karg-Elert Visits SMU

By early 1932 Bertha Cassidy had extended an invitation to Sigfrid Karg-Elert to perform at McFarlin Auditorium as part of his transcontinental tour. The concert seems to have been arranged rather hastily, as the first notice of it appears only on January 10, 1932, albeit in the most radiant of terms:

> The visit to America of the famous Dr. Siegfried Karg-Elert, organist and composer of Leipzig, will be utilized by a former pupil, Mrs. J. H. Cassidy of Dallas, for the purpose of bringing the noted musician to Dallas. Mrs. Cassidy, head of the organ department of Southern Methodist University, will present Dr. Karg-Elert in the McFarlin Memorial Auditorium on the night of Feb. 19, a Friday. Mrs. Cassidy will be assisted in her arrangements by the Texas Chapter of the American Guild of Organists. Dr. Karg-Elert's compositions for organ, voice, piano and the kunst-harmonium have been prolific. As a virtuoso of the organ he has been proclaimed by some to be the greatest since Bach or since what they understand Bach to have been.[73]

The tour, in which he was joined by his daughter Katharina, was not a successful one for the composer, who by this time was suffering from diabetes and had only one year to live. His diary of the performances, concerts for which he was much lauded before his arrival, reflects a man beset by frail health and nagging personal doubts. In his diary he describes his arrival in Dallas, but his account circa February 15–18 neglects any mention of his performance: "Here in Dallas it looks good: cacti in the street, plants in bloom around the houses, no snow as always up until now, and also no slush. The Cassidys are unpretentious, lovely people. They have a fine house—with an organ of course; some Germans were with them at the railway-station, and because the 'Adolphus' (our hotel) is too expensive and too far away, they have asked us to stay in the house of a dear lady from Koenigsberg."[74]

There are hints concerning his silence about the concert. A notice in the paper the morning of the concert politely suggests he was disappointed in the organ:

> Dr. Sigrid Karg-Elert, composer, pedagogue and organist of Leipzig, Germany, has made several changes in his invitational program . . .
>
> The announced program was one which the noted visitor arranged for his concerts in Germany. Since concertizing in Canada and the United States, the organist has found that the American organ is not adaptable for proper playing of Franck's Suite Brétonique in F Sharp Minor, Rossi's Due Pezzi Per Organ Portative, Bach's Echo in M Minor from B Minor Partiti. In place of these numbers, the program will include a group of his own compositions, titled "Three Impressions," Liszt's Benediction Dieu Dans La Solitude in F Sharp Major and Bach's Sonata in C Minor.
>
> Dr. Sigrid and his daughter, Kitty, arrived in Dallas Thursday and are guests of Mr and Mrs Harold Hart Todd. . . . The daughter acts as secretary and manager for her father, who does not converse in English.[75]

Karg-Elert made adaptations to the announced program at other locations, too, so these cannot be seen as an indictment solely of the Hillgreen, Lane organ, or even of American organ building in general, but of Karg-Elert's failure to understand the American organ situation.[76]

The media silence following his concert stands in stark contrast to the fanfare he was initially accorded. Perhaps reflective of the Dallas media's obsequious attitude toward its musical community, the only cogent review comes from a self-proclaimed organ "layman" who reminds the reader that "by this time you may have suspected that we have only a scant notion what we are writing about." Nonetheless, John Rosenfield Jr. observes:

> With good judgment that Mrs. Cassidy and her associates took the recital out of the field of commerce. We laymen of Dallas probably realize that the world of the pipe organ is an esthetic green pasture but, for some reason or another, we have never visited it. . . . It was for the specific purpose of sowing the thought that the pipe organ is an instrument of virtuosity and has a evolutionary literature that Mrs. Cassidy et al. brought this important organist to Dallas.
>   Nor was it as simple as all this. No two organs are alike and the mill-run of American outfits fall short of the resources of the European organ—so we are told. Dr. Karg-Elert, after inspecting the admirable device in McFarlin Auditorium, was forced to change his program to numbers that might be played [on that organ]. . . .
>   Although our education in pipe organ can not be accomplished at one sitting, we enjoyed Friday night, a thorough primer course.[77]

Whether the other 1,500 people in the invitation-only audience were as lukewarmly enamored with the sounds evoked from the organ that evening is unknown, for nothing else of substance was written about the program. An honest, if punitive, review by organist and composer Harvey Gaul of Karg-Elert's recital in Pittsburgh the next month perhaps sums up why this tour was disastrous for the composer:

> What is tone-psychology in Berlin is one thing, and what it is in Boston or Brookline (or Beltzhoover, for that matter) is another, and to the untutored ears of Pittsburgh the constant use of the tierce, the sesquialtera, the sesquioctava and the quint, all

super-coupled and all shriller than a two-foot piccolo is a degree of monotony at times hardly bearable.

Registration is purely a matter of taste (and inheritance) and what is one man's idea of tonal building is another man's hurdy gurdy. . . .

He opened badly with an extended improvisation called "In Memoriam," with a peculiar tempoed Bach sonata, and then came Liszt and some good Karg-Elert, and the virtuoso appeared and the recital began in earnest.

There was stupendous playing in the Karg-Elert "Partita," with a "Minuetto Melanconico," tremendously idiomatic and a "Toccata-Finale" that was a masterpiece of virtuosity. . . .

The composer's daughter accompanied him and accompanied is the word because she sometimes provided extra chords, making a four-hand arrangement of the compositions. She also assisted in registration.

A large audience was present (one didn't know there were that many organists in Allegheny county) and in many ways it was the most illuminating recital of recent years.[78]

Whether this was a fair assessment or not, it seems representative of critical views of his tour. That the Dallas press refrained from deprecations speaks more to its cultivating a civic persona worthy of such performers than its approbation of the actual music itself. That Dallas, through the impetus of SMU's organ department, could attract performers who stopped in New York City, Pittsburgh, and San Francisco speaks to its advancement since frontier-town days. Even a humble performance was worth celebrating in a town still with "cacti in the streets."

Mrs. Cassidy's Retirement

Bertha Stevens Cassidy, having guided SMU's organ department from its inception, announced her retirement in the autumn of 1933, effective at the end of the academic year, citing the "necessity for a diminishing of musical activities."[79] Holding the organist positions at First Baptist, Temple Emanu-El, and still teaching students "as many as fourteen hours a day," Cassidy, at the age of 57, had elected to retire from the school "in order to have more leisure."[80]

Her husband had become president of Egan Printing Company earlier that year, probably alleviating any financial concerns the family may have had and further impressing on her the duties of a society housewife of the era. Her "farewell recital to Southern Methodist University" was held in June 1934, in which she was joined by fellow faculty colleagues Walter Fried, violinist, and Harold Hart Todd, pianist, the solo organ pieces being among the more rigorous in her repertoire:

Prelude and Fugue in G minor	Bach
Fantasia on Chorale "Ad Nos"	Liszt
Adagio from Sixth Symphony	Widor
Finale in B Flat	Dupré[81]

Bertha Cassidy's musical dynamism continued in her retirement. In June 1935 she played the organ dedication at Tyler Street Methodist Church in a lighter program of transcriptions and character pieces;[82] later that year she rededicated the recently electrified Hook & Hastings organ at First Presbyterian Church in Palestine, Texas, where she was joined by soprano Mrs. C. H. Brick, presumably the wife of Mr. Brick, the sometime organ tuner at McFarlin.[83] Although retirement was not without leisure, her actual vacations warranted a 1937 newspaper notice entitled, "Mrs. Cassidy Returns, Resume Music Duties." Seemingly more interested in her return to work than in her artistic proclivities, "Mr. and Mrs. J. H. Cassidy have returned from a vacation in New Mexico and Arizona art colonies, and Mrs. Cassidy will take up her duties as choir director and organist for the First Baptist Church for the seventeenth year."[84] She returned to play at SMU at times, being invited by the University Women's Club to perform at McFarlin in November 1936, underscoring the good relations she still must have had with her colleagues there.[85] A retrospective article published in 1938 noted that

she had resigned because of her exhausting schedule in professional and club circles. With nineteen years of professorship
behind her, the organist still is busy as director of the choir at
the First Baptist Church—or, specifically, four choirs of 140
members. This is in addition to her extensive participation in
such clubs as the Daughters of the American Revolution, University Women's Club and the Dallas Woman's Club, all of which
she is serving as music committee member. . . .

Composition is one of Mrs. Cassidy's avocations. She has
published a junior choir book, songs for male quartets and
arrangements for girls' choruses.[86]

Mrs. Cassidy's penchant for composition seems to have been encouraged by Robert H. Coleman, an assistant pastor and "director of
congregational singing" at First Baptist Church.[87] Among his publications is *Coleman's Male Choir* (1928), which contains several of
her hymn settings, including one Christmas hymn, "Make Room for
Jesus," which is a collaboration between her and her daughter, Viola,
who wrote the text.[88]

James Harvey Cassidy, of Irish stock and an entrepreneur, served
as an executive of Egan Printing Company and a related business,
Cassidy Realty. It was perhaps because of his real estate acumen that
the Cassidy family moved at least four times in that many decades,
with each large home having sufficient space for the pipe organ.
Their final home, purchased in the mid-1930s on leafy Lakewood
Boulevard, became a center for society functions involving civic,
business, or musical affairs, with the Estey organ still a focus for
many events.[89] Census records suggest a family of financial means
with household staff up through 1940, possibly allowing both
Cassidys the freedom to pursue their own professional interests.[90]
However, the family's circumstances changed with Mr. Cassidy's
death in August 1941.[91] Bertha and Viola, who had lived with her
parents most of her life, moved into a home on Ellsworth Avenue
less than half the size of their previous house. No further mention
is made of the Estey organ, and the extant, modest bungalow house

on Ellsworth is hardly conducive to a domestic pipe organ. Without James Cassidy's income, perhaps the instrument was sold to raise funds. Bertha Cassidy continued to host club meetings at her new home at least until 1947, although they had become greatly reduced.[92]

In 1945 Cassidy retired from First Baptist Church. The *Dallas Morning News* wrote:

> Mrs. J. H. Cassidy will leave the console July 1 and call it a career. The highly respected church organist, choir director and pedagogue announced Monday that she will retire from the musical direction of the First Baptist Church July 1 and accept no other church position. Her successor has not been chosen. . . .
>
> Mrs. Cassidy was organizer and first dean of the Texas chapter of the American Guild of Organists. She was influential in bringing to Dallas fifteen years ago Dr. Siegfried Karg-Elert of Leipzig, late master of the console and called by some the greatest of this generation.
>
> "I promised myself to quit long ago," she explained. "I am long past the time I had given myself for active work. I think the way should be left open for the new and younger musicians."[93]

Perhaps her retirement had been hastened by the death the previous year of George Truett (1867–1944), for almost fifty years pastor at First Baptist. His successor, W. A. Criswell, wrote lovingly of Bertha Cassidy's tenure as organist:

> She has taken her work as director of our music program as prayerfully and as seriously as any of the God-called workers in our fellowship. After my coming here as pastor of the church, Mrs. Cassidy expressed a desire to retire from her heavy responsibilities because of her length of service and because of strenuous work. . . . She has been truly a great help and a worthy Christian co-laborer. Mrs. Cassidy thinks now that these beginning days are past and that in order to conserve her best health she should give up this work. It is with regret and with deepest

gratitude for what she has meant to me and to the whole church that we see her turn over the task to other hands.[94]

Dr. Criswell goes on to assure the congregation that the assistant organist will take over some duties, another person will take over the morning choir, and another will take over the evening choir.

In a 1948 celebration marking the thirtieth anniversary of the Texas Chapter of the AGO, Mrs. Cassidy was honored for her musical service, one of the highlights of which was her founding of the chapter. "The dean, Mrs. W. E. Bloomdahl, presided and paid tribute to Mrs. Cassidy, who responded with an account of how this chapter came into existence. . . . Mrs. Walter E. Alexander, representing former Cassidy pupils and members of the chapter, presented to the honoree a certificate of life membership from the Guild Headquarters in New York City."[95] In late 1950 Viola Cassidy, who had held a succession of local organ posts, including most recently at Ross Avenue Baptist Church, and was always a partner in her mother's musical adventures, died at home of cancer.[96] From 1952 until 1959, the School of Music honored the younger Cassidy's memory with an award presented to outstanding organ students, recipients having included Mary Elizabeth Moore (1952),[97] Mary Annette Hill (1955?),[98] Joy Anne Moore (1956),[99] Ruby Bloxum Eubanks (1957),[100] Barbara Marquart (1958),[101] and Howard Ross (1959).[102]

Following her daughter's death, and after four decades of life as a minor celebrity in a city striving for elusive cultural significance, the media went silent about Mrs. Cassidy in the 1950s. On June 27, 1959, Bertha Stevens Cassidy died at her home at age 83, her death certificate offering the clinical explanation that she died of "senility and malnutrition," a condition from which she had suffered for five years.[103] With no surviving children or relatives in Texas, and her previous wealth probably long depleted, it was an inglorious end to an illustrious career and life spent in service of the pipe organ, the Dallas organ culture, and the SMU organ department.

Her students, those who studied with her privately as well as those at SMU, were legion, and her recitals throughout the region brought organ music to small communities where she was an esteemed musical guest. Her musical tendencies had been formed by her era. She was no more progressive in outlook than Karg-Elert had been in couching the Lutheran chorales in the thick harmonies of Romanticism. The *Orgelbewegung,* already in its early stages in her late career, held no appeal to her, preferring as she did transcriptions, lush character pieces, and organs with sumptuous tonal palettes to play them. Her words eulogizing her colleague from First Baptist who had installed the Hillgreen, Lanes in McFarlin Auditorium, Will A. Watkin, at his death in 1934 could be applied to her own career: "His love was always for the old masters . . . and while he took much interest in modern music, he believed that the classical music, whether in orchestral form, in oratorios or what not, was basic. He was an accomplished performer himself and his playing of the pipe organ was always very poetic. His standards were always high and he never would cater to what he considered lower ones in an effort to meet the demands of popularity."[104] Mrs. Cassidy's standards were high. She remained devoted to the musical "classics" throughout her life, despite the changing tastes of later generations who might consider some of her repertoire illegitimately chosen to cater to "the demands of popularity." This is not how she viewed herself. She advocated indefatigably for Bach's music, received as it was through a Romantic tradition. Her affinity for Baroque music extended no further than the Leipzig master. Her industriousness and vivacity in campaigning for the organ paralleled the city of Dallas's own maturing cultural values, the city providing a hospitable environment for her and her students. She did not seek to generate concert organists even in an era when organists could draw thousands of paying customers to a recital; rather, her teaching never strayed far from sacred music, that her students might always produce the best music possible from week to week. In this she was successful, modeling as she did the practical concerns of the School of Music, which, like SMU, originated as a regional institution intending to produce competent professionals in every field. Her influence in the organ world was regional rather than national but found fertile ground in a young city's burgeoning church culture, craving as it did competent organists, which Bertha Stevens Cassidy and the SMU organ department were so ably to supply during the university's first generation.

Chapter 3

Dora Poteet Barclay

I f Dora Poteet Barclay exemplified the well-meaning provincialism of the faculty and students in the early days of Southern Methodist University, she also represented the professional potential that the university envisioned for all of its scholars. SMU initially courted Texas students, relying heavily on local enrollment. A native of Cameron, Texas, near Waco, having moved to Dallas by age 15, the young Dora Poteet was precisely the type of student on which the university counted to buttress its numbers and bolster its coffers when the institution was not much more than two buildings in a sea of Johnson grass. A musician of considerable abilities whose technical prowess at the organ had been evident from an early age, meticulously honed by fine local teachers, Poteet graduated in 1925 with a degree in organ performance after only three years. Not willing to countenance the loss to the department that Poteet's departure represented, Bertha Cassidy and the music faculty appointed her as an instructor the day before her graduation, ensuring that this local organist, trained in-house, utilized her prodigious abilities to the betterment of SMU's School of Music.

Dora Poteet Barclay. Picture property of Benjamin Kolodziej,
courtesy of Dan Garland.

Youth Nurtured in Music

Dora Poteet was born on October 4, 1903, and growing up her personality was as shaped by the genteel, refined, Southern character of
her maternal lineage as it was by the academic, intellectual nature of
her father.[1] In 1906 John Poteet was appointed to teach history and
civics in the Cameron public schools.[2] He also assumed the duties
of teaching and administering Milam County's "normal" preparatory
school for teachers,[3] where he taught English, grammar, arithmetic,
physiology, and civics.[4] Poteet fostered a domestic atmosphere of
intellectual curiosity that served his daughter well. By 1914 the family
had moved to Waco,[5] where Dora studied piano with her mother and
her aunt Mollie Moore, performing her first piano recital at age eight.
By age nine she was playing piano regularly at St. John's Methodist
Church.[6] Four years later, in the summer of 1919, William Kirkpatrick,
organist of First Methodist Church in Beaumont, gave Dora Poteet her
first organ lessons, and in September 1919, Austin Avenue Methodist
Church in Waco appointed her as organist, where, on her first Sunday,
she "play[ed] pieces of great difficulty," a feat that warranted coverage
in the local paper.[7] She continued piano study with Professor Grover C.
Morris at Baylor University. The *Waco News-Tribune* in a July 1920,
piece admiringly entitled, "Waco Girl Makes Enviable Record as Pipe
Organist for Church," portrays her as a "charming, modest and unassuming girl, thoughtful and considerate, and is very popular with her
own set as well as with older people. Her ambition to excell musically
has not encroached on her desire for a fine school record. She has
finished her second year in high school, having made an average high
enough all along to be exempt from all examinations."[8] According
to former student Dr. William Teague, Dora Poteet also studied with
Carl Wiesemann,[9] at the time organist at St. Matthew's Cathedral in
Dallas, organ professor at Baylor University in Waco,[10] and eventual
dean of the New York City AGO.[11] Although there is no other primary
source documentation of her study with Dr. Wiesemann, it is probable
that she studied with him at Baylor from the autumn of 1919 until the
family's move to Dallas in late 1920. The family's final move was

necessitated by John Poteet's acceptance of a position as a director
of the YMCA. Fifteen-year-old Miss Poteet began organ lessons with
SMU organ professor Bertha Stevens Cassidy in January 1921,[12] also
enrolling at Dallas's Bryan Street High School.[13]

A Student at SMU

Already in May of 1921 she performed in one of Mrs. Cassidy's
SMU studio recitals at Oak Lawn Methodist Church, playing James
Hotchkiss Rogers's Allegro con brio from his first organ sonata
(1910), an advanced student work.[14] By November 1921 she was
assisting Annie Byrd Whaling (who later became associate professor
of organ at SMU) with duties at First Methodist Church in Dallas.
Whaling resigned in April 1922, passing responsibility for the 1894,
eighteen-rank Hook & Hastings to Dora Poteet, of whom the *Dallas
Morning News* states, "At the resignation of Mrs. Whaling it was
learned that Miss Poteet had refused several paid positions in order
to remain at her own church. . . . She has studied organ at Beaumont,
Baylor University at Waco, and in Dallas under Mrs. J. H. Cassidy and
is recognized as one of the most talented young musicians of the city."[15]
She honed her skills as a piano accompanist during these months,
frequently playing for YMCA events, presumably at the behest of her
father.[16] Poteet's high school graduation must have been in the spring
of 1922, with her studies at SMU commencing the following autumn,
as she first appears in the university yearbook published at the end
of the 1922–23 academic year.[17] In June 1922, along with four other
students of Bertha Cassidy, she received the Certificate in Church
Playing, clearly the culmination of a successful high school organ
career.[18] The university usually awarded this certificate after two years
of practical training, akin to an associate's degree.[19]

In July 1923 she traveled to New York City with Bertha Cassidy
to study with Clifford Demarest (1874–1946) and Richard Keys
Biggs (1886–1962).[20] Biggs, a noted concert organist, composer, and
founder of the Detroit Chapter of the AGO, was organist of Queen of
All Saints Church in Brooklyn.[21] It is likely that Demarest, a founder

of the AGO and an illustrious pedagogue, taught Bertha Cassidy at the same time he taught Dora Poteet, as Cassidy also always claimed Demarest as one of her own teachers. Poteet's college years were brief, and there is little record of her endeavors beyond a few recitals. In February 1924 she is listed as a charter member of the university's Bach Club, the prerequisite for which was simply the "satisfactory playing of a Bach prelude and fugue."[22] Dora Poteet's graduating recital was held at First Baptist Church, Dallas, on Tuesday, May 12, 1925. She played a joint program with graduating organists Lenoa Wilibel Huguley and Ruth Abernathy, Poteet's portion featuring the Allegro risoluto from Vierne's *Second Symphony,* the Andante from Edward Shippen Barnes's *Second Suite*, Opus 5, and the Allegro from a Handel Concerto in G minor.[23]

An incident relative to this recital speaks to the interactions between the School of Music and the city. Mrs. Cassidy had arranged for WFAA radio to broadcast this recital. The school's dean, Paul van Katwijk, hosted a weekly *Music Hour* at that same time every Tuesday, broadcast from SMU, which Mrs. Cassidy assumed her students' recital would replace that week with no extra charge, not considering that WFAA would have to set up equipment at First Baptist. When the station sent a bill of $29.50 for off-site broadcasting to SMU later that summer, Dean van Katwijk made clear that he sanctioned no such extra expenditure, but that the responsibility was to be borne solely by Mrs. Cassidy. The ensuing correspondence reveals that, despite the unforeseen expense, the School of Music appreciated the "publicity obtained" from the radio broadcasts and sought to maintain a mutually advantageous relationship with the radio station, which, after the miscommunication was acknowledged, still insisted on its off-site broadcasting fee nonetheless. The university paid the invoice.[24]

Appointed Instructor in Organ

Dora Poteet graduated with a degree in organ performance from SMU in 1925, "making such a record that she was elected to the music faculty one day before she had received her sheepskin."[25]

The *Dallas Morning News* lauded her achievement: "One of the youngest assistant instructors in the music faculty at Southern Methodist University this fall will be Miss Dora Poteet, 19 years old, it was announced by a faculty member Monday. She was graduated from S.M.U. in June with the degree of bachelor of music. She will be assistant under Mrs. J. H. Cassidy."[26] The hiring of Dora Poteet (as well as Annie Whaling) illustrates the growth the organ department was experiencing, notwithstanding the relatively static enrollment in the School of Music in general.[27] The first organ major graduated in 1921, before which all organ students had been nonmajors. Following are the numbers of graduating organ majors between 1921 and 1927:[28]

Year	Graduates
1921	1
1922	0
1923	1
1924	0
1925	3
1926	5
1927	4

Publicity announcements aside, it is doubtful the position was of much prestige, as she was classified as an "instructor" rather than even the lowest rank of professor, and it certainly provided little income in the early years. Until her marriage in the 1940s, Poteet lived with her parents—not unusual for single women at the time. Accepting a position at the local university instead of continuing her education or seeking employment elsewhere would have been a natural course for her, as there were few regional opportunities for postgraduate performance training during this era. The organ department at SMU followed a traditional conservatory model that emphasized the practical musical skills and technique one could acquire sufficiently in undergraduate school given the academic strictures of the time. Further, the era certainly did not encourage women's advanced academic

study. Although Dora Poteet would have known male musicians holding advanced degrees (Grover Morris and Carl Wiesemann at Baylor,
for example), her mentor, Bertha Cassidy, had never received a degree
beyond her diploma from the Cincinnati Conservatory of Music, hint-
ing that further study was neither expected nor fitting for a young
woman. A "Financial Supplement to Report of Dean of Music" likely
issued in the autumn of 1926 and enumerating "collections" for
"several" of the music faculty shows Cassidy as having earned $1,816
in the nine months ending in August 1926, while Poteet brought in
a scant $324 in her first full year of teaching, the combined total of
which is significantly less than the $3,105 Mrs. Cassidy earned the
year before—her last as sole organ professor. The report also omits
Annie Whaling, suggesting that perhaps she did no teaching her first
year.[29] If Poteet's teaching was limited in the first year, she was still
musically involved elsewhere, not only at the Methodist church but
also as accompanist of the YWCA choir, an ensemble that undertook
concert tours and broadcast over the radio.[30] In 1928 she was appointed
an organist at the Scottish Rite Cathedral, a position Cassidy had held
and in which both Whaling and Poteet increasingly assisted.[31]

The lure of New York again beckoned, and in mid-August 1927,
Poteet departed Galveston to journey via steamer up the Eastern
Seaboard, having arranged to study with Hungarian-born organist
and composer Dezso d'Antalffy (1885–1945).[32] Hardly a household name in subsequent years, at the time d'Antalffy maintained
a respectable reputation as a concert performer, having studied
composition with Max Reger and organ with Karl Straube in
Leipzig, with further studies with Marco Enrico Bossi in Bologna,
after which he taught at the Academy of Music in Budapest.[33] His
multifaceted career entailed stints as a composer of dramatic music
for plays, vaudeville shows, and silent movies; he composed an
oratorio for the opening of Radio City Music Hall in 1932.[34] At the
time of Poteet's study with him, he played at the Roxy Theatre. But it
must have been his classical reputation that had enticed her to study
with the virtuoso.

D'Antalffy had taught briefly at Eastman School of Music in the early 1920s, and from 1927 to 1929 at Union Theological Seminary.[35] She must have studied for less than a month, because she returned to Dallas "about the last of September to resume her duties at the university and at the Methodist Church."[36] The Dallas paper ran a short notice on October 2, 1927, announcing her return: "Dora Poteet, Dallas organist and instructor of organ in the school of music of Southern Methodist University, has returned from New York, where she has coached this summer with Dezso d'Antalffy, Hungarian virtuoso, formerly of the Royal Conservatory of Budapest. Mr. d'Antalffy is also a composer of note, Miss Poteet says, and has written many numbers for the organ. Some of these Miss Poteet studied with the composer and plans to present in concerts which have been booked for her in Dallas and other cities of the Southwest."[37]

As Concert Organist and Teacher

Dora Poteet's concert engagements began to accumulate as her reputation grew. Scarcely two weeks after her return from New York she performed the dedication of the Pilcher organ at the Methodist church in Caldwell, Texas. As promised, this program included a work by d'Antalffy—namely, his "Festival Bucolica,"[38] which, in the words of a reviewer from the *Musical Courier* in 1922, is "a very brilliant showpiece, but requiring a player who has plentiful technic."[39] In the next year, Poteet performed at least two more of the noted composer's pieces. In a Sunday afternoon concert at McFarlin Auditorium in April 1928, she played his "Sportive Fauns," a programmatic work that a reviewer in the *American Organist* recommends that "those of us who cannot boast a fluent technic will avoid."[40] In November she performed d'Antalffy's "Madrigal" on the new organ at the Adolphus Hotel in Dallas,[41] which the same reviewer characterized as "an experiment in notes rather than beauty."[42] This program also included Mozart's Fantasia in F, and the *Cortège* and *Prélude* of Vierne.[43] Poteet programmed Vierne frequently, her recitals from these years often featuring the Final from his *First Symphony*[44] and the Allegro Vivace[45] from an unspecified symphony. Her concert selections nonetheless still exemplified the tastes of the era, often including light pieces such as Wheeldon's *The Minster Bells*, Russell's *Up the Saquenay*, and Nevin's *Will o' the Wisp*, as well as transcriptions by Wagner and Dvořák.

Yet even in her early career, her proclivity toward authentic organ music is evident. At a December 30 studio recital in McFarlin (that was followed by Poteet's lecture on "Organ Accompanying"), six students performed portions from Guilmant's *Third Organ Sonata*, two Bach preludes and fugues in G major and C minor, Karg-Elert's *Sicilian Corenti*, a toccata by Edward d'Evry, and Melchiorre Mauro-Cottone's *Christmas Pastorale*.[46] In a 1933 recital at SMU, Poteet performed the "Sinfonia" from Bach's cantata "Wir Danken Dir, Gott"—the first time in the archival record that an SMU program utilizes an untranslated title in the original language, an infrequent practice in an era when musicology was in its nascent stages and concern for authenticity was negligible.[47] In this year she added the Liszt "Prelude and Fugue on B-A-C-H" to her repertoire; one can imagine the confusion of the *Dallas Morning News* editor who alphabetized the piece "A., B., C., H."[48] By 1934 she had learned the Dupré "Prelude and Fugue in G minor" and Guy Weitz's Symphony for Organ, which she debuted in a joint recital with Robert Markham, her counterpart at Baylor.[49] Cassidy had initiated regular Wednesday and Sunday recitals in McFarlin Auditorium, events that Poteet employed to her advantage in exploring new (or historic) literature, debuting Mendelssohn's complete *Fifth Sonata* as well as Joseph Bonnet's *Variations de Concert* in 1934.[50]

In a February 1935 recital at SMU, Dora Poteet played a Corelli transcription and Bach's Prelude and Fugue in D, presumably BWV 532, as the reviewer stated that it "began brilliantly and highly militaristic, then proceeded to a somber, stately strain." Showing her increasing affinity for the French school, she also played Franck's Choral in B Minor, to which the reviewer inarticulately responded that "it proceeded from one movement to the next in adequate rendition, showing skill on the part of both the composer and the organist who interpreted it."[51] Her own musical personality is evident already in the 1937 course catalog, which specifies that advanced students are to study the "'Dorian' Toccata; Mendelssohn: Sonatas V and VI; Franck: *Pièce héroïque* and *Cantabile;* Karg-Elert: *Cathedral Windows, Impressions* . . . Bach Fantasia and Fugue in G minor, "St Anne's Fugue" . . . Franck: *Trois Chorals*; Widor: Symphonies II and V; Vierne: Symphony I; works of Dupré."[52] This is not to imply that significant organ literature had not been learned by SMU organists prior to this point. Certainly Mrs. Cassidy regularly played and learned major Bach works and the occasional Mendelssohn sonata move- ment, as well as the Liszt "BACH" and "Ad Nos," the latter of which became Dora Poteet's signature piece. Nonetheless, the new literature she performed as the decade proceeded demonstrates a progressive attitude toward performance much more akin to that of the modern era, whereas Mrs. Cassidy's approach to programming was firmly beholden to the nineteenth century.

In addition to the duties of an organ instructor and performer, Dora Poteet spent the first half of the 1930s exploring other avenues of professional musicianship. She formed a duo piano partnership with Elizabeth Gay, a local pianist trained at the New England Conserva- tory. Early performances together occasioned WFAA radio to broad- cast their collaborations regularly from 1930 until 1932.[53] Poteet further burnished her credentials in the summer of 1934 when she earned the AAGO certification.[54]

Dora Poteet attended the AGO convention in June 1935, in Rochester, New York, where she played, probably unofficially, for members of the East Coast organ elite. On her return an article in the local paper acclaimed that "Miss Poteet also had auditions with a number of outstanding organists of the country, among them William E. Zeuch, Frank Wright, Walter Peck Stanley, Marshall Bidewell, Charles M. Courboin, Bernard Laberge and H. W. Gray. All spoke highly of her playing, Mr. Bidwell and Mr. Laberge being especially complimen- tary."[55] To have impressed Mr. LaBerge, the noted Canadian impresario who founded the concert management company now known as Karen

McFarlane Artists, Inc., was a feat that paid dividends for her burgeoning recital career. Through her acquaintance with these men she was
invited to perform for the 1936 AGO convention. The *Dallas Morning
News,* in announcing her prestigious invitation, explained further: "Miss
Poteet traveled in the East last summer and played before many of the
country's leading organists. It was through their efforts that arrangements were made for her appearance on the forthcoming program."[56]
Unfortunately, there is but scant record of her performance, with the
exception of a brief article in the Dallas paper:

> Dora Poteet, young Dallas organist and organ instructor at
> Southern Methodist University, returned recently from Pitts-
> burgh, Pa., where she appeared on the program of the national
> convention of the American Guild of Organists. Miss Poteet
> played the evening of June 24 and received numerous comments
> of a decidedly favorable nature. Her selections were Liszt's
> Prelude and Fugue on Bach and Bach's Fugue in D Major.
>   She went to the convention a comparative unknown, but indi-
> cations are that she may shortly be invited for a whole program
> at the convention, so delighted did the convention officials seem
> with her playing. Among the organists present who praised her
> work were E. Power Biggs and Arthur W. Poister, as well as
> Herbert C Peabody, chairman of the convention.[57]

In fact, her program functioned as an extended prelude recital to the
Annual Service, held that year at East Liberty Presbyterian Church
and performed on the church's 1931 Aeolian-Skinner. In addition
to the aforementioned pieces, she also played Bach's choral prelude
on "Erbarm dich mein, O Herre Gott" and the Adagio from Widor's
Fifth Symphony as the final number preceding the processional hymn.
(F. Carroll McKinstry of Springfield, Massachusetts, played the actual
service.)[58] No longer relegated to the status of a minor local celebrity,
the convention success propelled her not only into a busy recital career
but also to consider her own merits and deficiencies as an organist.

     The convention achievement bolstered her career. Bertha Cassidy
had retired in the summer of 1934, leaving the organ department in

the hands of Annie Whaling and Dora Poteet. Evidently the arrangement had been more of a partnership, as neither had been promoted
to head of the department. However, the comparative merits of the
two women relative to their service to the School of Music may be
gleaned from a brief announcement at the initiation of a recital series
in autumn of 1934 in McFarlin: "Mrs. H. M. Whaling, Jr. and Miss
Poteet, both of the faculty at Southern Methodist University, and
students of the organ department, will be presented in recitals, which
will be about thirty minutes in length. Miss Poteet is an organist of
some prominence in the State. In addition to being on the faculty of
the university, she is organist and choir director of the First M.E.
Church of Dallas and has served as organist for the Scottish Rite
Cathedral during the last six years."[59] Perhaps here what remains
unsaid is as illuminating as what is written; there is no mention made
of Annie Whaling's accomplishments or qualifications. In the two
and a half years since Cassidy's retirement, no doubt political expe-
diency at least partly negated promoting the youthful Poteet over the
elder Whaling, the wife of an SMU vice president and minister at the
prestigious Highland Park Methodist Church, despite the younger
woman's qualifications. Whaling and Poteet had worked together
since young Dora was 16 years old, when she had inherited the organist position at First Methodist Church from Whaling. Any evidence
of rivalry between the two women would have been unlikely to enter
the historical record, and the nature of their relationship has been
lost to history. Nevertheless, when Whaling abruptly resigned in
early 1937 and retired to Houston with her husband, Dora Poteet was
appointed "acting head of the organ department," a position which,
after it was made permanent, she held the rest of her life.[60]

    Perhaps eager to expand her credentials, in early 1937 she arranged
to study in France with Marcel Dupré at the acclaimed American
Conservatory in Fontainebleau, France.[61] Along with companion Helen
Nolde, Dora Poteet set sail on June 5, 1937, from New York to Europe,
where she played organs in Germany and Switzerland before arriving
for the commencement of studies in Fontainebleau on July 1.[62]

Fontainebleau, Dupré, and the Summer of '37

During the summer of 1937, one last calm enveloped Europe before the winds of war beset the continent. The American Conservatory, founded by Walter Damrosch in 1921 and with the subsequent cooperation of the French government, sought to offer a uniquely French musical education to capable young musicians. In the early years there was much to offer for young organists in particular, from its first director, Charles-Marie Widor, to faculty such as Camille Saint-Saëns and Marcel Dupré. That summer, Maurice Ravel was concluding his tenure as the school's director and composition professor, already suffering from the illness to which he succumbed by year's end. Poteet, however, greatly profited from study with the illustrious pedagogue and composer Nadia Boulanger:

> One of the prime attractions of Nadia's 1937 composition class at Fontainebleau was "the possibility of the collaboration of M. Igor Strawinsky," as the catalogue put it. In addition to counterpoint, fugue, and the principles of musical structure," all integral parts of the composition course, Nadia also taught harmony, keyboard harmony, the history of music, musicology, and "general pedagogy." Her classes occupied at least ten hours a week of her time, with private lessons and discussions—offered in addition to most of the students in the group courses—accounting for at least another 2½ hours a week per private student. All this she crammed into the two or three days a week that she spent at Fontainebleau.[63]

Whether Dora Poteet actually studied with Boulanger is unknown, as she only spoke of Dupré in reference to her Fontainebleau studies. However, as Boulanger was thoroughly involved in all aspects of teaching, there is no reason to believe that Poteet did not benefit from Boulanger's expertise. A notice in the *Corsicana Daily Sun* in May 1937, from information certainly gathered from Poteet herself, states that she "will take a course in general pedagogy under Nadia Boulanger and classes in improvisation and history and interpretation of organ music."[64] Perhaps this was simply an "organist's bias," preferring to consider only private study with one of the monumental figures of the organ world worth mentioning. It is likely that Poteet's contact with Boulanger was merely in the general classroom, without personal interaction, and therefore she did not consider it compelling enough to include Boulanger among her teachers. According to her students, Poteet seldom mentioned her study with Dupré, so few facts can be ascertained from her two months' study with him. Nonetheless, third-hand accounts offer a glimpse into a time that shaped her approach to organ playing as both a performer and pedagogue.

According to former student Russell Brydon, Dora Poteet prepared her repertoire a year prior to her study with Marcel Dupré.[65] Her first lesson, or lessons, depending on the account, were spent playing for Dupré to a taciturn response, which increasingly concerned her. After some length of time agonizing under his silences, she inquired as to his response to her playing, to which he replied nonplussed, "Where did you learn your technique?" She answered that she had learned her technique from Mrs. Cassidy. Dupré, gratified by her playing, insinuated that he had nothing to teach her.[66] Former student Howard Ross asserted that Dupré had remarked, "My dear, I cannot help you. Your playing is perfect!"[67] Even given the propensity for a story to embellish itself through the years, there is no doubt that Dupré considered her a brilliant pupil, either the best American he had ever coached, or the best woman, or possibly the best American woman, depending on who tells the narrative.[68] Whatever the nuance of the superlatives, Dupré greatly admired her and considered her a worthy student, even condescending to perform on what by that time was the "tub" of an organ at McFarlin Auditorium in 1948, all for the sake of "my Dora."[69] Their relationship was a congenial one. One former student recalled her mentioning that she had memorized his *Variations sur un Noël* but forgot to memorize the opening theme, a faux pas the French composer found hilarious.[70]

Upon her completion of the program at Fontainebleau, he presented her with an autographed picture that he inscribed to his "exceptional" student, Dora. She received a diploma "with highest honors."

The admiration was mutual and, even if she failed to express many of the details of her experience with future students, for the remainder of her career she never failed to promote Dupré's music and, by extension, the French music he taught and introduced to her. The only regret of this sabbatical was the death of Louis Vierne that occurred on June 2, 1937; the news, reaching Poteet while onboard the ship bound for France,[71] was particularly disappointing as she had already made arrangements to take lessons with him, or planned to do so.[72] By the time she boarded the *S.S. Europa* on September 5 to sail back to New York, the French manner of performing and approach to teaching had, at least as she understood it, been profoundly embedded in her musical persona.[73]

Her hometown newspaper, no doubt inspired by pride in a local girl made good, recounted that the highlight of her trip to Germany, Switzerland, and France was studying "pipe organ under Marshall Dujri," which one can suppose is "Marcel Dupré" after several convolutions of Texan dialects.[74] Her first important recital after her study with Dupré was on January 18, 1938, in McFarlin Auditorium. An article advertising the concert proclaims:

Miss Poteet has been presented often at S.M.U. in recitals with other members of the faculty, but, because of the interest aroused since her return from Europe, she is conforming to many requests in giving an entire program. Her study in Europe during the summer was with Marcel Dupre, famous French organist and composer, at Fountainbleau, where she received the diploma with the highest honors ever won by anyone in the organ department. . . .

Her program for Tuesday, which is open to the public, will include two Bach compositions [Toccata, Adagio and Fugue in C and "Rejoice Now, Ye Christian Men"], Mozart's Fantasia in F in Dupre's arrangements, the Allegro from Widor's Sixth Symphony, Cesar Franck's Chorale in B minor, two modern American numbers by Harvey B. Gaul and H. B. Jepson and Dupre's Variation sur un Noel.[75]

Certainly Dupré's influence is stamped upon this program. From his own massive "Variations," to his arrangement of the Mozart, to the Widor and the Franck, which she likely studied with him, she no longer played the evanescent compositions so characteristic of the musical palate in prior decades. Her playing had been transformed in such a marked manner that it was perceptible even to a reviewer for whom an organ concert was only a "rare opportunity":

> Since her last program Miss Poteet has been occupying herself with further study in France where she spent several weeks in the summer working under the renowned French organist, Marcel Dupre, who gave several recitals in Texas this fall. From him she absorbed much with varied results. Her brilliant, individual style of playing has been lessened to a degree but at the same time her conception of the master works for her instrument has been broadened and deepened considerably.
>
> Miss Poteet's technical equipment is of the highest order, naturally, punctuated with manual dexterity and fleetness, flawless footwork, skillful manipulation of the mechanics of the instrument. She is an artist and a musician in everything that she does. Among her happiest gifts is excellent registration, whether orchestral and majestic or cute and clever, but invariably interesting. This was most forcibly demonstrated in the Dupre "Variations sur un Noel" which closed the program.[76]

Aside from Dupré's purported exclamations to the contrary, it appears as though he did offer her instructions for improvement, in this case something that resulted in a lessening of her "individual style" of playing, at least according to this reviewer. Whatever the case may be, even though she had always possessed a flawless technique that was enhanced by daily piano study, her exercises with Dupré resulted not only in her successfully being able to stretch a tenth on the keyboard but also in her having to purchase a larger set of gloves![77]

Years of Professional and Personal Growth

At the end of the academic year in 1938, SMU promoted Dora Poteet from assistant to associate professor, officially appointing her to the role as head of the organ department—a role in which she had served on an acting basis since 1937.[78] A department that had consisted of three professors a few years before now employed only one, perhaps an indication of the state of organ study in decades to come. According to an internal memo in January 1940, she was among a group of six professors teaching from "15 to 20 hours" a week; only three professors in the School of Music taught more hours per week (averaging twenty-five), with ten professors teaching significantly fewer hours; the next tier down averaged only three weekly teaching hours.[79] By 1939 she also secured the organist and choirmaster appointment at Trinity Methodist Church, a post that had been occupied by Mrs. Cassidy many years before.[80] The extra responsibilities translated into some financial gain. The university charged $90 per student, per semester, for two private lessons a week with Miss Poteet, or half that for a single lesson.[81] The 1940 census, like those prior, included among its enumerated factors the annual income for each person in each household, each home delineated according to city block. The Poteet household consisted of parents John and Nettie, plus Dora. John's income for the year prior was $780 and Nettie's was $0, but Dora's was $2,000. For comparison, among the dozen households on her block, only one person—an accountant—earned more than Dora.[82]

In 1941 the Texas Chapter of the AGO elected her as dean.[83] During the summer of 1940 she continued studies with Dupré via letter, offering "her pupils the benefit of her recent studies under his guidance when classes are resumed in September. This will include outlines of methods given her by correspondence from Marcel Dupre in Paris."[84] She showcased the technical prowess perfected under Dupré in a four-week concert tour during that she "received unstinted praise," performing at Albert Riemenschneider's request at Baldwin-Wallace College and at Oberlin College, as arranged by Arthur Poister.[85] Her faculty recital at SMU in January 1941, found her playing "a well-balanced program of Schumann, Vierne, Reger, Franck . . . [that] concluded with two movements of the *Suite Bretonne* and the Carillon by Marcel Dupre." She had "opened the program with the epic Fantasia and

Fugue in G minor of Bach. All the dramatic power of the work was sounded, and the fugue was taken at an exciting tempo that is well beyond most organists. . . . The organ becomes something a great deal more responsive than a mere mechanical instrument under the hands of Dora Poteet."[86] During the next few years she concertized regularly, accepting engagements throughout the United States, including at Rockefeller Chapel in Chicago,[87] Brown Memorial Presbyterian Church in Baltimore, Wilson College in Chambersburg, Pennsylvania, and Girard College in Philadelphia.[88] As a contribution to the war effort, in 1943 she played for "an audience of 1,700 students, sailors and marines . . . various organ selections at the Louisiana Polytechnic Institute, Ruston, La., Thursday, also broadcasting over Station KWKH of Shreveport. The presentation was part of a program planned by the Navy V12 Unit," a program in which SMU and other universities participated in order to train potential commissioned officers.[89] In 1944, in addition to accepting a new position at the Episcopal Church of the Incarnation in Dallas, she continued her studies at the Church and Choral Music Institute at Northwestern University in Chicago, where she coached with Dr. David McKay Williams.[90] Having grown to 205 students in the 1943–1944 academic year, the SMU School of Music authorized the initiation of graduate studies the following year, certainly adding to her workload in the ensuing years.[91] In May 1947, almost ten years after her triumphal performance at the AGO convention in Pittsburgh, she was invited to play at the annual AGO Spring Festival in New York City, performing Bach, Handel, Schumann, Reubke, Vierne, Nanney, and Dupré.[92]

On February 9, 1948, Dora Poteet married William Archibald Barclay at First Presbyterian Church in Fort Worth.[93] An organist and pianist of some acclaim himself, and professor of organ at Southwestern Baptist Theological Seminary in Fort Worth, Barclay had studied at SMU but graduated from Baylor, coaching in the summers in New York at Columbia University and at the Guilmant Organ School with Ernest Hutcheson and William C. Carl.[94] The Barclays were of differing stripes, one most comfortable in the classical tradition, the other at home in the free spirit of Gospel music.

Dora Poteet Barclay at Broadway Baptist in Fort Worth. Picture property of
Benjamin Kolodziej, courtesy of Dan Garland.

Their respect seemed mutual; once, after a "grand improvisation on
gospel hymns," Dora remarked, "Isn't it wonderful Bill can do that?
Not many organists can!"[95] William Barclay was celebrated for his
radio and television broadcasts, in which he specialized in jazz-in-
fused renditions of Southern Gospel tunes. After the marriage Dora
Poteet Barclay settled in Fort Worth, commuting to SMU to teach and
assuming organist duties at St. Andrew's Episcopal Church.

Concerts on Campus

Promoting a musical culture had always been a guiding principle
since the founding of the university, when Robert Hyer rented cars
to ferry students to the festive musical gala at the Scottish Rite

Cathedral downtown and local churches graciously provided practice and performance venues to the students before the university
had infrastructure to support concerts. Now that SMU had its own
musical facilities, the School of Music sought to attract audiences
to its campus through varied, often international, fare. Russian
pianist Vladimir Horowitz played at McFarlin in 1932,[96] Sergei
Rachmaninoff played an engagement there in 1936,[97] the Philadelphia
Orchestra under Eugene Ormandy in 1937,[98] Polish piano virtuoso
Artur Rubenstein's first Dallas concert was there in 1939,[99] and
acclaimed German soprano Lotte Lehmann sang in the auditorium
in 1940.[100] Bertha Cassidy had done her part in the early years to
present the organ in public concerts. Palmer Christian, professor of
organ at the University of Michigan, played a solo recital in McFarlin
in 1927,[101] and her sometime-teacher, Sigfrid Karg-Elert, disappoint-
ingly performed there five years later. The organ faculty and students
regularly performed public recitals, many of which were broadcast
on the radio. After Dora Poteet was promoted to acting organ department head in 1937, she was proactive in arranging for visiting artists
to perform at McFarlin, whether sponsored by the university directly
or by ancillary organizations, in this case usually the AGO. Arthur
Poister played a program of Handel, Clerambault, Bach, Franck,
Karg-Elert, Clokey, and Widor's entire *Sixth Symphony* in December 1935, only months after Miss Poteet had impressed him with her
playing in her New York auditions.[102] Harold Friedell, teacher at the
Juilliard School of Music and Union Theological Seminary's School
of Sacred Music, performed in McFarlin on April 27, 1938.[103] Virgil
Fox, while still head of the organ department at Brown University,
under the auspices of the Texas Chapter of the AGO, concertized at
SMU in February 1942, playing Reger's *Fantasie on the Chorale,
How Brightly Shines the Morning Star*, Middelschulte's *Perpetuum
Mobile*, Bach's Passacaglia in C minor, and Dupre's Prélude and
Fugue in G Minor.[104] E. Power Biggs's recital the following year
was characterized by the "precision, clarity and brilliance" that "has
not come from McFarlin's organ in many a long day."[105] Vierne's

student and Mormon Tabernacle organist Alexander Schreiner played a "traditionally correct" concert of Bach, Biggs, and Vierne the same year.[106] But the pinnacle of these distinguished musical events, and the swan song of the prematurely aging Hillgreen, Lane organ, was Marcel Dupré's recital on December 7, 1948.

Marcel Dupré Performs at SMU

By 1948 Marcel Dupré was at the height of his career, having played 1,500 recitals in Europe and managing to perform fifty to a hundred concerts on each international tour.[107] As propitious as this event could have been, the Hillgreen, Lane instrument was only marginally suited to the task. Not even 25 years old at the time, the organ had suffered ciphers and mechanical problems. Its tuning was so precarious that Barclay often refused to allow students to practice on the instrument between the time of its tuning and a major concert.[108] William Teague, who studied with Dora Poteet in the late 1930s before studying at the Curtis Institute of Music, assessed the organ's condition at the time: "The auditorium was a dreadful room, and the organ was a dreadful organ . . . it was a thick sounding organ. I remember David Craighead, who was also with us at Curtis, played in Dallas on his first tour at SMU. I asked when he got back, 'What did you think of the organ at SMU?' He said, 'I felt like the whole place was filling up with dark blue smoke.' It was an opaque sound."[109] The horseshoe console was beset by mechanical problems: pistons functioned anti-intuitively, vexing every harried visiting organist, and only two mixtures were present; the Dolce Cornet on the Swell was barely perceptible, and the Mixture on the Great was synthetically derived. Tonal challenges aside, the heavily draped auditorium hindered sound projection, and the instrument had always lacked the dynamic power to fill the room—a deficiency that had been addressed through the years by various methods of amplification, the first of which was installing a set of microphones in 1929.[110] The instrument was in no condition to host any illustrious organist, much less one of such caliber and discernment from France.

Marcel Dupré on the evening of his concert at McFarlin Auditorium.
Courtesy of Walter Davis.

Walter Davis, a student of Barclay from 1946 to 1951, served as a
docent that evening, keeping students from wandering about but observing
the performance himself from the front row. He recalled Mrs. Barclay's
utter horror and embarrassment when, upon his arrival at the organ
for practice, Dupré removed his handkerchief to wipe off the keys.[111]
Madame Dupré did little to assuage her host's sense of social inferiority

when, on a shopping trip to haute couture Neiman-Marcus, Madame Dupré observed that the fashions were "introduced in France, three years ago."[112] Before the performance the organ students met Dupré, who, at least in the minds of impressionable students accustomed to Southern hospitality, exhibited a haughty froideur by not extending his hand in greeting. The concert was played with minute perfection, Dupré even utilizing the tibias without tremolos.[113] Donald McDonald, another of Dora Poteet Barclay's students before he enrolled at Curtis, recalled Dupré's aversion to that organ, saying, "If it were not for my dear Dora, I would not play."[114] The organ's predicament notwithstanding, the event seems to have been a success, with an audience of 1,200 present to hear him play Bach's Passacaglia and Fugue in C Minor; his *Vision*, Opus 44; Liszt's *Variations on Weinen, Klagen, Sorgen, Zagen*; Eric DeLamarter's *Prelude on a Theme in Georgian Style*; Franck's B minor Choral; Messiaen's *Le Banquet Céleste*; and his own Prelude and Fugue in C major, Opus 36. The recital concluded with a "Symphonic Improvisation on a Given Theme."[115] He played the Bach Toccata and Fugue in D minor and the Widor Toccata as encores. Rual Askew, the reviewer for the *Dallas Morning News*, extols the French virtuoso:

> M. Dupre's own Vision, Symphonic Poem, Opus 44, somehow dominated the initial portion of the program by its tenuous and complex construction. A somber and searching utterance, the work is perhaps best appreciated and understood by the academic musician.
>
> Apparently an artist whose mood dictates a particular performance, M. Dupre Tuesday evening displayed his famous light touch that only occasionally seemed fleeting and impatient. This quality was most apparent in his two concluding encores . . . [which] mesmerized his listeners evenly and grandly and elicited their heartiest approval.
>
> M. Dupre also extemporized on three themes, submitted in envelopes, by three audience members, Dr. Paul van Katwijk, dean of SMU's school of music; Dr. Hans T. David, SMU's noted musicologist, and Jack Kilpatrick, composer-member of the university music faculty.

The most completely inspiring projections of the evening were
Delamarter's haunting Prelude on a Theme in Gregorian Style,
Franck's Second Chorale in B Minor (with its anticipations of the
D Minor Symphony), Messaien's mystic "Le Banquet Celeste"
and M. Dupre's own thrilling C Minor Prelude and Fugue.[116]

The concert provided a once-in-a-lifetime opportunity for Dallas
concertgoers and for the organ studio. The next morning, Mr. Davis
hastily copied the French master's registrations for posterity, before
the daily humdrum of organ practice inevitably expunged them from
the organ's memory, just as Dupré certainly eagerly expunged his
experience of that organ from his own.

Marcel Dupré's recital specifically, and the development of the organ
department through these years generally, may have been indicative of
the struggles of a fledgling university in a town that lacked the historic,
social, and cultural heritage of the great American cities on the East
Coast, much less those of Europe. Southern Methodist University had
been established in the lofty tradition of the great universities of the east,
setting forth its own vision to develop into a premier educational institution in Texas. Yet, in the early years at least, this noble goal always
seemed slightly out of reach. Professors were largely drawn from the
local or regional talent pool, as was the case of Bertha Stevens Cassidy,
with an increasing number being drawn from its own graduates, as was
the case of Dora Poteet Barclay. Far from representing diverse geog-
raphies, the student body remained mostly regional in nature. Because
its buildings were sturdy, generally reflecting historic architectural
traditions, they were expensive and their construction had to be paced
over the course of years, compelling a reliance on the generosity and
hospitality of the surrounding community, a consequence of which was
a healthy town-and-gown symbiosis in the early years. But neither the
city nor the university could hasten the process of cultivating a reputation. Perhaps Askew, the *Dallas Morning News* reviewer, appraised
Dupré's Symphonic Poem with some prescience as "best appreciated and understood by the academic musician."[117] Of these, Dallas
possessed few. This realization had certainly motivated Mrs. Cassidy

Dora Poteet Barclay at McFarlin Auditorium. Rotunda Collection,
SMU Archives, DeGolyer Library, SMU.

to seek opportunities for further study in New York, England, and Germany—an attitude that she had instilled in Dora Poteet Barclay at least by the time of their trip together to study with Clifford Demarest in 1923. Barclay likewise throughout her career continued to expand her education in New York, Chicago, and Fontainebleau.

Dupré's Dallas appearance highlighted the disparity between the Old World and the New. The French virtuoso represented a sophisticated culture that developed over centuries. The organs, as the Cavaillé-Coll he regularly played at Saint-Sulpice, exemplify the apex of one tradition of organ building, incorporating the sights and aural sonorities of centuries-old pipes and casework into something new yet decidedly ancient. American organ building, although in debt to its European progenitors, was largely unencumbered by the sonorities and mechanics of Old World organs, preferring industrialization and innovation. The United States had been shaped by experience rather than tradition, which perhaps was its ultimate genius. In organ building this manifested itself in the brilliant development of new technologies such as electric action and new sounds, exemplified in the work of E. M. Skinner. Although from the same era, the Hillgreen, Lane organ in McFarlin Auditorium was no such specimen, epitomizing size and accoutrements before aesthetic beauty. There remain organs from the 1920s that represent timelessness and the best of the organ industry at the time, but the McFarlin organ represented a strand of organ building in which novelty superseded history, efficiency displaced artistry, and practicality supplanted discipline.

Despite aspirations to the contrary, Dallas was still characterized by a frontier mentality. Karg-Elert embodied the typical European mind when he expressed astonishment at cacti growing in the midst of unpaved, muddy streets. Whether they were consciously aware of it or not, both Mrs. Cassidy and Mrs. Barclay in their own ways bolstered the standards of organ playing and building at SMU. Dupré's recital was a painful reminder to Mrs. Barclay how far the organ department had yet to come. Without a fine concert and teaching instrument, the department would always be relegated to the subordinate tiers of the organ world.

Chapter 4

Optimism and Transition

On Friday morning, May 11, 1951, Southern Methodist University's board of trustees, under the chairmanship of Bishop A. Frank Smith, met to hear an address by President Umphrey Lee and to attend to official school business, after which time they adjourned to the recently completed Perkins Chapel to hear Dora Poteet Barclay play the dedication of the new Aeolian-Skinner organ. This afternoon service was followed by a formal recital later that evening in which Mrs. Barclay performed a program of Bach, Rinck, Dupré, Nanney, Vierne, Purvis, and Reubke on the firm's No. 1167, a thirty-four-rank instrument situated in the sumptuous neo-Georgian architecture of the university's new chapel. The organ was the third on campus, following the two Hillgreen, Lane organs languishing in McFarlin Auditorium. The Aeolian-Skinner organ represented a new, historically informed yet progressive musical vision for the university's organ department. Unlike the murky, "opaque" quality of the auditorium organ, the new, moderately sized Aeolian-Skinner boasted mixtures and mutations to clarify contrapuntal lines and to enhance polyphonic transparency while harboring a considerable complement of color timbres, including two celestes and a Clarinet. Since the first organ was installed on campus, Hillgreen, Lane's reputation had been eclipsed by other builders, including the prestigious Boston-based Aeolian-Skinner. Bertha Stevens Cassidy's selection of the former firm to install the school's premier instrument had encumbered, embarrassed, and hindered the organ department for years, despite how stoically Dora Poteet Barclay had borne her burden. When it came to selecting a new instrument for the campus, Mrs. Barclay undoubtedly motivated the building committee to commission one of the nation's most illustrious builders.

Perkins School of Theology

The end of World War II portended unmitigated growth throughout American academia, and SMU was no exception. Returning veterans were spurred into receiving a higher education by the GI Bill of 1944, with SMU having to construct temporary buildings "for classes and offices, for housing, and as a student center" to accommodate the swelling enrollment.[1] In 1944 the School of Theology counted 152 students, but by 1946 the number had increased to 238, burgeoning to almost 300 ministerial students by 1949.[2] The acute need to enlarge the facilities resulted in the planning for a theology quadrangle encompassing six buildings, including a library, dormitories, and administrative/classroom facilities, the centerpiece of which would be a chapel. The Georgian architecture that had inspired the campus's first edifice, Dallas Hall, would be promulgated in the new buildings, particularly in the chapel with its redbrick, graceful arches and columns, decorative filigree, and generous, clear-glass windows.[3] The ambitious construction project was underway by late 1948, the university having secured notable architect Mark Lemmon to design the buildings "to harmonize with present structures on campus."[4] The entire project, estimated to cost as much as $3 million, was funded largely by donations from Joe and Lois Craddock Perkins, who bestowed their name to the former School of Theology. The new Perkins School of Theology, with its eponymous chapel, evidenced a continuing legacy of a family whose philanthropy had long supported SMU.

Aeolian-Skinner, Opus 1167

Joe and Lois Perkins hailed from Wichita Falls, a small Texas town near the Oklahoma border, making their fortune in the oil business. By 1913, before SMU opened, the couple had made a donation to the nascent university. Their liberality extended to the world of the pipe organ; in 1928 they had donated to their home parish of First Methodist Church, Wichita Falls, a fifty-rank, four-manual Reuter organ—certainly one of the largest instruments in the state.[5] That SMU's Perkins Chapel would house a fine pipe organ, and that Joe and Lois Perkins would pay for it, seemed a foregone conclusion, the cost of a fine new instrument adding only fractional expense to the overall project. Yet Mrs. Leila Peyton, an oil heiress and devout Methodist from the small Central Texas town of Mexia who claimed to be neither a "poet [nor] musician," expressed an interest to School of Theology dean Eugene B. Hawk about contributing something to the new construction "in a musical way."[6] She had apparently floated this idea early in 1945, but the political expediencies of dealing with donors delayed the process until December of that year, at which time Dean Hawk wrote to her:

> Well, it seems we have a break in the organ matter. Doctor Lee [Umphrey Lee] was talking to Mr. Perkins about it and he said he would be delighted for you to provide the organ in the chapel if you desire to do so. A month or two ago we took up this question of making proper arrangements for this instrument and the architect is shaping the building so as to feature the organ and it will likely be enjoyed by a wider range of people than any other organ in Dallas or the Southwest. You think the matter over. . . . I am confident the organ too will serve a number of generations.[7]

The deliberations of the committee that selected Aeolian-Skinner to build the chapel organ are not part of the archival record, but the committee consisted of local organ builder William Redmond, Dora Poteet Barclay, and Dr. Fred Gealy, a professor of New Testament in the School of Theology, amateur musician, and regular organist at the chapel during the 1950s. Together they developed a fairly conventional stoplist in conjunction with G. Donald Harrison.[8] Aeolian-Skinner was a prestigious firm at the apex of its professional development, Harrison having recently completed the organs at St. Mary the Virgin, New York City, in 1942 and the Mormon Tabernacle in 1948, with notable projects at Grace Cathedral in San Francisco and Trinity Church on the Green in New Haven among his previous credits, while major installations at Symphony Hall in Boston and the Cathedral of St. John the Divine in New York were underway during these years. The contract for the new organ was signed by Umphrey Lee and Harrison in August 1948, promising delivery of the thirty-four rank, $29,985 organ by September of 1950.[9]

Mark Lemmon, a Texas native, already had achieved a reputation as an architect in classical styles by the 1920s, having designed the neo-Gothic sanctuary of Highland Park Methodist Church on the SMU campus in 1927. He had forayed into more modern styles in his design of the Texas Hall of State in Dallas's Fair Park in 1935, but for SMU, for whom he planned a total of eighteen buildings, he returned to the neo-Georgian style when he designed the Fondren Science Building in 1949, a style he continued at the theology quad-rangle.[10] He was as respected in his trade as G. Donald Harrison was in his own, and perhaps conflict was inevitable, the first hint of which appears in the autumn of 1949. A disagreement over the nature of the interior surfaces, of visual concern to the architect and acoustical concern to Aeolian-Skinner, resulted in Dean Eugene Hawk implor-ing Mr. Lemmon to address acoustical concerns that Joseph White-ford, then assistant to Mr. Harrison at Aeolian-Skinner had expressed to Dora Poteet Barclay, reiterating that "we want to do the things that should be done to the end that the organ may be most effective. It would be a serious mistake not to make a careful study of this matter so that corrections would not have to be made later on."[11] Dean Hawk likewise implores Mr. Harrison (who had not returned some of Lemmon's correspondence) to deal proactively with Mr. Lemmon, to "agree on plastering, etc., so as to work out the best installation."[12]

He politely rejects Whiteford's suggestion to bring in an acoustician, saying, "We have not had in mind bringing a man here to make a study of the acoustics of the building."[13] Nonetheless, an acoustical engineer hired at Lemmon's behest had apparently affirmed the architect's desire for less-hardened surfaces in the room. In response Whiteford hired his own engineers from MIT to survey the acoustical properties of the chapel, ultimately affirming Aeolian-Skinner's contention that the surfaces needed to be hardened and certain ceiling angles be mitigated.[14] As he paternalistically attempts to mediate this dispute, Dean Hawk graciously chides the organ builder that "these engineers should be clearly informed that we are not building a music hall primarily, but a chapel for worship. The acoustics should be of such a nature as to readily carry the human voice, and I see no reason why this cannot be done and at the very same time have a treatment that will permit the very best service from the organ."[15] Eventually, Aeolian-Skinner and Lemmon could reach no satisfactory solution, forcing Dean Hawk to write to President Umphrey Lee:

> The Aeolian-Skinner Organ Company and Mr. Lemmon have not been in agreement as to the plastering for Perkins Chapel. . . . I wonder just what we should do in this matter. The consulting engineers were secured at the expense of Aeolian-Skinner. Mark Lemmon is out of the city until Thursday morning. I talked with George Reynolds of the staff in his office. He stated that they have been pleased with the treatment given the Highland Park Presbyterian Church and the ceiling is of acoustical plaster, which is not the hard plaster suggested in the enclosed letter. . . . Mark seems to be obstinate about making changes and certainly we should give the Aeolian-Skinner people no grounds for claiming that the organ cannot give good service because of the way the building was treated.[16]

Although Lemmon had conceded to a request from Joseph Whiteford, by now vice president at Aeolian-Skinner, to create openings into the nave to provide better sound egress than the divided-chancel layout then allowed, he was rather firm that any façade pipes be pewter colored, hoping that a "zinc natural finish" would accomplish the effect.[17] Harrison countered with a proposal to install grilles instead of actual façade pipes, the expense for which had risen exorbitantly due to the requisitioning of zinc by the government, ostensibly a result of the Korean conflict.[18] Fortunately, this aesthetically questionable proposal was rejected and Aeolian-Skinner ultimately provided zinc façade pipes.[19] The acoustical matter drops from the record, and the only evidence suggesting the victor is the dry acoustics that prevailed in the chapel before its renovation in the late 1990s.

The particulars worked out at a high level among the university's president, the Perkins School of Theology's dean, the architect, and Harrison and Whiteford at Aeolian-Skinner were left to the local installers to execute and, if need be, to change. In this case Aeolian-Skinner's Texas installations were handled by Thomas Jackson Williams, his son Jimmy Williams and daughter-in-law Nora Williams, and Roy Perry, organist at First Presbyterian in Kilgore, Texas, incumbent of Aeolian-Skinner, Opus 1173. This team would go on to install numerous Aeolian-Skinner organs through-out Texas, but the Perkins Chapel organ, along with the instrument nearby at Highland Park Methodist (Opus 1231), was among their first. Aeolian-Skinner would secure a contract, design the organ, build the constituent elements, and ship them to the team's loca-tion. The Williamses provided the localized technical expertise that included wiring, soldering, and specialized tools, while Roy Perry handled voicing matters. Discussing her time installing the Perkins Chapel organ, Nora Williams observed that "Perkins Chapel . . . came along right after we started with the company. . . . [Dora Poteet Barclay] sure could get the job done. She was very nice and easygo-ing with us."[20] The Boston headquarters paid the group ten percent of every job as well as reimbursement for incidentals, from which they could hire laborers as needed.[21] They bore the burden of daily responsibility for the installation and complaints that began to accrue as it became clear that the organ would not be complete by the theol-ogy quadrangle's dedication.

The Williams family of New Orleans. *From left*: Nora Williams, Jimmy Williams, Sally Williams, and T. J. (Thomas Jackson) Williams during the 1966 revision of the Aeolian-Skinner, Opus 1173, First Presbyterian Church, Kilgore, Texas. Photo courtesy of the East Texas Pipe Organ Festival, Kilgore.

The usual conflicts that arise when installing an organ must have perturbed the normally equable Dean Hawk, for in June 1950 he delicately communicates to G. Donald Harrison his "hope [that] the organ construction is progressing so that it can be installed in September or October. I believe September has been designated as the time it will be needed. We have the feeling that it will be one of the very best organs in the city of Dallas for a chapel the size of the one we are building."[22] By August it had become clear that the organ would not be installed during the contracted time frame, and Hawk, who seems nonplussed by the situation, conveys to Whiteford his disappointment:

> In a previous letter your Company stated that the organ would be ready for installation in January. President Lee and I are quite concerned about the installation. During Ministers' Week, February 5–9, 1951, there will be some eighteen hundred visitors to our campus from various sections of the country. At that time we will dedicate the plant, consisting of seven buildings, and costing approximately $3,750,000. It will mean much to our program and especially to the donor of the organ and those who have made this possible if the organ could be used during the Week. I think also it will mean something to your Company. We will greatly appreciate your giving this matter your special consideration. We sincerely hope that the organ will be installed and ready for use by the first of February.[23]

The response from Aeolian-Skinner underscores the age-old rift that develops between two parties of differing goals—one artistic and one practical. Whiteford replies:

> We certainly are doing everything possible to get the organ to you including a six day week with as much overtime during the week as is possible from the labor force we have. You can be assured that we are most anxious to do the finest piece of work for you. . . . I am afraid, however, to be entirely realistic we cannot reasonably contemplate completion of the organ for this period.
>
> I do wish there was something we could do about it but, in a way, in the manufacture of an artistic product there is hardly a matter of choice in the speed with which it can be built if the work is to be of the highest artistic standard. It simply cannot be rushed through the factory. The craftsmen we employ are never pressed for sheer production and consequently it is often

very difficult for us to estimate exactly when an organ will be completed. . . . I am sure you would not want to take a chance on compromising the successful result of the instrument for the sake of its delivery.[24]

Indeed, the instrument would not be complete on that day in February 1951, on which 300 professors along with 2,100 onlookers witnessed Ernest C. Colwell, president of the University of Chicago, dedicate the new buildings to the delight of Joe and Lois Perkins, who demurely declared, "The size of the donation never excited Jesus."[25] The work on Aeolian-Skinner, Opus 1167, would continue for another three months.

A Twofold Dedication

SMU authorities must have contented themselves that the organ would remain unfinished until the spring of 1951, and planned accordingly. Perhaps the long-suffering Dean Hawk's frustration at the delay was mollified by his perception that the challenging interactions between architect and organ builder would result in an instrument aesthetically well suited for its environment. That is what he conveyed to the donor, Leila Peyton. In March Dean Hawk assured her that all was proceeding well, stating, "I have been talking with Mr. Williams and the other men who are installing the organ. They assured me that this will be the one organ in Dallas. They feel it is going to be almost perfect in its tone and quality. It seems that the chapel and organ were really built for each other. I felt you would be delighted to know this."[26] He then speaks to plans for the dedication concert: "I have talked with Doctor Gealy and also with Doctor Lee about the recital for the afternoon of the board meeting day. They are of the opinion that Mrs. Dora Poteet Barclay would be a very appropriate choice for the recital. We could have two or three selections by the Seminary Singers and it should be a most interesting program."[27] He then encourages the diffident Mrs. Peyton to consider participating in the dedication liturgy by presenting the organ to the university community.

The arrangement of the day of the dedication exemplified the dual role the organ would play in the theology and music schools, both as a liturgical instrument and as a concert organ. The dedication service the afternoon of May 11, 1951, consisted of the organ dedication liturgy from the current *Book of Worship*, with Walter Ward delivering the invocation, Bishop A. Frank Smith performing the Act of Dedication, and Umphrey Lee offering the dedicatory prayer. (Nothing indicates whether Mrs. Peyton formally presented the organ to the university.) Dean Hawk was liturgist for the service while Dora Poteet Barclay presided at the organ, playing a brief recital at the end.[28] Having first demonstrated its liturgical utility, Mrs. Barclay then performed the actual dedication concert at 8:00 that evening:

Toccata in F Major	Johann Sebastian Bach
Sonatina from the Cantata, "God's Time is the Best"	J. S. Bach
Chorale Prelude, "Rejoice, Ye Christian Men"	J. S. Bach
Prelude and Fugue in G Major	J. S. Bach
Rondo	Rinck
Variations on a Noël	Dupré
Intermission	
Adagio Molto Expressivo e Cantabile from Sonata in E Minor	Nanney
Naiads	Vierne
Dies Irae	Purvis
Finale from the *Ninety-Fourth Psalm*	Reubke[29]

By now Reubke's *Ninety-Fourth Psalm* was one of Dora Poteet Barclay's signature works. To perform it on a well-appointed, modern instrument with suitable reeds and console assists must have been a relief from her experience with the fatigued Hillgreen, Lane in

McFarlin Auditorium, even though that instrument was larger. That Bach constitutes such a considerable portion of the program demonstrates how musical tastes had changed since the era of Mrs. Cassidy. Each of the four pieces represents a different musical style: an effusive toccata to open the program, a contrasting, meditative cantata movement transcription, a capricious and virtuosic chorale prelude, and a Prelude and Fugue, in this case probably BWV 541.[30] This day represented in microcosm SMU's organ program during the 1950s. The new organ was situated in an edifice dedicated to the glory of God, which, in the words of Dean Hawk, had not been conceived as a concert hall. The organ department might have needed a concert instrument, but they got a liturgical instrument in a sacred space instead, and with this they were content.

Perkins Chapel in the mid-1950s. Rotunda Collection, SMU Archives, DeGolyer Library, SMU.

Perkins Chapel
Southern Methodist University, Dallas
Aeolian-Skinner, Opus 1167 (1951)[31]

GREAT
16 Quintaten
8 Diapason
8 Bourdon
4 Octave
2⅔ Twelfth
2 Fifteenth
Fourniture IV

SWELL (enclosed)
8 Geigen Diapason
8 Stopped Diapason
8 Viole de Gambe
8 Viole Celeste (t.c.)
4 Octave Geigen
4 Flute Octaviante
Plein Jeu III
16 Fagotto
8 Trompette
4 Oboe Clarion
Tremolo

CHOIR (enclosed)
8 Cor de Nuit
8 Dulciana
8 Unda Maris (t.c.)
4 Koppelflute
2⅔ Nazard
2 Blockflute

PEDAL
16 Contre Basse
16 Bourdon
16 Quintaten (Gt)
8 Octave
8 Flute (ext. 16′ Bd.)
8 Quintaten (ext. Gt)
4 Choral Bass
16 Bombarde
8 Trompette (ext. 16′)

COUPLERS
Swell to Great 8
Choir to Great 8
Swell to Choir 8
Swell to Swell 16, Unison Off, 4
Swell to Great 16, 4
Swell to Choir 16, 4
Swell to Choir 16,
Choir to Choir 16, 4
Choir to Choir 16,
Choir to Great 16, 4
Choir to Great 16
Swell to Pedal 8, 4
Great to Pedal
Choir to Pedal

COMBINATION PISTONS
Great: 6

8 Clarinet	Swell: 6
	Choir: 6
Tremolo	Pedal: 6
	General: 6
	General Cancel
	Great to Pedal reversible

MECHANICALS
Swell pedal
Choir pedal
Crescendo Pedal with light indicator
Sforzando Pedal with light indicator

This organ was situated in chambers on facing sides of the upper chancel.

Concerts and Creative Uses

The new chapel, now wholly functional with the completion of the organ, found itself in demand for services, teaching, practice, lectures, and other events. The chapel fell under the purview of Perkins School of Theology, so the daily worship services of the ministerial students took priority. Furthermore, ancillary worship events began to coalesce as the chapel appropriated its own identity. Perkins Chapel became a popular wedding venue, the first wedding being held on June 16, 1951, and officiated by President Umphrey Lee himself.[32] In the first decade of the chapel's existence, weddings were held on Saturdays, Sunday afternoons, and any day of the week that was mutually convenient; eventually, the popularity of the building as a venue necessitated offering weddings only on Saturdays. Until the late 1990s, when the position was formalized, organ students shared wedding-playing duties with organ professors, allowing them to gain service-playing experience in addition to the social problem-solving skills required of any organist who must communicate with brides and their families in their music selection process.

Scheduling constraints necessitated that only organ majors would study and practice on the Aeolian-Skinner, while other students still had to contend with the Hillgreen, Lane.[33] Despite the complexities of scheduling around the many classes and services that the chapel would host, most events featuring the organ would now be held in the chapel instead of McFarlin Auditorium, and organ events in the auditorium were drastically curtailed.[34] The next year, 1952, saw an abundance of musical events in the chapel. In February E. Power Biggs performed a solo recital,[35] while Mrs. Barclay reprised her dedication concert for the Music Teachers National Association convention.[36] Thomas Webber played for the Texas Chapter of the AGO the next month,[37] and in April a concert of ensemble music for organ featured works for strings and organ by Handel, Piston, and Poulenc, with organists Mary Elizabeth Moore, Rule Beasley, and Eugene Ellsworth, a member of the music faculty.[38] That same year, organist William Watkins (no relation to the Dallas Hillgreen, Lane representative) performed, with Edwin Arthur Kraft performing in 1953.[39] In 1955 Clair Coci "brought some expert poetizing and several spellbinding moments to the American Guild of Organists' recital series . . . the brunette organist's Dallas debut also attracted an almost capacity audience that remained in Perkins Chapel until Miss Coci had performed four encores."[40] The next year, Marilyn Mason's recital exemplified the renewed appreciation in modern North American composers and "contemporary repertoire, expressing a particular interest in living Americans."[41] Esteemed organist Alexander McCurdy, whose acquaintance with Dora Barclay was nurtured through her sending students to study with him at the Curtis Institute of Music, even came to play at Perkins Chapel in 1956, although not to perform on the organ. The Schulmerich bell-making firm had recently installed an Arlington-style carillon in the steeple at Perkins Chapel, and McCurdy, whose organ training was supplemented by studies in carillon at the University of California at Berkeley and at Bok Tower Gardens in Florida, performed a recital on this artificial carillon device.[42] The notable organists who could now perform at SMU were legion; however, that the organ department

had now reached a certain caliber was less evidenced in the organist stars it could attract than it was in the quality of students it could
produce, and recitals by SMU students and graduates would now
showcase young, homegrown talent.

Donald McDonald and William Teague were two of Dora Poteet
Barclay's students from the 1940s whom Alexander McCurdy recruited
to study at the Curtis Institute of Music and who subsequently enjoyed
performing, teaching, and church music careers. A conclave of the
AGO in December 1952, over which AGO president S. Lewis Elmer
presided, featured William Teague at Perkins Chapel. Teague, praised
for his "musicianship and showmanship,"[43] was rapidly becoming a
successful concert organist, having recently accepted the positions of
organist and choirmaster at St Mark's Episcopal Church in Shreveport
and on the music faculty at Centenary College.[44] In a memorized
recital, Teague played music of Handel, Bach, Willan, Langlais,
Dupré, and Vierne.[45] McDonald, a Waxahachie, Texas, native who
recalls riding the Interurban Railroad to Dallas to study with Dora
Poteet in the 1940s, and at the time a student at Union Theological Seminary, played a concert of Bach, Widor, Bingham, Ducasse,
Langlais, and Duruflé in the chapel in January 1954. A newspaper
review lauded his performance: "The Texas Chapter of the American
Guild of Organists had to look no farther than its own state citizenship
for one of its most compelling and sweetly persuasive recitalists in
several seasons. Donald McDonald, a native of Waxahachie and an
SMU alumnus . . . [played] the second recital on the annual series at
Perkins Chapel Tuesday night. He created an excitement rare for such
an event, and brought spontaneous bursts of applause from a usually
reserved audience, this time the capacity of the chapel. McDonald has
a magic touch, a wonderful sense of form and a rhythmic drive."[46]

Of these organ students, SMU and Dora Poteet Barclay
could be proud. They were local and had received their training
with Mrs. Barclay but had been recruited to the East to develop
their potential. Yet even students who remained local began to
accumulate professional successes, raising the standard of organ

performance and church music throughout the area. Barbara Marquart was one of Mrs. Barclay's last students, and she continued graduate studies with Barclay's successor, Robert Anderson. She would serve at St. Vincent's Cathedral (Episcopal) in Bedford, Texas, for many years, and as an adjunct instructor in the SMU organ department, assisting Robert Anderson. Russell Brydon was organist and choirmaster at Church of the Incarnation in Dallas, developing a notable church music program that continued through subsequent decades. Howard "Buddy" Ross, at the Episcopal Church of the Transfiguration in Dallas, likewise fostered the growth of church music in this major suburban parish. Walter Davis played the first daily worship service at Perkins Chapel before engaging in a career that took him to Ohio and then to South Texas. Whether SMU's graduates remained local or traveled elsewhere, this decade offered a first glimpse of the SMU organ department's emerging national reputation.

Recollections of Dora Poteet Barclay's Students

Mrs. Barclay's students were unequivocally and intensely loyal to their teacher, their abundant respect for her tempered only by their appreciation for her humanity. She could be friendly and engaging, or at times appropriately distant with her charges. Barbara Marquart, who studied with her from 1954 to 1959, remembers a woman who was never harsh or raised her voice, never expressing anger, yet suitably aloof. Marquart remembers Barclay as matter-of-fact in her organ instruction with a mild temperament. Barclay missed both Marquart's junior and senior recitals in Perkins Chapel, but apparently foregoing her students' recitals was a routine occurrence, the evaluation of which would be left to another professor.[47] Presumably, this was largely a result of her having moved to Fort Worth after her marriage in 1948, presenting difficulties for transportation, rather than ambivalence toward her students' efforts. Donald McDonald remembers her inimitable patience with him as a young student working through the

Eight Little Preludes and Fugues.[48] Howard Ross remembered her compassion when, after complaining to her about the brackish drinking water in Dallas during a drought, she brought him a container of clear water from Fort Worth.[49] Walter Davis affirmed that she was reserved toward her students at first but "warmed up once you got to know her." He remembers fondly her addressing him in a lesson shortly after World War II (and shortly after her marriage), saying, "Walter, can you get me some boxes of baking soda? I can't find any, and I have to cook for Bill!"[50] Her kindness even extended to packing a lunch for William Teague and personally seeing that he safely made it on the train to Philadelphia for his audition with Alexander McCurdy in 1939.[51]

However Dora, the name by which her students referred to her, had a moody side. Peggy Bie wrote of one such experience:

> For the most part she was distantly friendly at lessons, always with great dignity and competence, but lesson time was strictly business. She really "threw the book at me" once in my very early career as a new organ major in 1953. . . . I was learning Bach's "Dorian Toccata," and had only played it for her once previously. I missed one pedal note! . . .
>
> Suddenly there was a big crash, and something big and hard hit my head and bounced down both manuals, making a tremendous noise! I was startled and turned around to see what had happened.
>
> Dora was sitting to my left and slightly behind me. She had thrown a hymn book, and it had hit me, hard! As I looked at her in utter surprise she set the stage for all future lessons. She yelled in absolute stern fury—you missed the note last week. Don't you ever, Ever, EVER dare return to a lesson without having absolutely fixed everything I pointed out to you in a previous lesson. . . .
>
> I lay my speedy progress on the instrument directly to that moment! But it didn't harm our relationship a bit.[52]

Walter Davis also addressed this aspect of her personality, saying, "We were all afraid of her at first. She could get angry,"[53] and

Russell Brydon similarly maintained that "she had a violent temper."[54] Manifestations of her temper seem to have been directed at aspects of a musical performance rather than at the particular person, however. Lessons rarely started on time, but they could continue for hours.[55] Her approach to her own playing was the same as her pedagogical approach; she was thorough, meticulous, exacting, and unforgiving of technical mistakes, whether belonging to her or her students.

She believed firmly that a solid organ technique was predicated on a secure piano technique. Russell Brydon maintained that the secret of her success was that "for each lesson, students transposed Hanon exercises by ½ step at the piano." These exercises were not played fast, and the fingers were lifted high and then depressed straight down. Mrs. Barclay practiced this herself for thirty minutes a day.[56] Further, William Teague remembered that her wrist was always flexibly and efficiently motionless, and she deployed an intentional thumb-under technique.[57] She herself had studied piano from an early age and presumably had consolidated her piano and organ technique by the time she studied with Dupré in 1937. In the absence of a suitable instrument, she practiced manual parts on her piano at home, earning a formidable reputation as a technician. Virgil Fox, upon his visit to SMU, even inquired about her fingering for a certain passage,[58] and near the end of her life H. W. Gray had requested she write a book on organ technique.[59] Her students unanimously maintained that her playing was practically flawless, a result of her claim that "she could practice longer without turning the page than anybody else!"[60] William Teague speaks of this perfection by citing an instance in which he heard otherwise:

> She was very strict and had an incredible ear. She could detect the slightest mistake. All the times I heard Dora play, I heard her split [miss] only one note, and never heard her play a wrong one. Splitting that one note, the first note in the right hand of the A Minor Chorale of Franck, threw her into a funk for

six weeks. She could not abide a mistake that could've been prevented. She had been a pupil of Dupré and graduated from the conservatory at Fontainebleau with the highest honors of anyone who had studied with him at that point. Dora never turned the page until the page she was working on was absolutely perfect.[61]

Her students likewise attested that Dora Poteet struggled with what later generations might deem "performance anxiety." She inculcated an unwavering perfectionism in her students—the same unrelenting perfectionism that propelled her own career to great heights. Her efforts to achieve perfection were undoubtedly motivated by her fear of public failure, a struggle many performers have shared. Dora Poteet Barclay confided to Walter Davis's mother that "I have always just wanted to crawl down into that organ pit and play without being seen."[62] Her students recalled her reticence to travel elsewhere to perform, motivated mostly by a fear of performance.

If Barclay had to contend with some manner of performance anxiety, as some of her students suggested, this would be manifest in both her teaching and performing. Her attention to musical excellence and detail, and her pride in being able to "practice longer without turning the page than anyone else," mitigated against her commanding a vast repertoire, which most of her students agreed was limited.[63] Yet the pieces she did play, she chose carefully and knew thoroughly. She allowed students to only select pieces to study that she had in her own repertoire, and the selection, favoring the romantics, was not particularly comprehensive.[64] Although she performed Bach frequently, her programs do not indicate a comprehensive knowledge of his oeuvre. Barbara Marquart mentions never having heard of her playing or teaching any of the *Clavierübung,* focusing rather on selected chorale preludes and the major Preludes and Fugues and other large-scale works, favoring the Franklin Glenn, Riemenschneider, and Dupré Bach editions.[65] Walter Davis remembers her lamenting that she never learned the complete organ works

Student Walter Davis in a lesson with Dora Poteet Barclay.
Courtesy of Walter Davis.

of Bach.[66] Dr. Teague suggests her repertoire was more encompassing than has been presumed, some evidence of which is her knowledge of all the organ works of Franck.

Barclay's experience in France nurtured her interest in French composers, although she was not particularly an exponent of contemporary music or living composers, playing their music presumably in spite of their contemporary status. She frequently performed Maurice Duruflé's Suite pour Orgue, Opus 5, and Dupré's *Variations sur un Noël* before they were well-known; she taught Vierne's Symphony No. 2, although conspicuously always omitting the last two movements![67] More elementary students generally played the same repertoire, usually including Boëllman's *Suite gothique*, Henri Mulet's *Tu es Petra*, and some of C. Hubert H. Parry's chorale preludes.[68] The Liszt *Ad Nos* and Reubke's *Ninety-Fourth Psalm* were staples of her German repertoire, which, with the exception of some Bach, was limited. Some students were given the Gleason organ method, while more advanced players concentrated on repertoire.[69] She used Nielsen's *Pedal Studies* with some students.[70] She never played from memory or encouraged her own students to do so, although one student from the mid-1950s with a prodigious memory, Mary Hall, elicited fame for playing her student recitals without music—a first for the SMU organ department.[71]

Dora Poteet Barclay's playing is of its era, a time before performance practice studies had been applied cogently to organ performance. Her surviving performances may seem idiosyncratic to some modern ears. An undated recording of her performing the Prelude and Fugue in G major, BWV 541, in Perkins Chapel demonstrates a conservatively registered prelude at an unhurried tempo with a consistent application of legato and a few unusual caesuras at the end of phrases.[72] In the final measures, she adds the manual and pedal reeds. The fugue dances along at a brisk tempo, still sufficiently legato. Episodic material in the fugue is played on a secondary manual, with liberal use of the swell box, before she effects a gradual crescendo to the end. It is not true that her baroque playing was all legato. William

Teague explains that she employed a "leggiero approach to Bach, not really legato," and that her very clean articulation was a result of a consistent application of various degrees of leggiero.[73] A recording of her performing Bach's "Toccata, Adagio and Fugue" on the TCU Möller indicates her different articulations.[74] The opening of the toccata employs a sharp staccato, but subsequent sections are moderated almost to legato, with registration changes and swell box manipulations delineating the form. The adagio section manifests Russell Brydon's contention that her playing lacked "sentiment."[75] The solo line is registered with a high-pitch mutation to which is added a rapidly spinning tremolo, accompanied by a soft flute. This alternates with a large flue taking the solo line with a nonundulating string accompaniment, all with the abundant use of the swell box, with the Grave section at a lugubrious pace and gradually crescendoing until the end. Although she employs rubato in the requisite places and takes great concern for dynamics, whether through registration changes or from the use of the swells, her control and discipline is still prioritized over emotion. The fugue, taken at a rapid tempo and employing all manner of registration changes, demonstrates a careful use of leggiero alternating with subtle, almost legato, slurs. Interestingly, these recordings manifest numerous minor "note splits," which, while in no way detracting from her performance, suggest that the disease that was to take her life was already manifesting itself in her playing.

A Panoply of Personalities

One of Dora Poteet Barclay's students, Peggy Carol Bie, whose junior recital at Perkins Chapel in June 1954 included works by Weitz, Franck, Vierne, Mendelssohn and Bach,[76] would gain international notoriety several decades later when, in the course of her studying and playing in Cold War Germany, she made the acquaintance of a Turkish *Gastarbeiter* automotive technician, Hüseyin Yildirim. She would sponsor Yildirim's emigration to the United States in the mid-1980s, only to testify on his behalf when he and notorious spy James Hall were collectively convicted of espionage against the United States in 1989.

Bie lamented that her completed doctoral dissertation, dedicated to American pianist William Mason, was confiscated by the CIA, which was convinced she was assisting espionage efforts through a system of microdots in the music. Bie, who had been employed as an organist in both the United States and Germany, would follow Yildirim from prison to prison, camping in her RV, until he was finally extradited to Turkey in 2003.[77] Bie died in 2010.[78]

Dr. Eugene Ellsworth, a Union Theological Seminary graduate in organ, theory, and sacred music, having previously taught at Wagner College on Staten Island, arrived at SMU in the autumn of 1949 to teach music theory, replacing recently deceased, first-generation faculty member Harold Hart Todd.[79] Dr. Ellsworth, although hired to teach music theory, would involve himself in the local organ community. Earning the fellowship certificate from the AGO, he was organist and music director at East Dallas Christian Church (1949–1966) and then Midway Hills Christian Church (1966–1978) and served as dean of the Texas Chapter of the AGO from 1955 to 1957. Dr. Ellsworth performed organ recitals regionally[80] and lectured on organ topics.[81] Dr. Ellsworth's unique professional training in sacred music would lead to SMU's establishment of the bachelor's degree in sacred music starting in the 1951 academic year. This cooperative venture between the Perkins School of Theology and the School of Music comprised a curriculum dedicated to the "history of church music, liturgical music, hymnology, administration of church music, choral techniques, materials, conducting, etc." and would be guided by Dr. Ellsworth and Dr. Fred Gealy at the theology school.[82]

Rev. Dr. Fred Gealy, a professor in the School of Theology since 1940, would find himself drawn to matters of organ installation and performance. Holding degrees in theology from Allegheny College, Boston University, and Union Theological Seminary, further studies took him to Europe. Ordained in the Methodist Church, from 1923 to 1936 he taught in Japan before returning to the United States.[83] At SMU his teaching specialty was missions, informed by his years abroad; yet he always fostered an interest in church music and organ performance. He wrote modestly of his musical pedigree:

> My degrees are all in the field of theology proper, music being rather an avocation. However, I have spent so much time during the years working with church choirs, and now giving courses in Hymnology and in the Church Choir in the School of Theology of S.M.U., that I sometimes feel just like a professional musician. I may say that my own musical instruction has all been in piano and pipe-organ. From the organ I advanced to choir direction, and then to the conductors-ship of an oratorio society. For ten years in Tokyo, Japan, I conducted an oratorio society, giving two concerts a year, and conducting such major choral works as Creation, Elijah, Messiah, the Brahms' German Requiem, the Bach Magnificat and Christmas Oratorio. At present I am organist and choir director of the Univ. Park Methodist Church.[84]

Gealy's official work may only have been peripherally related to the organ, but he kept busy in the organ community. In addition to serving as organist at University Park Methodist Church in Dallas from 1951 to 1956, where he oversaw the installation of a new Möller organ,[85] he played for services and many weddings at Perkins Chapel throughout the 1950s. He served as dean of the Texas Chapter of the AGO from 1951 to 1953 and as chaplain of the Dallas Chapter from 1969 until 1970.[86] He almost certainly was on the committee that selected the Aeolian-Skinner for Perkins Chapel in 1945. He would direct the Seminary Singers, the chapel's resident choral ensemble, throughout much of his tenure on the faculty. Barclay student Walter Davis, whose father taught at Perkins School of Theology and for whose funeral Gealy preached, remembered Dr. Gealy as a competent service organist with the limited repertoire one might expect from an organist with multiple professions and specialties.[87] Gealy contributed significantly to the eventual development of the MSM program.

Gealy's connection to M. P. Möller seems to have been nurtured through their collaboration on Möller's Opus 8107 organ for University

Park Methodist Church. Nonetheless, correspondence between Gealy and the firm seems to indicate the intentions Möller might have had for future work at SMU. Gealy's favor must have been worth earning; that his musical opinions were respected in the SMU music community is implied in a letter from Möller's Texas representative Gordon Young to Gealy in 1949:

> While Mr. Ridgely and Mr. Daniels from Möllers were here we called on Dr. Umphrey Lee and Dr. Orville Borchers [SMU School of Music dean] relative to doing something about the McFarlin auditorium organ and we are now in process of making a complete study of the situation so that something may possibly be worked out. I expressed to Dr. Lee at that time our high regard for your work at Southern Methodist University and told him of signing the contract with your church. I am sure that both Borchers and Lee will consult with you on this and naturally we shall appreciate any reference or recognition which you may care to make in behalf of Möller.[88]

Despite Möller's hopes to the contrary, their firm's presence at SMU would remain negligible, their only contribution being the construction of a new, stop-knob, classical console to replace the dilapidated Hillgreen, Lane horseshoe-style console at McFarlin Auditorium in 1953.[89] The newspaper waxed lyrical about the $10,000 console, donated by Mr. and Mrs. George P. Cullum, extolling the device as containing "all the parts of an organ except the pipes and bellows—namely the manuals (keyboards), foot pedals, mechanical and electrical system and cabinet work."[90] Even such a magnanimous upgrade failed to stave off the old organ's decay, and with the completion of the new music building a few years later, the Hillgreen, Lane was virtually abandoned, relegated to appear only at graduations, ministers' week, and occasional community services.

Möller's efforts were not completely fruitless. While living in Fort Worth, Dora Poteet Barclay had served as organist and director of music at St. Andrew's Episcopal Church, where she was instrumental

Barclay student Peggy Bie at the new Möller console in McFarlin Auditorium in 1958. This was taken from a cached copy of Peggy Bie's website.

in installing Möller, Opus 8546, in 1953, an organ of three manuals and twenty-nine ranks.[91] Her apparent affection for the similarly sized Perkins Chapel Aeolian-Skinner had compelled her originally to seek a bid from Aeolian-Skinner, but the shop's wait time discouraged her, and Möller built the instrument. The company reciprocated by honoring her as "an outstanding artist of the organ" in a 1956 brochure.[92]

Dora Poteet Barclay's Final Years

The Texas Chapter of the AGO sponsored her in a recital on February 4, 1958, at Park Cities Baptist Church in Dallas, where she performed a program of Bach, Schumann, Jongen, Vierne, Messiaen, Duruflé, and Liszt[93] on the IV/62, Reuter, Opus 1179, built in 1956.[94] Barbara Marquart reported that this event was "a wonderful concert, spectacularly played."[95] The professional recording of the affair showcases an artist at the height of her command of the organ, with effervescent and insatiable rhythmic drive coupled with delicate shadings of timbre, all carefully regulated by her characteristic discipline.

On Sunday, February 7, 1960, Dora Poteet Barclay played a concert at St Mark's Episcopal Church in Shreveport at the request of her former student, William Teague. Her program included Bach's "Wir danken Dir," the Fantasy in G major, selections from Widor and Vierne, and the Liszt *Ad Nos* Fantasy and Fugue. She later recalled her feet not responding with their characteristic nimble dexterity to the pedal trills in this piece.[96] William Teague had invited her to perform this recital after hearing her play in Wichita Falls but recalled her reluctance, the cause of which was unbeknownst to him at the time:

> I heard her play for a regional convention up at Nita Akin's church. She played the "Ad nos" and it was just stunning. After the program I said, "You must come play this same program at St Mark's," and she said, "Oh, I don't think so." (I didn't know she was already having trouble, so was insistent with her.) She said, "Oh, I'll do it for you." Her paralysis started in her feet, and she was having to repedal everything, which I did not

realize. She came to St. Mark's and played, and that was her last recital. Unfortunately, the Contra Ophicleide ciphered during the "Ad nos" and ruined the recording. I tried to get her to go back in after we got the cipher stopped and record the "Ad nos" again, but she just could not do it.[97]

The unmistakable symptoms of Lou Gehrig's disease (ALS), progressive neurodegeneracy, had already set in. An appointment at the Mayo Clinic confirmed the diagnosis, certainly a cruel circumstance for anyone but particularly for one who depends on their fine motor skills to apply their vocation.[98]

As her body was ravaged by disease, her mind continued unabated, seeking to teach music as she had always done. William Teague realized this and lovingly proffered his assistance:

She became more and more paralyzed, and was finally confined to bed. I would go visit her, and once asked her husband, "Bill, is there anything I can do for Dora?" Well, this was during the time when I had my radio broadcasts from St Mark's. He said, "Why don't you bring the tapes over once a month and let Dora coach you on the pieces?" I thought this was a wonderful idea, so once a month I would write her a letter telling her what I was preparing, then would take the tapes over for her to listen to. One time, toward the end, she was in the bed and I could tell she was getting very agitated. Finally she said, "Oh, turn it off. Has this been broadcast?" and I said, "Yes." She said, "Oh, GOSH!— You didn't mention my name, did you, as your teacher?" I said, "No." And she said, "Well don't if you're going to play like that! You don't remember anything I taught you. You realize you're playing pieces that you studied with me. Besides, you recorded these too late in the evening. If you'll go back and start the tape, I can tell you what time of the night it is by your playing!" She was that sharp. We listened to the tape again, and she was right. Little things happened, like a missed ending to a phrase, a smeared note, or a rushed note. She said, "The later you go, the worse you play. You're not alert. Now get the score. I don't have enough life in me to teach this again. I told you exactly what to do with it in 1939. I can tell you are not using my fingering or my pedaling, now get the score and mark it. You go back and learn this right and bring it back the next time." I did, of course. And that was the last time I played for her.

After that she only had occasional lucid moments. I asked her husband to, if she had a lucid moment, please give her my love and ask her if there was anything I could do. He called me back in the afternoon and said, "Dora did have a period where she was lucid, and said there is something you can do for her. She asked that you play for her funeral, and she gave me a list of everything to be played." She died that night.[99]

Dora Poteet Barclay died on Bach's Julian-calendar birthday, March 21, 1961, at her home. A funeral was held at First Presbyterian Church in Fort Worth, where William Barclay was music director, on Thursday afternoon of that week.[100] As requested, William Teague played the "Saint Anne" fugue (BWV 552b), Brahms's chorale prelude, "O Welt, ich muss dich lassen," Widor's Toccata, and Handel's "I Know that My Redeemer Liveth" with a soloist.[101] Another memorial service was held later that same afternoon in Dallas at Hillcrest Mausoleum Chapel, at which SMU president Willis Tate presided. Of her he said, "Mrs. Barclay was worshipped by her students, many of whom, through her inspiration and guidance, have proceeded to professional success and prominence as organists."[102]

To honor Dora's legacy, the Dallas and Fort Worth Chapters of the AGO released a commercial recording of her concert at Park Cities Baptist Church from 1958. Entitled the *Dora Poteet Barclay Organ Recital Memorial Issue,* proceeds from the 1,000-pressing disc would benefit the newly established Dora Poteet Barclay Award, initially a fifty-dollar prize presented to SMU junior or senior organ students with at least a B average.[103] The Meadows School of the Arts at SMU continues to bestow the Dora Poteet Barclay Award to exceptional organ students to this day. E. Clyde Whitlock, in his jacket notes for the album, pens a worthy tribute to the Texan organist:

It is not given to many people in this life to have an important influence upon the music of three major Christian communions,

Dora Poteet Barclay at Broadway Baptist Church in Fort Worth.
Picture property of Benjamin Kolodziej, courtesy of Dan Garland.

but such was the destiny of Dora Poteet Barclay. In fulfilling her responsibilities as Chairman of the Organ Department of Southern Methodist University, as well as her many years as organist-choirmaster of Episcopal churches, and also in the Presbyterian Church of which she was a communicant and where her husband is a Minister of Music, her influence will be felt and remembered for many years.

Probably no organist of the Southwest had as influential a career throughout as long a period of time as did Dora Poteet Barclay. She excelled as concert organist, church organist, and teacher. . . .

Many organists professionally engaged throughout the country trace their standing to study with Mrs. Barclay during her thirty year tenure at S.M.U. . . .

In organ recitals on the afternoon of Easter Day, 1961, Mrs. Grenier at the Washington Cathedral and Mr. Ryan at St. Thomas in New York, each played a number dedicated to Mrs. Barclay's memory, works they had studied with her.[104]

The M. P. Möller firm, in issuing a 1956 booklet entitled *The Artists of the Organ and The Organs of the Artists*, extolled her pedagogy and performance:

> Mrs. Barclay's knowledge and application of the French method of organ playing have placed her in the vanguard as a teacher. As chairman of the organ department at Southern Methodist University, she has produced many fine organists which include some of the outstanding artists in the concert field today. Notable among these are William Teague and Donald MacDonald, both of whom received their foundation work from Mrs. Barclay and later received scholarships from the Curtis Institute of Music, Philadelphia.
>
> Mrs. Barclay has the distinction of having played to the largest audience ever to attend an organ recital in Fort Worth. Later at St. Andrew's a new Moeller organ was installed and her first recital was played on this instrument to a congregation that filled the church. Approval of her artistry was immediate. Moeller points with pride to Dora Poteet Barclay—an outstanding Artist of the Organ.[105]

Barclay represented the consummate native Texan musician, of which there had been few exemplars. She trained in the university at which she was to teach successfully for over three decades, a professional longevity typical of a time long past. Also characteristic of another era were her extensive musical successes in spite of her rather parochial pedigree, studying with local organists until settling at SMU for an undergraduate, essentially conservatory, education. She neither had advanced academic degrees nor was known as a scholar, as these would only be deemed professional requirements for university music professors in subsequent decades. Performance study with her "beloved maître,"[106] Marcel Dupré, albeit briefly for one fleeting summer, provided just enough exoticism on her résumé to lend her career any requisite professional credence. Yet even Dupré intimated that she had come to him as a complete and mature musician. His influence on her was real, particularly in her repertoire, but her playing seemed fully formed by that time, a tribute to both her musical acumen and her Texas teachers, with due credit to her occasional summer coaches in New York City. *Dallas Morning News* critic E. Clyde Whitlock evaluated her extensive legacy, observing that her influence was felt far beyond SMU: "Dora Barclay's death removed from Texas one of the finest executant artists ever associated with the State's musical life. She was regarded with respect as a musician, with honor for her high professional ideals and attainments and with affection as a person."[107] Her concern for musical excellence garnered her a formidable reputation in her early career, but an editorial in the *Fort Worth Star-Telegram* suggested that the actual constitution of her success was that "Dora Poteet Barclay cared enough to take the time to get everything right," a care evidenced not only in her musical performance but also in her relationship with her many students who would remember her fondly while continuing her legacy.[108]

Chapter 5

New Directions
Robert Theodore Anderson

The postwar era marked a discernable economic, social, and political reconfiguration of American society largely unprecedented in the prior generation. The Great Depression compelled the country to confront scarcity while Franklin Roosevelt's New Deal policies sought to bring about "relief, recovery, and reform" to a nation crippled by economic malaise.[1] World War II reinvigorated the industrial capacity of the United States at the expense of a great many lives lost overseas, while the subsequent Cold War divested the country of any remnants of international isolationism. The technological innovation required to defeat fascism, then sustain military parity with the Communists, brought about new professions and new ways of living. The GI Bill not only assisted returning veterans in their education but also provided low-interest loans that facilitated purchasing homes, and "suburbia" entered the American lexicon for the first time. Cheap land, tract housing, and inexpensive automobiles facilitated such development, spurred by corporate growth that increasingly preferred a nonurban setting.[2] In North Texas the suburbs surrounding Dallas experienced exponential growth from 1950 to 1960. The northern towns in particular benefited from the new Central Expressway, a north-south artery linking downtown to Richardson, Dallas's contiguous northern neighbor, by 1956. Technology giants Texas Instruments and Collins Radio established themselves in Richardson by the mid-1950s, presaging the corporate centers the northern suburbs became by the 1960s and 1970s.[3] That city grew from a population of 1,289 in 1950 to 16,810 by 1960, while another suburb, Garland, grew from 10,571 in 1950 to 38,501 in 1960.[4] Both the growth and the redistribution of the populace necessitated that mainline denominations adapt their parish governance to the domestic patterns of their membership. The Methodist Church (USA), formed in 1939, grew by one million members between 1950 and 1960, and these suburbs were fertile ground for new church plants.[5] Perkins School of Theology counted 300 students enrolled in 1949, peaking at 415 students in 1958.[6] New churches, it seems, sought not only ministers but also ancillary support staff—notably, professionals to administer parish education and sacred music programs.

Developing the Master of Sacred Music Program

Southern Methodist University recognized the need for sacred musicians, or "ministers of music" as documents of the time prefer to call them, to be as dexterous in their pastoral skills as they were in their musical and administrative abilities. In 1951, under the auspices of the School of Music and with the cooperation of Dr. Fred Gealy of Perkins School of Theology, the university initiated a bachelor of sacred music degree program, the curriculum for which included coursework in "history of church music, liturgical music, hymnology, administration of church music, choral techniques, materials, conducting, etc."[7] The degree was hindered by a lack of accompanying theological instruction, a fact recognized by Dr. Gealy in 1953. While writing to counsel a pastor who had written for advice on behalf of a prospective student, Paul Ofield, Gealy assessed SMU's relative inability to train church musicians:

I think you know how inadequately we are equipped at Perkins to prepare a man for the musical ministry. Of course, there is a

School of Music in the University which could give a general and intensive musical background, and we have the one course really in Perkins on hymnology, which I do. But we do not really work here in problems of choir directing and so forth. He could get a Master's Degree in Religious Education here and some music on the side, but frankly we are not equipped to give a man the sort of education musically which he needs to get a good position as a minister of music in a church of any size. The demands are constantly increasing, and if a man is to make a career of church music he just about has to go to the School of Music at Union Theological Seminary or to the Westminster Choir School at Princeton. . . . Of course, we like to have musical persons in Perkins. That helps to make our program good. But we must honestly say that our work is very definitely pointed towards the Bachelor of Divinity degree. A student coming here for any other purpose is therefore likely to be a bit disappointed.[8]

This lacuna in the curriculum troubled both Dr. Gealy, a musically minded theologian, and the Perkins School of Theology dean, Merrimon Cuninggim, who was prepared to address the problem. Dean Cuninggim invited Robert Guy McCutchan, editor of the 1935 *Methodist Hymnal*, to teach as visiting professor during the spring 1954 and 1955 terms,[9] underscoring his commitment to the study of sacred music.

In May 1955 J. W. and Nita Akin of Wichita Falls pledged $2,000 per year for four years to support the initiation of sacred music studies,[10] a gift Dean Cuninggim qualified as "the real beginning of our development of a first-class program for training of Ministers of Music."[11] This gift subsidized a Consultation on Church Music, organized that November by Dean Cuninggim and Dean Orville Borchers of the School of Music to gather "competent counsel from leaders in the field of Church Music across the country" in order to ascertain how the university might best establish a "Program for the training of Ministers of Music."[12] This deceptively modest "consultation" featured some of the most prominent church and university musicians nationwide, including Earl Harper, director of the School of Fine Arts, State University of Iowa; Mack Harrell, an instructor at the Juilliard

School; Ruth Krehbiel Jacobs, president of Chorister's Guild; David Jones, a professor of music at Princeton Theological Seminary; Austin Lovelace, minister of music at St Luke's Methodist in Oklahoma City; Hugh Porter, director of the School of Sacred Music at Union Theological Seminary; and John Finley Williamson, president of Westminster Choir College. Representatives from SMU's theology and music schools included Dora Poteet Barclay, Fred Gealy, Eugene Ellsworth, and George C. Baker Sr., while Nita and J. W. Akin, whose philanthropy was made possible through oil ventures, were likewise in attendance at the conference they had sponsored.[13]

The panel affirmed that a full-time faculty position would be required to develop this new MSM program. By 1956 the search was underway, culminating in the hiring of acclaimed choral conductor and pedagogue Lloyd Pfautsch with the 1958–1959 academic year. Pfautsch was uniquely qualified for this endeavor, being a graduate of Elmhurst College and Union Theological Seminary, where his master's thesis explored "A Curriculum of Church Music for a Theological Seminary." That he had matriculated from Union Theological Seminary, whose model for sacred music graduate studies SMU had hoped to emulate, and that his thesis demonstrated thoughtful analysis of such a model, only added to his luster. The tension between musical and ministerial studies had vexed Pfautsch, as in his early years he equivocated between ordination (his degree from Elmhurst was in theology) and fulfilling his musical vocation as a singer, conductor, and teacher. He had been professor of voice and choral director at Illinois Wesleyan University from 1948 to 1958, having attained national recognition as a choral clinician.[14] Assembling a committee comprised of both deans and representative faculty from the music and theology schools, Pfautsch immersed himself in the task of developing and implementing a viable MSM curriculum, inaugurated in the autumn of 1959. By the beginning of the 1961 term, the MSM program had twelve students enrolled.[15]

The initial consultation in November 1955, to establish a groundwork for the MSM program, included four women among the twenty-nine participants, among which was Dora Poteet Barclay.

Lloyd Pfautsch. Rotunda Collection, SMU Archives,
DeGolyer Library, SMU.

Curiously, the abridged transcripts from two days of meetings suggest
Mrs. Barclay was a passive observer. She is not recorded as having
contributed anything, although the other women freely offered thoughts.
The correspondence among Borchers, Cuninggim, and Gealy during
these years indicates no consultation with Mrs. Barclay. Presumably,
as a member of the School of Music faculty, she had no connection to
Perkins School of Theology beyond use of Perkins Chapel as the main
performance venue for the organ department; further, that the MSM
lacked the traditional applied major of the master of music (MM)
may have obfuscated its value in the minds of faculty accustomed to

traditional academic delineations. Indeed, for a number of years after the MSM program had been initiated, faculty in the music school were occasionally blunt in expressing their opinion that the program catered to students who could not perform technically at a master's level.[16] When Lloyd Pfautsch arrived at SMU, Dora Poteet Barclay still held the post of professor of organ, but her influence was admittedly negligible. Pfautsch, however, knew the importance of the organ faculty to the success of his new degree program and immediately began his recruitment efforts, centered on the young accompanist from his days at Illinois Wesleyan University, Robert Theodore Anderson.

Robert Anderson

Robert Anderson was born on October 5, 1934, in Chicago, Illinois, to Albert Theodore (Ted) Anderson and Lillian Gertrude Anderson, both of whom cultivated a household whose children were steeped in musical endeavors. Both parents and his sister, Dorothy, sang in the Swedish Choral Club, and both Ted and his other son, Ron, played trombone in school. His mother's love for music motivated her to purchase a $425 Krakauer Bros. grand piano in 1931. Beginning piano study around age six, young Robert was always self-motivated in his practice, performing in regular studio recitals at the American Conservatory of Music from 1940 to 1951. The family held membership at Hyde Park Methodist Church, where he turned pages for his teacher, Mary Ruth Craven.[17] Marcel Dupré's performances during the summer of 1946, in which he was in residence at the University of Chicago teaching students and performing six recitals,[18] inspired the 12-year-old Anderson, and he began organ lessons with Frederick Marriott, organist at Rockefeller chapel from 1928 to 1953 and himself a Dupré student.[19] By age 14 Anderson was playing regularly at church. Excelling at Hyde Park High School, both scholastically and musically, he sang in the a cappella choir, even composing a song, "We Must Say Goodbye," for graduation in June 1951. He performed baritone solos in the choir's 1950 and 1951 spring productions.[20]

Robert Anderson began his undergraduate education at Illinois Wesleyan University (IWU), studying organ with Lillian Mecherle McCord, a graduate of the Guilmant Organ School, Illinois Wesleyan, and Union Theological Seminary.[21] McCord was a pedagogue of some repute and taught numerous prominent organists of the latter twentieth century, including Marilyn Keiser and Schuyler Robinson.[22] The respect between teacher and student was mutual, McCord thinking so highly of Anderson that she invited him to play a joint organ recital in May 1952, at the end of his first year in college, at Saybrook (Illinois) Methodist Church.[23] In 1952, along with five other music students, Anderson received the Presser Scholarship, awarded "on the basis of scholarship, musicianship and need by the vote of the entire music faculty at IWU."[24] For his junior recital in 1954, Anderson performed Bach's Prelude and Fugue in G major and Dupré's *Variations sur un Noël*.[25] The next year he was elected president of the Phi Mu Alpha music fraternity.[26] For his senior recital at IWU's Presser Hall, he played Mozart's Fantasy in F Minor, K 608, a Daquin *Noël*, the Prelude and Fugue in E minor of Bach, Roger-Ducasse's *Pastorale* and the Reubke *Ninety-Fourth Psalm*.[27] McCord's admiration for her student approached veneration; decades later she recalled her experiences with her young protégé, assessing him as

> a genius thru native ability, hard work, a good, good organization ability . . . generous in his opinions of others, an ideal of perfection in all he does, an enjoyment of driving cars and eating good food and of course a good cook and the best musician I've ever known who chose pipe organ to express the wonderful music down through the years. . . .
>
> He never quits learning, experimenting to get the sounds he wants and uses tension and relaxation to bring out different ideas different touches all incorporated in his mastery of the instrument, the subtlety of the music and the grandeur of the sounds under his complete control. The "digging in" with relaxation at the end of the phrase or whatever. He lets the music flow out under his guidance.[28]

The years at Illinois Wesleyan afforded him the opportunity to study composition with Union Seminary graduate Frank Bohnhorst, professor of organ and theory and composer in residence at IWU,[29] whose promising career was cut short by his untimely death at age 32 in 1956.[30] Although he had composed some student works as early as 1950,[31] mentored by Bohnhorst, Anderson honed his compositional facilities with his first choral work, "Sing Unto the Lord," composed in 1953 for soprano, alto, tenor, and bass (SATB) and organ. A Sonata for Oboe and Piano (1954) and Two Pieces for Flute and Piano (1952) also date from his IWU years.[32] Anderson collaborated with university choir director Lloyd Pfautsch while accompanying the university choral ensembles. Pfautsch was impressed by Anderson, recalling, "I had about ten students of the caliber of Bob Anderson in the choir. Can you imagine ten Bob Andersons running around your campus? One was a flutist, one a violinist; several were singers or pianists—a really good mix. At least six of them had perfect pitch. So I could do quite demanding works with the choir."[33] During his college years Anderson served as organist at Second Presbyterian Church in Bloomington, Illinois, and during the summers as organist at Fourth Presbyterian Church in Chicago.[34]

Robert Anderson graduated in June 1955 from Illinois Wesleyan and began studies at Union Theological Seminary in New York City, the natural trajectory for advanced sacred music studies at the time, particularly for someone whose primary teachers had all studied there. He commenced composition studies with Harold Friedell, also organist at St. Bartholomew's Church in Manhattan. Friedell guided Anderson as he poured his creative energies into composition during the Union years of 1955–1957, composing for organ a *Passacaglia on the Southern Folk Hymn "Saints Delight"* (1955), *Three Sketches* (1955), a *Toccata* (1955), *Two Chorale Preludes* (1955), Sonata I (1956) and *Two Extemporizations* (1956). In the realm of choral liturgical music, he also completed an SATB *Te Deum* (1957) and "Benedic Anima Mea" (1956); for two voices, "God is Our Refuge"

(1956);[35] and a multivoice setting of Darwall's 148th, "Rejoice, the Lord is King" (1955) that was later published.[36] He composed four a cappella SATB settings during 1955–1956—namely, an "Introit for Easter Day," "Let Thy Merciful Ears, O Lord," "The Eucharist," and "Hodie, Christus Natus Est." To this he added a smattering of secular and hymn-based choral settings, among them a "Bird's Courtin' Song" (1955) for SATB and piano.[37] Although Anderson succeeded in having some pieces published in the ensuing decades, he was never again as prolific in his creative output. After his return to Union for his doctor of musical arts (DMA) after studies in Europe, he studied composition again with Seth Bingham (Harold Friedell had died in 1958), enlisting Bingham's assistance in publishing a cantata, *Garden of Gethsemane*, which Anderson had written to fulfill requirements for final graduation from Union in 1961. Although Bingham's efforts were unsuccessful, he affirms that "it does not surprise me that your name as a player is getting around and that audiences like your compositions; I know you really deserve this success."[38] While at Union he studied organ with Robert Baker, a student of Clarence Dickinson. It was Baker who successfully performed Anderson's "Triptych" for the 1958 AGO Convention in Houston.[39]

In addition to serving Union Seminary as organist at James Memorial Chapel, Anderson was employed as organist and choirmaster at the United Church of Christ in Milford, Connecticut, from 1955 to 1957. He earned his AAGO certification in 1955, and the fellowship (FAGO) certification in 1957.[40] After graduating magna cum laude with his MSM degree in the spring of 1957, Anderson briefly returned to Chicago to coach with Heinrich Fleischer, who had assumed organist duties at Rockefeller Memorial Chapel after the resignation of Frederick Marriott, with whom he had coached throughout his undergraduate years.[41] Study with Fleischer allowed Anderson to burnish his credentials further in the Germanic repertoire, Fleischer having been a student of Karl Straube in Leipzig.[42]

Robert Theodore Anderson's Fulbright portrait (ca. 1957).
Robert T. Anderson Papers, SMU Archives, DeGolyer Library, SMU.

Fulbright Study with Helmut Walcha

Anderson departed in the autumn of 1957 for Frankfurt, where he
spent two years studying at the Hochschule für Musik with Helmut
Walcha, one of the foremost twentieth-century exponents of Bach's
music. Gradually blinded as a teenager because of a smallpox vaccine,
Walcha trained his ears to compensate, learning polyphonic music one
voice at a time. During the years 1956–1971, Walcha undertook a
stereo recording of the complete works of Bach a second time, the first
having been recorded in monaural during the late 1940s for Deutsche

Grammophone.[43] These earlier recordings had enraptured Anderson, who recalled,

> I remember well my reactions to the first Decca releases in the early '50s. I found a convincing, indeed extraordinary understanding of the idiom—an identification of Baroque keyboard style coupled with the sound of the old organs—something which I had not heard previously. In those days, I thought that organists were playing games with Bach—creating screwy "articulations" with hot-stove 16ths and legato 8ths; registration had no stylistic commonality. Walcha had a formula, but this seemed to be the thing that was needed at this time. Indeed, many of the great organists beginning their careers in the '50s were strongly influenced by Walcha. One could hear this in their early recordings. Walcha fit like a glove for me after McCord and Baker (Dickinson), Fleischer (Straube) and Marriott (Dupré).[44]

Anderson further recalls that Walcha had "no use" for Romantic music, and remained "devoted to Bach and Buxtehude and to polyphonic music in general." The lessons with Walcha on the Förster & Nicolaus organ at the Dreikönigskirche[45] were "very exciting," according to Anderson, as "most of us never cared to play wrong notes for Walcha so we practiced eight hours a day. Making sacrifices by practicing in a cold church was no different than I had experienced in Chicago winters. Nothing escaped his notice. Walcha's ear was the keenest I have ever known."[46] Lessons were scheduled once a week, all students beginning with the *Orgelbüchlein* and progressing through more significant works, a practice Robert Anderson continued in his own studio. Delbert Disselhorst, studying a few years later, recalled that Walcha's expectations were such that even large-scale works such as a prelude and fugue would be played in a lesson only two or three times before it needed to be mastered.[47]

A letter Anderson wrote to his parents in February 1959 reveals the palatable sense of reverence he held for Walcha: "Walcha played his last Bach Stunde at the university last night. He's giving them up for good now, after 20 years of continuous concerts during the winter seasons.

Helmut Walcha's students (*left to right*): Melvin Dickinson, Robert Anderson,
Margaret Leupold (Dickinson), Ursula Walcha, Helmut Walcha.
Robert T. Anderson Papers, SMU Archives, DeGolyer Library, SMU.

He will concentrate on special programs in the church. He says he feels
the effects of age (he will be 52), and finds it harder to keep his repertoire up well. He has, practically ready to play, 90 harpsichord works
(this counts the long Goldberg Variations—30 of them, (takes ½ hours
to play) as <u>one</u> work) and 160 organ works. His schedule is just fantastic."[48] Walcha's ability to learn music fast and retain it securely no doubt
inspired Anderson, and this work ethic was conveyed to his students.
Anderson also studied harpsichord in Frankfurt with Maria Jäger,
a professor with Walcha at the Hochschule.

Although his Frankfurt years were comprised primarily of studying
and hearing the great postwar composers and performers, Anderson
did perform concerts himself under the auspices of the American
Embassy in Bad Godesberg, the center of the American diplomatic
corps.[49] Although there is little surviving record of what or where he
played, except that he played "his own works as well as the traditional
repertory,"[50] Anderson was apparently not pleased with the limited

number of concerts, there being a couple in Frankfurt-am-Main and one in Bielefeld.[51] This was his first encounter with a broad range of historic European organs. Further, Walcha allowed him to deputize at the Dreikönigskirche, cultivating his service-playing and improvisational abilities.

Near the end of his Fulbright years, Anderson was anxious to arrange for doctoral study in the United States, and he was eventually accepted back at Union. Hugh Porter wrote to him, "We are extremely proud of the record you are making for yourself in Europe. We feel that what you are doing resounds to our credit as well as yours."[52] During the time Anderson was again in residence at Union, he resumed organ study with Robert Baker, began composition lessons with the aforementioned Seth Bingham, and worked as assistant to Julius Herford, a conducting teacher of Robert Shaw. Further, Anderson was active as a bass soloist in the area, continuing a tradition of vocal performance that he had begun in high school.[53]

Recruitment to SMU

At SMU Pfautsch lacked a "star" faculty performer to buttress the credibility of the new MSM program and to legitimize the degree to the faculty of the music school. Approaching graduation, Anderson had been courted by the University of Chicago, certainly an attractive situation, close to family and familiar to Anderson from his youth and childhood. Yet, at Pfautsch's instigation, he visited SMU in the autumn of 1959 to explore the possibility of accepting a position. After the visit Pfautsch wrote to him, outlining the advantages of SMU relative to the University of Chicago:

> Reactions of the people you met were all most encouraging and full of hope that you would join us next year. They now join me in the exciting prospect of having you participate in the growth and development of this MSM program. I think they are now convinced that we need someone here to attract people to our program as well as help in its establishment. . . .

> With the prospect of two new organs (fine arts and chapel) plus the practice organs, this in itself could be a most exciting experience for you as well as us. It would almost be like being able to design your own instrument.[54]

Pfautsch must rightly have concluded that Anderson's enthusiasm for participating in building a new program at SMU more than compensated for the attraction offered by the familiar organ turf offered by the University of Chicago. Pfautsch acknowledged that he "could not afford to get involved in a financial tug of war" with the University of Chicago, so he outlined another aspect of the proposal that would enhance its financial viability:

> The concertizing possibilities for you here in the southwest would be great and would not preclude your concertizing throughout the country . . . in fact, this we would want you to do . . . but the advantage in the southwest is that plane service is available to all of the important cities and involve good connections. You could play the morning service at chapel and be able to play a recital that evening in most any Texas city. We are an hour from Houston, San Antonio, Wichita Falls, etc. You know the size of the churches and their ability to pay. This would be a factor to keep in mind during salary considerations.[55]

Pfautsch's evaluation of the transportation situation in Dallas was perceptive if not prophetic, as the founding of Dallas Fort Worth International Airport in 1973 allowed even easier access to European capitals.[56] (Whether Anderson found the idea of Sunday afternoon flights to Sunday evening concerts, as suggested by Pfautsch, either desirable or practical, the record does not indicate.) The unexpected death of Norman Jacobs, assistant professor of music theory and education in December 1959[57] hastened the need for a replacement and afforded Pfautsch the opportunity to press for Anderson's hiring. To theology dean Cuninggim he proposed that Anderson also serve as organist for daily chapel services, providing remuneration from the Perkins School of Theology budget, an idea to which the dean was receptive. Pfautsch wrote again to Anderson in December 1959, with more encouragement:

> While I realize that the U of Chicago would be quite a professional "plunk" for you I hope you will consider what can be done here over the next decade. While many of my friends express amazement that I made the move to SMU and while I still am faced with certain frustrations in the general setup, I remind them that I knew that I was not moving to a ready-made situation but to what some call a musical frontier. Actually, I have been able to make many changes already . . . as a senior put it yesterday, the choral department has made such great strides in the past year. Of course, there is much to be done but that is part of the excitement and watching the reactions of the students is part of the satisfactions.[58]

There was still the matter of Dora Poteet Barclay, for whom Anderson had played an audition during his initial visit to SMU,[59] and who was still securely ensconced as professor of organ, her health condition notwithstanding. Pfautsch judiciously and diplomatically addresses Anderson's latent apprehension: "As far as Dora Barclay is concerned, she is merely the organ teacher and plays very little around school. At first, you would probably not be able to enter the organ instruction area, but as the MSM program grows this would become a necessity . . . and then too, she is not far from retirement age. I do not feel you need have any fear there. She [is] very nice to work with."[60]

Now Pfautsch had only to await Anderson's decision, complicated by the fact that at least one other institution, Milliken University in Decatur, Illinois, was also vying for Anderson's interest.[61] By April 1960 Anderson had communicated his decision to accept SMU's offer,[62] his position of instructor in theory and sacred music apportioned among the School of Music, for which he worked half time, Perkins School of Theology, which involved quarter-time teaching in the MSM program, and the chaplain's office, which paid a quarter of his salary relative to his Sunday morning duties at Perkins Chapel. He earned $6,000 his first year of teaching, or about $59,000 in 2021 dollars.[63] As Pfautsch had unambiguously put forth, this position reflected the need for another teacher of theory to replace Jacobs, so organ instruction was not included in deference to Barclay. Even so, Pfautsch writes elatedly in May 1960, "Everyone is delighted that you will be with us next fall. . . . With your coming, I would like to suggest that you consider another part of my proposed plans for our program. . . . I would like to suggest that you make some recital appearances within convenient environs . . . perhaps once a month. I have sufficient contacts now that would help in arranging for such recitals. We would, of course, expect the Churches to pay your expenses plus an honorarium so that it would be worth your while."[64] If Anderson had concerns about the lack of organ performance his new position seemed to entail, Pfautsch had clearly made known his personal willingness to assist him professionally by arranging organ concerts.

Music Facilities at SMU

Although the university had undergone a postwar building program, the music school benefited little from such attentions, and the music facilities remained dispersed among the aging McFarlin Auditorium, Atkins (now Clements) Hall, and Perkins Chapel, which was technically the domain of Perkins School of Theology, if not infrequently used for concerts and organ lessons. The new Mark Lemmon–designed buildings at the theology school increasingly housed music classes, their popularity enhanced by air conditioning systems.[65] The School of Music functioned out of multiple buildings in enforced exile. Umphrey Lee, president of SMU from 1939 to 1954, understood that the "long neglected School of Music, along with the departments of art and speech, had been seriously crippled because of inadequate quarters."[66] Further, he recognized the need for "a proper home for the School of Music, the university's 'step-child,' which he saw as 'suffering severely' for lack of space. 'This is very unfortunate,' he told the trustees in 1952, because the School of Music enjoyed an 'excellent reputation and an almost unbounded opportunity in the Southwest.' "[67]

Pfautsch had not exaggerated the lachrymose state of the conditions of the organs on campus. Certainly the Perkins Chapel organ was the flagship instrument on campus, built by Aeolian-Skinner in 1951, but it was still a modest thirty-something-rank instrument befitting Methodist ecclesiastical use rather than functioning as a true concert instrument. Its heavy use throughout the 1950s had aged it prematurely to the extent that Pfautsch suggested to Anderson that a new chapel organ might even be a consideration, to which Anderson designed a stoplist for a new, larger chapel organ that he audaciously suggested would reside in a different chapel—"not Perkins Chapel!"[68] The Hillgreen, Lane instruments in McFarlin Auditorium had deteriorated to such a state that Arthur Poister, who had performed at SMU in 1935, in a letter of congratulations to Robert Anderson on his appointment to SMU, consoled him saying, "I do hope you are never called upon to play a recital on the organ in Macfarland auditorium! That is the world's worst!"[69] The music facilities were languishing behind the rest of the university, to which Umphrey Lee "pointed out that remarkable opportunities existed for this school in a metropolitan center such as Dallas, and SMU would have to either properly exploit them or be content with a minor role in music in the Southwest. He concluded that there were two options: SMU could continue with a separate school of music, or it might enlarge into a school of fine arts that encompassed art, theatre, and dance."[70] Dean Orville Borchers had managed to hire some eminent faculty in the mid-1950s to redeem the school's lagging reputation. György Sándor, Hungarian pianist and student of Béla Bartók, as well as Alfred Mouledous, a protégé of Walter Gieseking and for many years pianist of the Dallas Symphony Orchestra, were among the more eminent hires of the time,[71] while Mack Harrell, a baritone at the Metropolitan Opera, instructor at the Juilliard School of Music and a Columbia Records artist, began teaching in September 1957,[72] and Louise Bianche would arrive a few years later to develop the Piano Pedagogy Department, the first of its kind in the nation.[73] The university administration having decided to pursue a course amalgamating all the arts disciplines in a single school initiated an ambitious building program to modernize old facilities and build new ones.

The first phase, a renovation of McFarlin Auditorium in mid-1961 inspired by a gift from the family of the late Mr. and Mrs. McFarlin, included modernized air conditioning, new seating, and a "modern acoustical system and complete face-lifting," the Dallas Symphony Orchestra taking up residence shortly after completion.[74] This renovation saw the removal of Mrs. Cassidy's old studio, elevators being installed where the organ had been. Bob Sipe, later an executive at Aeolian-Skinner and an organ builder in his own right, remembers removing the old Hillgreen, Lane and reconstituting parts of it to build a practice organ for Atkins Hall.[75]

McFarlin Auditorium having been refurbished for other purposes, the university broke ground in May 1962 on the Josephine Selecman Forbes Music Building on the south end of campus nearer Perkins School of Theology. This building was part of a new arts complex that eventually included the Virginia Stuart Meadows Museum, dedicated to collecting the paintings of the old masters, particularly the Spanish school represented by Goya and El Greco, and occasioned by a $3 million gift in 1962 of thirty-six oil paintings by her husband, Algur H. Meadows, chairman of the board of the General American Oil Company.[76] In 1964 many of these pieces were discovered to be forgeries; yet Meadows donated more money to ensure the Meadows Museum would be able to purchase authentic works and cultivate its reputation as a premiere art museum in the United States.[77]

The School of Music, now the Division of Music, benefited from the 1965 completion of the music building, attached to the Owens Arts Center that featured

nine attractive classrooms, equipped with desks and tablet chairs of latest designs, have been especially arranged for the teaching of music history, music education and music theory. Music history classrooms have new hi-fidelity phonographs and Ampex tape recorders which make the encounter with great music unusually exciting. . . . The music library contains scores, reference materials, and recordings. . . . Private lessons in applied music are taught in twenty studios, while students have the opportunity to use twenty-three practice rooms as they prepare for these private lessons. Completion of the rehearsal hall wing in the Fine Arts Center will add over fifty additional practice rooms along with band, choral and orchestral rehearsal space.

Five organ practice rooms are now available with two more rooms to be included in the rehearsal hall wing. Two new practice organs will arrive before the end of this year, and three more are scheduled for installation next spring.

The real gem, however, is the Caruth Auditorium, which sound engineers say is the most perfect concert hall in the United States.[78]

Perfect concert hall or not, with Caruth Auditorium Lloyd Pfautsch was able to fulfil his veiled 1959 promise to Robert Anderson that he would have free reign to design SMU's first modern organ dedicated solely to teaching and performance, and to this task Anderson dedicated himself from the beginning of his tenure.

Aeolian-Skinner, Opus 1438

Fortuitously for Pfautsch's pledge, the administration during these heady years was guided by SMU's fifth president, Willis Tate Sr., in office from 1955 to 1975[79] and partial to the school's musical endeavors. His wife, Joel Estes Lichte Tate, graduated from SMU in 1932 with a degree in organ and piano,[80] studying with Annie Byrd Whaling[81] and later serving as organist at Government Hills Methodist Church in San Antonio and First Methodist Church in Houston.[82] So supportive were the Tates of the organ department that in 1984 the family bestowed $500,000 to endow a faculty position in organ in honor of Joel Estes Tate.[83] Mrs. Tate's organ background certainly did not hinder the new organ's prospects. By early 1962

Dr. Willis and Mrs. Joel Estes Tate at home. Rotunda Collection,
SMU Archives, DeGolyer Library, SMU.

Anderson had begun seeking an organ company that could accomplish his vision for the new concert instrument.

University records provide only a modicum of background on the circumstances that led to the selection of Aeolian-Skinner. According to George Klump, assistant professor of organ from 1965 to 1969, Anderson had proposed to the administration that four organ firms be considered: Holtkamp, Austin, Möller, and Aeolian-Skinner, Anderson himself preferring Holtkamp.[84] Roy Redman, Fort Worth organ builder and longtime curator of organs at SMU, also remembers Anderson later expressing to him his preference for Holtkamp.[85] Former student John Hooker asserts that Anderson expressed admiration for the Holtkamp at the Chapel of the Good Shepherd at General Seminary in New York City, a three-manual, fifty-one-rank instrument installed in 1958, thinking that Holtkamp would be better able to build an organ of *Werkprinzip* design.[86] According to Klump, Walter "Chick" Holtkamp had developed a stoplist and a visual design of which Anderson was fond, and that ultimately guided him as he supervised Aeolian-Skinner's work. When SMU vice president Sterling Wheeler finally wrote to Aeolian-Skinner requesting a formal bid for the project on June 13, 1962, a request likewise was sent to "all three companies we have previously consulted."[87] Regardless how many firms may have been considered at the outset, it seems Aeolian-Skinner might have been the only serious contender. Unsubstantiated lore of the time suggested that the donors, Clarence and Bernice Hamilton, had favored Aeolian-Skinner due to the connection with Virgil Fox, and had steered Anderson in that direction, to which he conceded after ensuring a provision that he could be involved intimately in the voicing of each stop.

In February 1962 Anderson sent Thomas Potter, sales manager for Aeolian-Skinner, plans for the new Fine Arts Center hall, requesting some sort of proposal, to which Potter replied, "This building looks like it is going to be quite a fine place for sound, since it will be particularly for music. Very often a large auditorium is designed for multiple use that invariably means a great sacrifice in both space and acoustics for an organ. What I am trying to say is that if there had to be a choice as to which instrument we would build, we would really prefer to build the one for the Recital Hall!"[88] Apparently, this oblique reference was also the first of many subsequent instances of Anderson attempting to devise a plan for a new instrument in McFarlin Auditorium. The McFarlin possibility must have been an ephemeral thought, for attention returned quickly to the new recital hall. By March 14 Aeolian-Skinner had sent a proposed stoplist for a sixty-rank, three-manual instrument costing $81,500.[89] By the end of the month, Joseph Whiteford had sent Anderson a preliminary "sketchiest of sketches" for the new instrument, although, "Not knowing what the building structure will be like, I may have gone off the deep end, but the idea appealed to me to mount the whole business on a cantilevered reinforced concrete slab."[90]

Caruth Auditorium
Southern Methodist University, Dallas
Aeolian-Skinner, Opus 1438 (1965)[91]

GREAT

16 Quintaten
8 Principal
8 Gedeckt
8 Gemshorn
4 Octave
4 Rohrflöte
2 Flachflöte
Mixture IV–VI
8 Trompete

SWELL (enclosed)

16 Contra Viole
8 Rohrflöte
8 Viola de Gambe
8 Viole Celeste
8 Flute Celeste II
4 Principal
4 Nachthorn
2 Octavin
Plein Jeu III–IV
Cymbale III
16 Bombarde
8 Trompette
8 Hautbois
4 Clairon
Tremulant

PEDAL

32 Grand Bourdon (electronic)
16 Principal
16 Subbass
16 Quintaten
16 Contre Viole (Sw)
$10\frac{2}{3}$ Grossquinte
8 Octave
8 Gedeckt
8 Quintaten (Gt)
8 Viole de Gambe (Sw)
4 Choralbass
4 Koppelflöte
Mixture IV
32 Contra Bombarde
16 Posaune
16 Bombarde (Sw)
8 Trompette
4 Rohrschalmei
Tremulant

COUPLERS

Great to Pedal 8
Swell to Pedal 8, 4
Positiv to Pedal 8, 4
Swell to Great 16, 8, 4
Positiv to Great 16, 8
Swell to Positiv 16, 8, 4

POSITIV (enclosed)
8 Principal
8 Holzgedeckt
4 Principal
4 Spillflöte
2⅔ Nazard
2 Octave
1⅗ Tierce
1 Sifflöte
Scharf IV
8 Krummhorn
Tremulant

COMBINATIONS
Great: 8
Swell: 8
Positiv: 8
Pedal: 8
Generals: 12

MECHANICALS
Swell expression pedal
Crescendo Pedal
Nameplate divisional cancels

REVERSIBLES
All pedal couplers, including 4'
    Swell off
Tutti I
Tutti II
32' Contra Bombarde
32' Grand Bourdon
Pedal reeds silent
Great reeds silent
Swell reeds silent
Positiv Transfer

Anderson edited the March specification from Aeolian-Skinner and countered with one in late June, after the project had been approved for further due diligence by SMU. Anderson's changes largely involved nomenclature; "Prinzipal" becomes "Principal," "Bordun" becomes "Gedeckt," "Oktave" becomes "Octave," "Terz" is changed to "Tierce," and "Scharff" is now "Scharf." More substantively, he also requests a 16' Gedeckt Pommer on the Great, moving the Quintaten to the Positiv, adding a 5 1/3′ Rohrquint, 2′ Principal (the original proposal had only a 2′ Flachflöte), and a 16′ Dulzian with wooden resonators. To the Swell he requests a Cornet III (2 2/3′, 2′, 1 3/5′), and on the pedal he wishes for an 8′ Spitzflöte.[92] On July 9 Anderson proposed further additions, including a Pedal 32′ Bombarde, a Fourniture IV, Tertian II, and Cymbale III on the Great, and an 8′ Principal on the Swell, raising the cost to $103,425.[93] On August 1, 1962, university president Willis Tate signed the contract for the revised specification for Aeolian-Skinner, Opus 1438.[94]

Robert Anderson adhered to consistent principles in this phase of the instrument's development, the primary being his faithfulness to a *Werkprinzip* design in which each division is spatially and tonally a coherent unit, the secondary being concern for sound egress. In a letter to the building's architect in March 1963, Anderson urged "the following principles as guiding points":

1. The pipework of each division should be located somewhat as a unit, with the larger pipes at the rear, so that the interesting sight-pattern will not be obscured, or a feeling of over-heaviness attained at the front. Crucial in this regard is the 16′ pedal Principal (metal). It should not block egress of tone from the SWELL organ. . . .

2. Though the SWELL is a large division, must it be located centrally? If this is an absolute must, it will be. However, I wonder if such a focal point should be made of an essentially unartistic sight? It seems to me that full egress of sound could yet be achieved if it were located to the side, and a balance achieved with the other pipework.[95]

Although these are guiding principles rather than specifics, those involved with this project acknowledged that Anderson had a tendency to micromanage, a penchant he largely outgrew with later organ installations. The architect having conceded to moving the Swell from its central axis location, in a "console memo" to

John Hansen of the Aeolian-Skinner Engineering Department in April 1964, Anderson enumerated a number of additional issues for which he sought assurances—namely, that there would be an adjustable bench, the music rack would be of solid wood, there would be no tracker touch, and the nameplate would be of engraved stainless steel rather than a decal.[96]

In May 1964 he penned a seven-page tome to Joseph Whiteford communicating his own tonal philosophy, remarking that "I feel very deeply about organ design and am very keenly aware of strengths and flaws in the instruments I play. . . . I think we can build a very successful organ for our eclectic needs."[97] Before itemizing the stoplist, providing in exact detail the sound he wished to achieve from each stop, he notes:

It is my concern to make an organ of this size serve two basic needs: (first) to be a good classic organ of three manual divisions and pedal, and (second) flexible enough to play the 19th and 20th century literature. It is well known to us that the most difficult music to register faithfully on our organs is the French music of the Baroque. Unless we build huge instruments, it is hard to incorporate some of these characteristics. I know firmly that the German literature comes first in my thinking about design. I am not one to play Bach Preludes and Fugues on one registration; I find a three-manual breakdown as Schnitger used ideal for what I like to do. This means we don't want to borrow a manual to use for pedal upperwork; that we don't want lots of stops, particularly pedal, which don't fit into the tonal picture desired; that we don't want one or more divisions buried so as to take a back seat inappropriately in the tonal scheme as we know the classic organ. I don't think we have any of these disadvantages to encounter here. . . .

Though they are marvelous and gripping sounds, I find that the tear of our French reeds obliterates the charm and intensity of the flue chorus when these reeds are drawn in for full effects in classic music. I think we need both sounds—German trumpets and French choruses.

I have noticed in Europe that the articulation as achieved in unnicked pipes is always more prominent in the upper-work than in the 8' (and 4') registers. I dislike intensely over-clucking 8' Gedeckts (especially in our dead rooms!). One very rarely noticed articulate speech as such in the European churches. Too much cluck makes the stops useless in Romantic music, and unmusical in classic literature. I hope we can work carefully with the flutes and principals to achieve the most musical result for this room.[98]

Only a little further into this epistle can one sense the source of Anderson's concern: Roy Perry, the acclaimed regional voicer for Aeolian-Skinner. Anderson writes candidly to Whiteford, "I must tell you quite frankly some observations about the local and current organs around here that Roy has finished." Although he acknowledges that Perry's "flue voicing is mostly quite beautiful," he follows with a litany of concerns:

We have mostly dead rooms, and the 8' flutes cluck far too much. The scale of the Gambe extension 16' in the Swell is invariably too big and loud. The Sherman organ is the worst culprit (Austin College). The Temple Emanu-El Choir Violon is more useful. The Pedal Contre Basses are too loud and I hate to use them except in very full combinations (with French reeds, etc.). . . . As an extension, the Pedal 8' is way too loud, cannot at all be used in the classic chorus or for the first pedal Principal sound (Subbass under) for the registration of the secondary chorus, as should be its function. When extended, the 4' Pedal Principal is also usually too loud. The 8' Pedal Bombarde extension (and 4') is way too loud and penetrating for use in early music. I often find the 16' reed also too much for use in baroque music.[99]

And if Whiteford thought Anderson's discourse concluded there, Anderson enticingly promises, "Now to some specifics," after which follows a host of voicing enjoinders and directives for a goodly number of the organ's ranks, including the tremulants, to which Anderson coyly inquires, "Do you know the tremulant on the Schnitger organ in Cappel?"[100]

Joseph Whiteford probably knew Anderson well enough so as not to antagonize him, and he responds to his concerns in a diplomatic letter on June 2, 1964, in which he contends the advice "is a great help because it tells us which way to steer the job."[101] Whiteford then admits that

> I think that most of the things you bring up are problems of finishing. As you know, Roy is a glutton when it comes to string tone and he likes his Principals loud. This is alright for the English music but certainly does present difficulties with the German. I agree that sometimes we overdo the chiffing in very dead buildings. This, again, is a finishing situation.
>
> I have revised my scaling somewhat smaller as a result of your letter and think this will work fine. . . .
>
> I think we have just the thing for the 8' Trompete. It will be on low pressure and we use a very high tin percentage in all Principal pipes.[102]

This was to be an "eclectic" organ, but it was to be so on Anderson's terms, his thinking being a result of his studies with Walcha and his (albeit at that point limited) exposure to the organs of Europe. Perhaps Walcha's influence in the matter cannot be overstated.

In fact, the Schuke organ at Walcha's Dreikönigskirche had been completed in 1961, and its planning had been underway when Anderson lived in Frankfurt. Also three manuals, at 47 "registers" it was eight registers smaller than SMU's instrument. From the 4' Koppelflöte, 10 2/3' Grossquinte, 2' Block/Bauernflöte and the 16' Posaune, 8' Trompete, and 4' Schalmei in the Pedal divisions of both organs, to the inclusion of a 16' Quintaten and 2' Flachflöte on the manual divisions, to the nearly identical Positiv/Oberwerk divisions and their conceptions within classic *Werkprinzip* designs, certainly the similarities were uncanny:

Schuke Organ
Dreikönigskirche, Frankfurt, Germany
Karl Schuke, 1961[103]

HAUPTWERK

16 Quintaten
8 Principal
8 Spielflöte
8 Rohrflöte
4 Oktave
4 Nachthorn
2⅔ Nassat
2 Oktave
2 Flachflöte
Mixture V–VI
8 Trompete

BRUSTWERK

8 Holzgedeckt
4 Blockflöte
4 Quintadena
2 Waldflöte
1⅓ Quinte
1 Octave
Sesquialtera II
Cymbel III
8 Regal
4 Regal
Tremulant

OBERWERK

8 Metallgedackt
8 Quintadena
4 Principalww
4 Rohrflöte
2⅔ Quintflöte
2 Oktave
2 Nachthorn
1⅗ Terz
1 Sifflöte
Scharff IV
16 Rankett
8 Krummhorn
Tremulant

PEDAL

16 Principal
16 Subbaß
10⅔ Quintbaß
8 Oktave
8 Gedeckt
4 Oktave
4 Koppelflöte
2 Bauernflöte
Rauschpfeife III
Mixture V
16 Posaune
8 Trompete
4 Schalmei
2 Cornett
Tremulant

Delivery, Installation, and Dedication

In late April 1965, trucks arrived at the newly completed Forbes Music Building with the first shipments of organ parts, in response to which Anderson writes to Whiteford, "I'm getting ready for a long, hot summer. Things look beautiful; console is fantastic. On Friday (May 7) we dedicate the Caruth Auditorium."[104] Hardly able to contain his excitement, Anderson proclaimed, "The console is the most beautiful of its size I have seen from the Company."[105] In mid-May Jimmy and Nora Williams, the Aeolian-Skinner representatives who had installed the organ at Perkins Chapel in 1951, began assembling the instrument in a process that continued through the early autumn. When it came time to voice, Roy Perry and Don Gillette were charged with the task, equally sharing console, listening, and chamber duties. Although Anderson approved of Gillette, he was clearly wary of Perry's results. At the end of a workday, Anderson listened to the results in Caruth, leaving specific (yet sometimes ambiguous) notes for Gillette and Perry with suggestions for voicing improvement. George Klump recalled with amusement many of these notes, but also that "once in a while, some improvement in a register or two of a particular stop was possible and, sometimes, Roy would admit to me privately that he [Anderson] was probably right."[106] Whiteford's assurances to Anderson that many of his specific tonal concerns could be addressed in the "finishing" stage seem not to have been a reality, as Klump continues, "In some cases, the scaling of the rank would not permit much more than Don and Roy had already gotten out of it."[107]

The acoustics for the new auditorium had been a concern from the outset, the elusive goal having been to create an "acoustically perfect" space both for speech and music. In so doing School of Music authorities had collaborated with Austin, Texas, acoustician Dr. C. P. Boner to "devise a system of electronically-operated shades covering the side walls of the Auditorium, which, when closed, provide an optimum reverberation period suitable to the dispersion of organ tone in its vast harmonic complexity. The shades may be opened as desired to accommodate other performing media, reducing the reverberation period."[108] By most accounts these shades managed to dodge acoustical success for most purposes, whether speech or music, and certainly complicated the task of final voicing. This creative collaboration was doubtlessly stressful for all parties, but by October 1965 the organ was ready for dedication.

The inauguration day itself, October 15, began with a dedication service at 4:30 P.M., presided over by Willis Tate and Chaplain J. Claude Evans, with Bishops William C. Martin and Kenneth Pope offering dedicatory rites. The assembly sang the doxology.[109] Afterward, Tate sponsored a banquet in honor of Clarence and Bernice Hamilton, the organ's donors. Clarence was a notable Dallas automobile dealership proprietor and Bernice was an organist for many years, playing at Central Congregational Church.[110] Tate lauded the couple as "staunch friends" of SMU when announcing "the magnificent gift" for which SMU was "deeply grateful" and which "will enrich the educational opportunity of all students who attend SMU and will give new stimulus to the arts in Dallas and the Southwest."[111] Eugene McElvaney, chairman of the board of trustees, amateur organist, and owner of a forty-eight-rank residence organ, flew home early from Japan with his wife in order to attend the event. Don Gillette and Roy Perry represented Aeolian-Skinner. President Tate's connection to Clarence Hamilton was personal, as he recalled, "If I attempted to express to you my love and affection and long-time relationship with our honorees tonight, we would never make the concert. C. S. Hamilton was the patron of athletics when I was in school and was kind of a father to me. These dear people have supported everything good at this University. Whether you admire the University's growth in scholarships or facilities, or endowment, or athletics, you can be sure that the Hamilton's had a part in that growth. And now they have made possible this magnificent organ in the Fine Arts Center."[112] The organ project was probably precipitated and encouraged by the wives of Tate and Hamilton, both of whom were dedicated organists.[113] Would the athletic-minded administrator Willis and capitalist Clarence have so enthusiastically supported this project without the encouragement and support of their musically minded wives?

Robert Anderson's dedication concert that evening showcased the organ in diverse styles, demonstrating the eclectic tonal philosophy

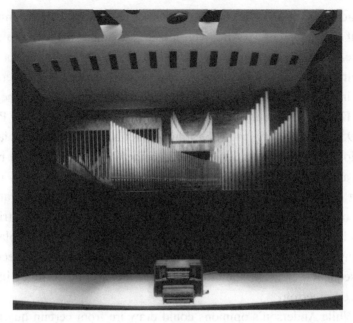

Caruth Auditorium's Aeolian-Skinner, Opus 1438. Robert T. Anderson Papers,
SMU Archives, DeGolyer Library, SMU.

Anderson had sought to capture in planning the specification and in
his careful voicing:

Johann Sebastian Bach	Toccata and Fugue in d minor, BWV 565
	"Wachet Auf!" BWV 645
	"Liebster Jesu," BWV 731
	"Kommst Du nun," BWV 650
Nicolas De Grigny	"Dialogue" from *Veni Creator*
Johannes Brahms	Fugue in a-flat minor
Norman Dello Joio	"Laudation"
César Franck	Prière, Op. 20
Marcel Dupré	"Preludio" from *Deuxième Symphony*, Op. 26
Maurice Duruflé	Scherzo
Wolfgang Amadeus Mozart	Fantasia in f minor, K. 608[114]

An advocate of all styles and a partisan of none, Anderson's commitment to contemporary American music is evident in the Dello Joio piece, commissioned by J. W. and Nita Akin of Wichita Falls and Aeolian-Skinner. The commissioning process, guided by Anderson, had initially sought new music from Samuel Barber, who declined.[115] But Dello Joio was no small coup, as he had received a Pulitzer Prize in 1957 and an Emmy in 1965 for his soundtrack to an NBC special.[116] Dello Joio wrote to Anderson in December 1965, after having been sent a recording, "The tape of the Laudation has arrived and may I say right off that your performance is a delight. The tempi, registration, and overall concept are all I could have wished. I second a friend who listened to the tape and said 'How good to hear an organ played so rhythmically.'"[117] Although Anderson programmed the piece at subsequent recitals, "Laudation" never seemed to find currency in the concert repertoire.

While Anderson's opinions could draw ire from certain quarters, reviewers throughout his career were largely sympathetic to him, the Dallas review for this concert being no exception. William Payne writes in the *Dallas Morning News:*

> With the expert musicology of organist Robert Anderson an accepted fact, the two identical concerts which he played Friday and Sunday on the new Hamilton Organ at SMU became more a demonstration of the capabilities of the instrument than the skill of the keyboard artist.
>
> Whether or not Dr. Anderson, head of the SMU organ department, planned the program with the deliberate intent of showing off the $100,000 organ in Caruth Music Auditorium, the selections he chose nevertheless served that purpose. . . .
>
> It was fitting, too, that Dr. Anderson chose as his second and final encore another organ workhorse, the Toccata from Symphony No. 5 for Organ by Charles-Marie Widor. It was this selection which brought the full house audience to its feet in an ovation which Dr. Anderson changed into a salute to the Hamilton Organ by turning to face the exposed pipes and applauding.[118]

Even the organ's design, the fruit of so many months of collaboration, received mention in Payne's article: "The exposed pipes provide a visual pleasure with their silvery color, the gold-faced brick behind the pipes and the huge teakwood swell box. The pipes themselves were arranged for architectural effect. . . . The Swell Box offered considerable interest for the audiences, since it is seldom that those listening to organ music have an opportunity to see this part of an organ in action."[119] (Hopefully Anderson was amused that the reviewer, later in the article, refers to his new instrument as the "Hammond Organ.") The Aeolian-Skinner would remain the centerpiece of the organ department for almost three decades, enduring the strain of daily usage better than it would be able to bear changing tastes.

Pedagogy, Faculty, Students

Robert Anderson assumed his post teaching music theory and sacred music in the autumn of 1960. By this time Dora Poteet Barclay had become bedridden, dying the next March. By the summer of 1961, Anderson had assumed charge of the organ studio and was now assistant professor of organ and theory.[120] The transition was not completely without tension, as some of Dora Barclay's students remained exceedingly loyal to her, viewing Anderson as too young a teacher and unseasoned of a performer to replace her. Peggy Bie, who studied with both, referred to Anderson as "dullsville," and some of Barclay's students later refused to send their own students to study with Anderson.[121] Nonetheless, he quickly refashioned the organ degree curriculum, evident in the 1961–62 catalog in which he specifies repertoire for each year of undergraduate study:

> First Year: Gleason, *Method of Organ Playing*; Dupré *Seventy Nine Chorales*; Bach *Eight Little Preludes and Fugues*; Bach-Riemenschneider, *The Liturgical Year*; movements from easy sonatas; hymn and anthem accompaniment.
> Second Year: Bach, Prelude and Fugue in E minor (The Cathedral), Fugue in G minor, Choral Preludes; Guilmant, Third

Sonata; Boellmann, *Suite Gothique*; Mendelssohn, Second
Sonata; church service playing.

Third Year: Bach, Toccata and Fugue in D minor, Dorian
Toccata; Mendelssohn Sonatas V and VI; Franck, Pièce
Héroique, Cantabile; Karg-Elert, *Cathedral Windows*, *Impressions*; works by American contemporary composers; registration and transcribing.

Fourth Year: Bach, Fantasy and Fugue in G minor, "St. Anne's"
Fugue; Karg-Elert, *Pastels*, *Choral Improvisations*; Franck
Chorals; Widor, Symphonies II and V; Vierne, Symphony I; works
of Dupré. Prepare a public recital.[122]

He also initiated an undergraduate course entitled Organ Survey
that he designed and taught throughout his career at SMU. This class
encompassed "history, literature, registration. A course designed to
acquaint the organ student with the development of the organ and
its literature. Emphasis will be placed upon stylistic principles of
registration. Required of all organ students in the Sophomore Year."[123]
This course presented the student with a historical and musicological
approach to organ performance (and building) that heretofore had
been the domain of scholars, not performers. The new organ studio
would indeed produce its share of performers, but these players
were expected to have a liberal rather than parochial view of their
profession. They would be scholar-performers, able to think critically
about historical trends and consider critically their chosen instrument
as it related to the greater world of art and music.

Anderson's influence brought a number of notable musicians to
campus during this decade, usually pairing a performance with a master
class for students. Notre Dame organist Pierre Cochereau played a solo
recital in October 1965, only two weeks after the organ's dedication,[124]
while Italian organist Luigi Tagliavini made his Dallas debut in 1965
at SMU.[125] Marie-Madeleine and Maurice Duruflé performed separate concerts at Caruth Auditorium in 1966; she played a solo organ
concert,[126] and he performed as soloist with the SMU symphony, playing the Poulenc concerto and the Saint-Saëns Organ Symphony along

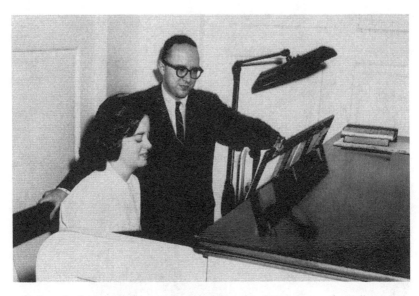

Robert Anderson teaching in Perkins Chapel in 1962. Rotunda Collection,
SMU Archives, DeGolyer Library, SMU.

with some of his own compositions.[127] Anderson remarked, "They loved
the Caruth Organ; I didn't have the guts to tell them that I was replacing the Positiv Cromorne—it was their favorite stop."[128] Anderson
recalled affectionately the Duruflés' involvement with SMU, which
was centered as much around that venerable local institution, the Highland Park Cafeteria, as it was around the Positiv Cromorne. Anderson
recalled Marie-Madeleine having dropped her pearls one evening in the
Kensington Room of the cafeteria: "Now if you can imagine a small
room full of people eating—how this could be interrupted by two
French people on the floor, under the table, picking up pearls scream-
ing French at one another!"[129] Anderson admired the couple—a respect
that seems to have been mutual. Anderson once remarked to her that
"we wanted an encore for her recital at SMU. She said, 'I never play
encores." I said, 'Could you play an encore?' She said: 'Oh yes, I could
play 20 encores.' I told her that one would be sufficient. What did she
play? The Dupré *Variations on a Noel*."[130] When Anderson plied her
with questions, including why she did not play from memory, she

André Marchal in the organ studio preparing for a concert. Robert T. Anderson
Papers, SMU Archives, DeGolyer Library, SMU.

responded that "Maurice kept changing their planned registration that
she was playing, and she thought she would get lost. In Caruth, Maurice
went from side to side pushing this pulling that."[131]

Marie-Claire Alain began a long association with SMU with her
first concert at Perkins Chapel in 1964,[132] returning the next year to
play in a "Festival of Arts for Celebration" with Anton Heiller and
Anderson. André Marchal performed on the Aeolian-Skinner in Caruth
during concert tours of 1966 and 1967.[133] Lady Susi Jeans, a personal
friend of Anderson's and a musicologist, lectured on "English Organ
Music of the 17th and 18th Centuries" in a 1967 event,[134] while Danish
organist Finn Viderø made an appearance in 1968.[135]

In establishing his new organ studio, Anderson was assisted by
adjunct instructors Paul Lindsley Thomas (1961–65) and Philip Baker
(1963–65), organist at Highland Park Methodist Church.[136] The organ

department flourished in these first years with the number of organ majors accounted as follows:[137]

Semester	Undergraduate	Graduate	MSM	Total
1960, Fall	12	1	2	15
1961, Spring	13	1	1	15
1961, Fall	10	1	6	17
1962, Spring	12	1	6	19
1962, Fall	17	2	7	26
1963, Spring	19	3	5	27
1963, Fall	22	3	3	28
1964, Spring	22	3	4	29
1964, Fall	17	3	2	22
1965, Spring	17	3	1	21
1965, Fall	13	7	8	28
1966, Spring	15	3	8	26
1966, Fall	12	7	8	27
1967, Spring	9	7	7	23
1967, Fall	14	5	7	26
1968, Spring	11	5	8	24
1968, Fall	13	6	7	26
1969, Spring	14	6	8	28

As important as the new concert organ would be to the increasing quality and breadth of the organ department, the enrollment numbers suggest that the organ was not a major factor in students' desire to attend SMU. In fact, the largest enrollment during this decade occurred in spring of 1964, a full year before the Aeolian-Skinner was completed; it seems that the faculty were the driving force behind the department's success during this era.

The teaching workload led to the hiring of the aforementioned Dr. George Klump as assistant professor of organ in the summer of 1965. A student of Arthur Poister and Clarence Mader, Klump had completed doctoral studies with David Craighead at Eastman, followed by a Fulbright scholarship to study in Vienna with Anton Heiller. Among Klump's students at SMU were Byron Franklin, Quentin and Mary Murrell Faulkner, Mary Helen Knight, and Rebecca Jean Alexander. When Don Gillis, dean of SMU's School of Music, left after only one year to become dean of the arts at Dallas Baptist College, Klump followed him to teach there in 1969. He and his wife, Barbara, who was associate organist at Highland Park Methodist Church, would eventually move to California, where he taught at Loyola Marymount University.[138]

Lloyd Pfautsch was appointed assistant dean to the School of the Arts in 1964, with Carlton "Sam" Young replacing him as MSM director. Trained as an organist and church musician, Young, a graduate of Cincinnati College of Music, the University of Cincinnati, and Boston University School of Theology, with additional study at Union Theological Seminary as well as in Vienna and Prague, had served as editor and director of music publications for Abingdon Press since 1959. By the time of his appointment to SMU, he enjoyed a formidable reputation as a hymnologist, composer, and church musician. During his tenure at SMU, Young would edit the 1966 edition of *The Methodist Hymnal*; later in his career, he would assume responsibility for editing the 1989 version of the same hymnal.[139] Under Young's guidance the MSM course of study developed to address concerns unique to church musicians and organists. The music division's required courses in music history and introduction to graduate studies neglected significant developments in Western sacred music, in response to which Young instituted the Church Music Seminar, a required course tailored specifically for church musicians but offered under the purview of the School of Theology rather than the School of Music. Under his tenure, and with the sympathetic assistance of Pfautsch and Anderson, the program began to produce performers who could satisfy the music faculty while proving to the theology professors that musicians could also think theologically.

Practice Organs

An organ department with so many students required a support structure of ancillary organs the university had been supremely ill-equipped to provide during the early years of Anderson's

Dr. George Klump, assistant professor of organ, at Caruth Auditorium.
Courtesy of Dr. George Klump.

tenure—a challenge he would address while simultaneously presiding over the installation of the Aeolian-Skinner. A Möller organ
had been donated by the Dewain Hughes family, and the repur-
posed Hillgreen, Lane studio organ, rebuilt as a practice organ in
1961 by Robert Sipe,[140] then of the Sipe-Yarbrough firm, was reno-
vated in 1967 as a tracker instrument of nine stops, in keeping
with Dr. Anderson's appreciation for the baroque tonal aesthetic.
Sipe-Yarbrough also built an additional four-rank unit organ of
fifteen stops in 1961.[141] In the spring of 1964, Anderson sought a
bid from Lawrence Phelps, then of Casavant, for practice organs,[142]
although a price comparison with European builders soon revealed
that overseas firms could offer better value; thus he placed an order
from von Beckerath for two three-rank catalog organs that arrived
in the summer of 1965 and two six-rank organs that were delivered in the summer of 1967.[143] In 1966 Sipe built a three-manual,
eleven-rank, electric-action unified organ with a swell box in

response to Anderson's desire to have an instrument that would allow students to practice on nontrackers.[144]

Since he was not to have a Holtkamp in Caruth Auditorium, he would have to settle for one in his organ studio in the new Owens Fine Arts Center. By early 1964 he had approached Walter Holtkamp Jr. about such an organ, to which Holtkamp replied:

> It seems to me that the Teaching Studio is akin to the Choir Rehearsal Room, in that you are trying to impart technique and the points of careful study, rather than performance.
>
> I have in mind a nice, three manual organ (one division enclosed), with independent Pedal. This is to be a straight organ. Each division should have about five stops and each division should be quite distinguished from the others. This is kind of like taking Walcha's <u>hausorgel</u> one step further. It has to be voiced so that the teacher or student (especially teacher) can use it for several consecutive hours without "aural fatigue." Actually, this should be more akin to the Practice Organ than the Concert Hall Organ.[145]

Unlike the hallmark haggling between Anderson and Aeolian-Skinner, the studio organ seems to have been built exactly to Holtkamp's design. This three-manual with a Swell division had five independent stops on each manual and six in the Pedal, with no borrowing or unification. Ultimately, the wrangling over minutiae might have resulted in a better instrument, and perhaps Anderson regretted his compliance, as by summer 1968 he had already begun to request a number of changes. There were minor console and winding problems, the location of the Pedal division near arm's level was resulting in numerous accidents with the pipes, the pedal fall was not to Anderson's liking, and at that point he wanted to replace the 1′ Principal on the Swell.[146] (Later, there would be more issues and suggestions.) The situation of the room was such that noise, climate control, and poor acoustics were always issues, and although Anderson showed partiality toward the organ, whether it avoids "aural fatigue" is a debatable issue among the organ students.

Southern Methodist University
Teaching Studio
Holtkamp Organ Company, Opus 1803 (1965)[147]

GREAT

8 Gedeckt
4 Principal
2 Hohlflöte
Mixture
8 Cromorne

SWELL

8 Quintadena
4 Füllflöte
2 Gemshorn
1 Principal
Zimbel

POSITIV

8 Copula
4 Rohrflöte
2 Principal
1⅓ Quinte
Sesquialtera
Tremolo

PEDAL

16 Subbass
8 Principal
8 Gedackt
4 Choral Bass
Mixture
16 Dulzian

COUPLERS

Great to Pedal
Positiv to Pedal
Swell to Pedal
Swell to Great
Positiv to Great
Swell to Positiv.

MECHANICALS

Swell expression pedal
Great-Pedal reversible

COMBINATIONS

Two levels of memory accessible via toggle switch.

Swell: 3

Great: 3

Positiv: 3

Pedal: 4

General: 4

Anderson's Burgeoning Performance Career

Although Robert Anderson spent the 1960s engrossed in the building of the organs and organ department at SMU, he still found time to perform and conduct master classes elsewhere, fulfilling Pfautsch's directive that "concertizing throughout the country [is something] we would want you to do."[148] From 1962 he concertized under the auspices of Colbert-LaBerg management, which later became the Lillian Murtagh Agency.[149] He was a featured performer at the 1963 Southwest Regional Convention of the AGO, playing at St. Mark's Episcopal Church in Shreveport, Louisiana,[150] as well as at the convention the next year in New York City.[151] The 1965–66 season saw him conducting master classes at the University of Michigan, Nebraska Wesleyan University, and Lindenwood College, while he performed concerts in Massachusetts, Michigan, Oklahoma, Washington, DC, Colorado, and North Carolina.[152] During his first official European tour, he performed eleven concerts in Germany, Denmark, Belgium, Holland, and England in the summer of 1967, the highlight of which was his performance at the International Organ Week in Nuremberg, playing Schoenberg, Mozart, Persichetti, Lübeck, and Bach. During the 1968–69 season, he returned to the Illinois Wesleyan campus for a master class and recital[153] and played concerts in Virginia, Georgia, South Carolina, New York, Wisconsin, Ohio, and California.[154] He remained active as a local performer, playing for the Christmas concerts at Perkins Chapel, teaching church music seminars sponsored by Perkins School of Theology,[155] and performing organ dedications, often on instruments that he helped design, including the Sipe-Yarbrough tracker organ at St. Stephen Methodist Church in Mesquite in 1962, an organ that heralded the baroque revival in North Texas. (This instrument was donated by Sue King McElvaney, wife of SMU Board Of Trustees chairman Eugene McElvaney.)[156]

As the 1960s closed, Robert Anderson was not yet even 40. In addition to teaching a full load since at least the autumn of 1962, developing the curriculum for the organ department and feverishly facilitating the construction of new organs on campus, he partook

Robert Anderson at Caruth Auditorium. Robert T. Anderson Papers,
SMU Archives, DeGolyer Library, SMU.

in a full schedule of concerts and teaching throughout the country.
In a 1990 convocation address to the division of music students, he
offered the following advice:

> Learn to set goals and keep them—larger goals, such as the
> successful completion of your work with us, and smaller ones,
> such as what will I accomplish today or even in this hour?

Organize your time—it will disappear. Give yourself some lead
time and get things planned and accomplished early. Set high
standards for yourself and watch things grow; often you will not
see this growth, if you are a performing musician, as easily as
your teachers see it. Discipline yourself and avoid outside influ-
ences which might hinder you. . . . Do your own thing, and insist
on the full utilization of each day. Don't waste time sleeping
unnecessarily long, watching TV or such. You will be busy—
that's what an SMU education in music is all about. . . . You'll
need careful planning to do all this well. This is the life of a
musician.[157]

As can be said of most significant personalities, Anderson had his
detractors. Not every student flourished under him, yet no one could
doubt his unyielding work ethic and dogged determination to accomplish goals. He set high standards for all his students and expected
them to achieve at a high level. His credibility was never in question,
his own vivacity and dynamism lending personal credence to his defi-
nition of the "life of a musician."

Chapter 6

A Flourishing Establishment

In many ways the 1960s saw the fulfilment of what the organ department at SMU had aspired to become since the days under Dora Poteet Barclay, who had shepherded the program from that of a training school for church organists to a department with loftier goals and performance standards. Robert Anderson had bestowed international repute on the program, its character solemnized in the quality of majors who had begun to matriculate and its collection of pipe organs, centered around two Aeolian-Skinner organs and a small host of rehearsal instruments, finally legitimizing the campus as a center of organ studies. The Sacred Music Department, under the leadership of Lloyd Pfautsch and then Carlton Young, navigated the precipitous territory between the academic rigors demanded by Perkins School of Theology and the performance acumen expected of graduates of the School of the Arts, with each school incipiently suspicious of the other. Nonetheless, the cadre of international performing organists who now visited SMU on a regular basis, teaching master classes and performing concerts for the entire university in the "perfect acoustics" of Caruth Auditorium, imparted the sense that the organ department may finally have attained the elusive reputation of the more established East Coast schools.

A New Dean for the Meadows School of the Arts

The latter half of the decade manifested latent tensions within the Meadows School of the Arts, as it was known after 1969 following a significant bequest by philanthropist Al Meadows. If SMU president Willis Tate was personally supportive of Anderson's projects, administration closer to the organ department was less so after Kermit Hunter replaced Orville Borchers as dean of the School of the Arts in 1964. Hunter, a West Virginia native, studied at Ohio State University and the Juilliard School of Music before assuming jobs in the newspaper industry, with a chamber of commerce, and as a business manager of a professional baseball team, in addition to stints as an organist and choirmaster in a Methodist church, before he was called for duty in World War II. Having been discharged at the rank of lieutenant colonel, he subsequently studied drama at the University of North Carolina at Chapel Hill, after which he began a career of writing outdoor plays, an endeavor in which he earned passable success. After teaching drama at Hollins College, he would come to the newly constituted School of the Arts at SMU.[1]

Lloyd Pfautsch, having relinquished his position as director of the MSM program in 1964 to Carlton Young, was now associate dean of the School of the Arts, his workload encompassing teaching, conducting the choral ensembles (both community and university), and tending to university bureaucracy. A staunch supporter of Anderson and the organ department, Pfautsch would suffer under the ink of the playwright-dean's hands. Hunter wrote a memo to Willis Tate in June 1966 expressing frustration with Pfautsch, whom he characterized as "a letter-signer, a chairman for faculty meetings, and in general a kind of musical piddler, infinitely more wrapped up in writing choir music and directing choruses than in operating the music division."[2]

A couple of months later, Hunter complained to Tate about Anderson, whom he had reprimanded for suggesting to Gene McElvaney, chairman of the board of trustees and a fellow member of the AGO, that he "investigate the food service at SMU," a request that properly should have gone through the dean's office. According to Hunter, Anderson was "abashed" about it and Hunter expressed the expectation that "Bob will see to it that he stays in his position as organist."[3] The Sacred Music Department fared little better under the scriptwriter, whose melodrama-infused missives to President Tate were frequent and rancorous:

> I wish you would also understand . . . that sacred music, no matter how it gladdens Methodist hearts and souls, is a tangent in the musical world. SMU is red hot on tangents, and weak on water down the main line (in music, I mean). We are gung-ho in organ, in sacred music, in choirs and all the paraphernalia for worshiping, but I am having to fight . . . to get a string program going, and we almost lost one of our best piano people to Texas until I talked him into staying, and we have no one to manage the voice program.[4]

Hunter's complaints about the preferential treatment garnered by the organ and sacred music programs gained little traction; Provost H. Neill McFarland even admonished Hunter to curb his vitriol against Lloyd Pfautsch, the architect of the Sacred Music Department and, through his hiring of Anderson, the organ program as well:

> Numerous times in memos and oral comments you have spoken disparagingly of Lloyd. I have known Lloyd for many years but I have never met the person whom you describe in this fashion. . . . Correctly or incorrectly, many of us, including the President, have the highest regard for Lloyd and consider him to be one of the most valuable people on this campus. His coming here marked the start of new excitement and creativity. He has thrilled us by his imaginative programming of special events, by his unfailing good taste and sense of touch, by his compositions for

special occasions, and by his personal warmth. Without a doubt he is one of our most effective public relationship people.[5]

Hunter's vituperative comments were by no means limited to choral or sacred music; elsewhere he found cause to disparage both the previous dean, Orville Borchers, as a "Prussian,"[6] and Dallas Symphony Orchestra conductor Donald Johanos, "who likes no one on earth quite as avidly as he does Donald Johanos."[7] Such was the acrimonious political environment that prevailed through the end of Hunter's tenure in 1976. In the midst of Hunter's persecutions, President Tate spared no opportunity to laud and support Anderson personally, as in this note from November 1967:

> Your organ concert was a highlight of the musical season at Southern Methodist University and another brilliant performance to add to your artistic achievements. I was impressed with the range and quality of the organ since the new stops have been added, and I can assure you that Mrs. Hamilton, who was my guest for the evening, was also delighted. Especially I appreciate your gracious remarks directed to her about the Hamilton gift and what it means to us at SMU. Thank you for your thoughtfulness and for your contribution to the cultural life of the University.
> Sincerely,
> Willis M. Tate
> President[8]

The support Lloyd Pfautsch and Robert Anderson received from the SMU administration during those days exemplified leadership's firm convictions of the benefits of strong organ, choral, and sacred music departments. Hunter could and would, however, offer support to the organ department when it suited his purposes.

Caruth Auditorium and Aeolian-Skinner

Only three days after the October 1965 dedication of Aeolian-Skinner's Opus 1438 in Caruth Auditorium, Robert Anderson had already initiated a plan to improve and enlarge the instrument, which had exhibited a number of deficiencies in voicing and design.[9] By December 1965, barely two months from the dedication and the same month it was featured on the cover of the *American Organist* magazine, he wrote to Donald Gillett and Roy Perry that

> none of us, including the visitors, are particularly happy with the Great 8' and 4' Principals—you know I spoke about this before. More serious, perhaps, is that the Pedal 8' Octave is too loud. It cannot be used as a Trio Sonata bass, and approaches being unacceptable as a foundation for the Secondary Chorus. Losing the 8' Quintaten borrow, as we will with the new Rauschquinte II, it must be softened. I also think that we can louden the Great 4' Rohrflöte a bit. The other matters concern certain notes here and there which are uneven. Merry Christmas![10]

C. S. and Bernice Hamilton would assume the $7,800 bill to install an 8' Regal on the Swell with half-length resonators that might "double as a Vox Humana (the early French one is much like the German type,)" a 16' Fagott on the Great that would also duplex to the Pedal division, a 2' Blockflöte on the Positiv, and a Rauschquinte II and Mixture IV in the Pedal, although these additions would not be installed until the summer of 1967.[11] After Jimmy Williams recused himself from the assignment "in that he has been working on another job under difficulties and delays," Aeolian-Skinner engaged Robert Sipe to perform the work.[12] Anderson had acquainted himself with the organ so thoroughly by the summer of 1967 that his earlier list of minor improvements and complaints had multiplied exponentially, enumerated in a letter to Aeolian-Skinner before he left for a European tour that summer. From regulating the speech of the reeds on the Swell and Great to improving the velocity of the combination action, installing pin brackets on the Great Gedeckts, softening the Swell Cymbale III, and addressing problems with the pedalboard, which has a tendency for "squeaking violently and intermittently," there was no shortage of improvements to be made. During the summer of 1968, Aeolian-Skinner "went all the way to Europe" for a new Krummhorn better to suit Anderson's taste.[13] At this point Anderson apparently had not yet considered replacing the organ, as during the summer of 1969 he requested a quotation from Aeolian-Skinner to install a Trompette en Chamade.[14]

According to George Klump, the balance between the manual and pedal divisions created the most problems in the final stages. Klump remembered that "Aeolian-Skinner had not really changed any pipe scalings significantly since E. M. Skinner had left the company. While RTA had insisted on a straight Pedal division—and it was for the most part—it generally overpowered the manuals, which always came off as thin sounding by comparison."[15] Anderson pressed Gillette and Perry to soften the mixtures until both men had to warn Anderson that they would not be responsible for the organ should they have to consent to his further demands. Even after Anderson conceded the issue, Harold Gleason, present in the auditorium for a recital by his wife, Catherine Crozier, remarked that "the mixtures always sounded like they were coming out of a box somewhere, sort of like a dog with its head in a sack."[16] Matters of aesthetics notwithstanding, the host of issues manifested the common problems endemic to the later years of Aeolian-Skinner.[17] John Tyrrell, president of Aeolian-Skinner from 1960 to 1966, and afterward chairman of the board, would later address the factors that precipitated the decline of the firm:

There were continuing financial worries . . . every year's results were as disappointing as the last. . . . There were deaths and retirements of some of our leading factory personnel, bringing production in some departments to a temporary halt. Several instruments of the late 1960s actually contain pitman chests built by Casavant, and for a time it seems as if every major installation had English ivory manual keys that warped. Talk about headaches!

All these things had to be pondered, as well as continuing financial worries—maintenance and the operation of two older buildings, losses of major proportions on several big instruments, and a search for new money. Questions were being raised by outsiders concerning the direction the company might take, particularly in view of the several recent changes of leadership.[18]

Anderson was no doubt one of these "outsiders" who raised questions about the company, although there is no archival evidence to suggest that he ever codified his concerns in writing. Yet Aeolian-Skinner would seek to leverage his reputation to buttress their own. In January 1969 Vice President Thomas V. Potter wrote to Anderson with a veiled but discernable sense of desperation:

> I think things are really looking up for the Company now. I was just out to the plant, into which we are currently moving, and it is just magnificent to see the facilities and the space we will have, the fulfillment of a dream that many of us have had for a long time. You will really have to come see us. . . .
>
> What with Roy Perry's leaving us, we do have some fence-mending to do in your part of the country and anything you can do in our behalf would be deeply appreciated. You and I have talked enough about the situation down there in the past that you must be aware of how confident we are that business will soon pick up in that area for us and will even improve.[19]

That the Caruth organ might have been one of the aforementioned instruments on which the company stood to lose money only augmented the financial burden with a potential political liability. Dean Kermit Hunter obliquely referenced such concerns in a fundraising missive in 1971 to address deficiencies in the auditorium ahead of, among other events, the national convention of the AGO in 1972:

> The Aeolian-Skinner Company did not do an outstanding job when they installed the organ as far as the looks of the instrument were concerned. They later admitted this, and also admitted that they were not unaware of the situation. They agreed that when we get ready to make certain additions to the organ which we felt were necessary, they would undertake to re-do the whole instrument and add considerably from their own pocket, the result being that if we could spend approximately $30,000 for additions and improvements, they would undertake to do about $50,000 of work and thereby correct their omission and inadvertent bad planning of five years ago. We thought this seemed like

a tremendous bargain, and we were therefore trying to work out some means of getting the organ re-done, the stage floor rebuilt, and the organ cable buried.[20]

Robert Sipe, now president of Aeolian-Skinner, had agreed to numerous of Anderson's changes, including replacing the 16′ Principal, 10⅔′ Quinte basses, and the 16′ Subbass, revoicing the Mixture IV and Gedeckt in the Pedal, and replacing the 8′ Principal, 4′ Octave, 2′ Flachflöte, Mixture IV–VI and the 4′ Rohrflöte on the Great. On the Positiv they would replace the 8′ Principal, 4′ Principal, and Scharf IV–V. The firm would also alter the configuration of some ranks within the caseless "flower box" arrangement primarily to aid tonal egress and to improve visual presentation. Perhaps this generous offer was an act of liberal corporate altruism, or perhaps the company, approaching a financial point of no return, needed the immediate infusion of cash such a contract would bring. Anderson's motivation was academic and musical, revealing his own development as a professor of organ, noting that "these additional stops are mainly needed to aid the organist in the performance of the French literature which is an integral part of student training"[21] French music was less of a concern to the inexperienced student fresh from two years of Fulbright study with a notable German organist than it had become to the increasingly seasoned teacher—who at age 37 in 1972 was the youngest recipient of the Alumnus of the Year award from Illinois Wesleyan University.[22]

Faculty, Students, and New Directions

James Tallis had joined the music faculty as associate professor of organ in the autumn of 1968, holding degrees from Eastman School of Music and Union Theological Seminary. A student of David Craighead and Robert Baker, he had received a Fulbright grant in 1963–1964 to study organ in the Netherlands with Cor Kee and harpsichord with Gustav Leonhardt.[23] Having previously taught at Hastings College in Nebraska and Hope College in Holland, Michigan, not only did Tallis bring some knowledge of the nascent field of early music, but

A class with Marie-Clarie Alain during the late 1960s. Robert T. Anderson
Papers, SMU Archives, DeGolyer Library, SMU.

his wife, Joan, would also prove an asset to the community.[24] A vocal-
ist and organist, her recitals, often in conjunction with her husband,
would regularly specialize in exploring authentic performance practices in seventeenth- and eighteenth-century vocal and harpsichord
works.[25] Anderson was reportedly delighted at Tallis's acceptance of
the position at SMU, an appointment that entailed initiating a graduate program in harpsichord.[26] Tallis had already assembled a formidable studio at his previous teaching positions, and his arrival at
SMU portended a buttressing in the numbers of organ students. To
hear Anderson speak of it, quantitative growth was never a driving
concern; he preferred a streamlined studio, hoping "that the department would never grow beyond the need for two full time faculty
members plus graduate (or postgraduate) teaching assistants."[27]
Tallis's addition to the faculty, and the students he would certainly
bring with him, would simply allow the organ department to exercise

James Tallis. Courtesy of Kathy Tallis Watson.

more admission selectivity. Nonetheless, a brain tumor would bring the young professor's life to a premature end at age 37 in September 1969, before Anderson's hopes for Tallis's contributions to the department could be realized.[28] Anderson had deeply respected Tallis, reportedly crying at his desk when informed of the news.[29] Barbara Marquart and

John Hooker, recent SMU graduates, were hired as adjuncts to teach Tallis's students. His only published work for organ, "Sonatina," was printed posthumously.[30]

In June 1970 the faculty senate ratified the appointment of Dr. Larry Palmer as associate professor of organ and harpsichord.[31] Tallis had brought a renewed appreciation for early music and the harpsichord, and Palmer's appointment likewise represented an investment in the intersection between performance and scholarship. Born in 1938 in Pennsylvania to Rev. Gerald and Esther Palmer, Palmer's youth was spent in Crestline, Ohio, where he played oboe and piano, participated in choir and marching band, and studied organ with Mabel Zehner of Ashland College as he prepared for admission to Oberlin. There his teachers included Leo Holden and Fenner Douglass, the latter of whom was known for his "advocacy of mechanical-action organs and interest in an historically-informed approach to the performance of music," a philosophy that "meshed more nearly" with Palmer's own interests.[32] The beneficiary of Oberlin's new program designed as "an experiment in international education," Palmer, along with the entire Oberlin junior class, would be sent to Salzburg in 1958–1959 to study at the Akademie für Musik und Darstellende Kunst (Mozarteum), an opportunity that had afforded him harpsichord study with Isolde Ahlgrimm in Vienna. Later, he would study for two summers with Gustav Leonhardt in the Netherlands. He subsequently earned graduate degrees from Eastman School of Music and had already established his reputation not only as a performer but also as a scholar. In addition to his early music interest, he had published *Hugo Distler and His Church Music* in 1967, the first biography dedicated to the twentieth-century composer. By 1969 he had been appointed harpsichord editor for the industry periodical the *Diapason* and had taught at Norfolk State College and Saint Paul's College, both in Virginia. As Anderson had done a decade before, Palmer would bring a cosmopolitan and innovative perspective to the organ department, shaped as he was by his European experiences. Meanwhile, Anderson was promoted to full professor in September 1971.[33]

The School of Music, which had begun as not much more than a girls' finishing school but had gradually transformed itself into a conservatory, had now become the multidisciplinary Meadows School of the Arts, in which the technical aspects of performance were enhanced by a general, university-wide liberal arts education. Serious musicology had advanced throughout the 1940s and 1950s in American universities, spurred by the founding of the American Musicological Society in 1934 and the publication of its *Journal* beginning in 1948. Musicological study would rapidly transform pedagogy and performance practice, which by the 1960s saw a flourishing of early music ensembles eager to perform "authentically." Kenneth Gilbert established an early music program at McGill University in 1960, the same year Howard Mayer Brown reinstituted a Collegium Musicum at the University of Chicago. Probably of more importance to the administration at SMU, Cecil Adkins had established an early music program at North Texas State University (now University of North Texas) in 1963.[34] By 1973 SMU would offer a graduate course in the Performance Practice of Early Music, teaching the "interpretation of Baroque keyboard music and the history of national styles in harpsichord making";[35] the following year they offered a Collegium Musicum as an ensemble elective,[36] and in 1976 they added a course dedicated to continuo playing.[37] In 1975 Palmer dedicated the university's new two-manual, three-register Kingston harpsichord, which "exemplifies the finest trends in harpsichord making today. In every important detail it is faithful to the spirit of the eighteenth-century instruments."[38] By 1977 the Early Music Society of Southern Methodist University could be found performing Spanish music of the Renaissance and Middle Ages in the galleries of the Spanish-themed Meadows Museum.[39] Thus would Larry Palmer's addition to the faculty poise SMU to venture with academic integrity into the field of early music study and performance.

The organ studio had begun to merit national stature as its students accumulated competition successes. George Baker, who had begun study with Robert Anderson as a high school student, later completing his undergraduate degree at SMU, won the AGO competition in Buffalo in 1970, the Grand Prix de Chartres in 1974, and later the International Improvisation Competition in Lyon, France, in 1979.[40] Baker, whose teachers included Marie-Claire Alain, Pierre Cochereau, Jean Langlais, and André Marchal, toured extensively in the 1970s, one review depicting his playing as being characterized by "a distinctly personal kind of expression, usually slight but very effective." An acclaimed concert improvisor in the French tradition, a reviewer openly lamented for there to have been more "organ disbelievers at this performance; they would have walked away knowing what organ music can be, and wanting more."[41] Helmut Walcha sent one of his German students, Wolfgang Rübsam, to study at SMU, largely to "prolong the graduation date in Frankfurt," thereby forestalling Rübsam's obligatory military service. Of his time in the SMU organ studio Rübsam recalled, "Here I discovered organ repertoire the world over, from early music to Messiaen. Every week I studied a new huge, often very difficult work of Reger, Franck, Langlais, Dupre . . . and the list goes on and on. In Dallas, I practiced six hours daily. Never before had I covered more repertoire in one year. The Masters Degree I earned there was surely the one 'golden life key' that changed everything in my career and contributed tremendously to my winning the Grand Prix de Chartres, Interpretation, in 1973—the first German to do so."[42] Other students would join the pantheon of laureates during this era. Robert Bates won the Fort Wayne and San Antonio competitions in 1976, eventually receiving the Prix de virtuosité from the class of Marie-Claire Alain in 1978.[43] John Chappell Stowe won the 1978 National Open Organ Playing Competition of the AGO,[44] while Bruce Bengtson spent the spring of 1975 accumulating prizes at the Fort Wayne, San Antonio, and Los Angeles Mader competitions.

The national convention of the AGO in Dallas in June 1972 featured SMU prominently.[45] Anderson chaired the steering committee of the convention, engineering the organ department to be featured prominently. His protégé George Baker "stunned the entire convention with perhaps the best recital of the whole week" according to the reviewer in the *Diapason*, who averred that Baker's "recital produced

Marie-Claire Alain teaching at SMU in conjunction with the 1972
national AGO convention. Robert T. Anderson Papers, SMU Archives,
DeGolyer Library, SMU.

more audience excitement than anyone else did. His formidable
program was played entirely from memory with complete assurance."[46]
If Baker earned the reviewer's praise, Anton Heiller's performance in
Caruth garnered less enthusiasm, having "produced what for us was
the dullest program we have heard him play in years. . . . We had
the feeling that he was uncomfortable with the instrument itself,
and that he was less than excited by having to play it."[47] Heiller seems
to have had a problematic relationship with the organ, as Anderson
had already observed in December 1965 that "Heiller was not over-
whelmed, but then, it isn't tracker!"[48] The question must be raised as
to why Anderson had assigned him to play a program at Caruth instead
of at a venue with a suitable tracker. The Dallas AGO, certainly at
Anderson's instigation, had likewise commissioned an organ work
from Vincent Persichetti (*Parable VI*, Opus 117) to premiere at the
convention. Harboring a proclivity for the music of the Juilliard
pedagogue, Anderson had just recorded his *Shimah b'koli*, Opus 89,
on an installment of Aeolian-Skinner's King of Instruments series of
LPs, in this case a program of twentieth-century music recorded on

the 1970 Aeolian-Skinner/Sipe organ at Zumbro Lutheran in Rochester, Minnesota. Never reticent to elicit affirmation from composers to whose music he was drawn, Anderson managed to have the tape sent to the composer for comment, to which he received a response in July 1972, Persichetti writing, "A. S. [Aeolian-Skinner] did finally send the *Shimah* record and I am delighted to have it. I enjoy your careful and telling playing and do hope you will not neglect this part of the country so that I can hear you sometime."[49] David Craighead had played the premier of this *Parable* in Dallas, a piece that the reviewer characterized as a "semi-12-tone style . . . filled with rambling and aimless pointillism punctuated by clusters and chords that verge on the tonal (triads are audible). We are not convinced the material supports the length of the piece, or that the musical ideas are very strong."[50] A curmudgeonly reviewer notwithstanding, Persichetti acknowledged Anderson gratefully: "Thanks to your effort I have 'Parable,' an organ piece that I am very happy about."[51]

The Dallas Musica da Camera, directed by Larry Palmer and, on that day at least, comprised of clarinet, soprano, viola, cello, harp, and harpsichord, included Palmer's rendition of the Bach "Chromatic" Fantasy and Fugue, BWV 903, whose "handling of the [piece] displayed depth of understanding about the music and the harpsichord."[52] Although hardly an exemplar of an "early" music concert, especially in that two of the pieces represented living composers, the performance demonstrated that the harpsichord could hold its own at a convention dedicated to the organ.[53] Organists could choose to remain after the convention for the International Organ Seminar, sponsored by SMU, featuring Anton Heiller and Marie-Claire Alain, who, with Tagliavini, had become fixtures around the music school in the last decade. This trio, along with Anderson and Palmer, would teach daily courses.[54] Alain, a personal friend of Anderson and a frequent visitor to Dallas, would eventually receive a doctorate honoris causa from SMU "in recognition of her consummate artistry and service to her profession."[55] Of the several hundred honorary doctorates presented by SMU to major leaders in the fields of industry, law, theology, business, and arts since 1918, Alain remains one of only five musicians (Samuel Adler, 1969; Gustav Leonhardt, 1983; Eduardo Mata, 1990; and Robert Guy McCutchan, 1935) to be so honored.[56]

A Push for Renewal

Whether brought about by the expected contingencies of aging equipment or by his own penchant for continual learning and adaptation, Robert Anderson issued a memo in the autumn of 1974 outlining the status of the organ program and his vision for its future. Addressed to no one in particular but suitable for any university bureaucrat who should inquire, the letter reports on the "revision and up-dating of the organ facilities at Southern Methodist University." He forthrightly proclaims that "SMU has perhaps the greatest organ department in the United States. If we are to maintain this excellence, it is necessary for us to consider what we can do to up-date the equipment; plan for the present and future needs. Though our facility was very advanced when it was built, it is fast becoming obsolete," after which Anderson issues a plea to purchase a new mechanical action organ for Caruth Auditorium, without which "the leading schools have surpassed us." He advocates for the Caruth Aeolian-Skinner to be moved to McFarlin, replacing the Hillgreen, Lane, further mentions work needing to be done to the Holtkamp in the organ studio and the need to purchase mechanical action practice organs, and proposes renewing or replacing the organ in Perkins Chapel.[57]

Anderson's seemingly abrupt coveting of a tracker-action organ stands in stark contrast to his ready acceptance of the electropneumatic Aeolian-Skinner only a decade before, yet his own views simply had followed the universal favor generally accorded *Orgelbewegung* principles at the time, at least as far as those ideas had come to be understood in academia. The European firms of Beckerath and Flentrop had taken an early lead in the tracker revival in the United States, with Beckerath building the four-manual, mechanical-action, encased organ at Trinity Lutheran Church in Cleveland in 1957. A few of the universities installing Beckeraths included Depauw (1969),

Yale (1971), Stetson (1971), Montreat (1971), and the University of Houston (1974). Flentrop had installed a landmark instrument at Harvard (1957), followed by St Mark's Cathedral in Seattle (1965), both of which exhibited neobaroque sonorities intriguing to some unaccustomed ears. Flentrop's university instruments included those at Yale (1962), Oregon (1968), Northwestern (1968), Northern Illinois (1969), the University of California at Santa Barbara (1972), and, probably most notably, a small organ for North Texas State University in Denton (1969). Charles Fisk was coming into his own, having built the organ at King's Chapel, Boston (1964) and the monumental seventy-eight-rank instrument at Harvard University (1967). Andover had built an organ based on classical principles as early as 1958 at Rice University; Robert Noehren, a leading exponent in historical design, had built a sixty-three-rank instrument in 1962 for the University of Northern Iowa, and Fritz Noack had constructed two organs for Yale (both 1968), two organs for Westminster Choir College (both 1971), and single instruments destined for Eastern Michigan (1966) and Brandeis (1967) Universities. Within Texas, Otto Hofmann promoted historic principles in his instruments, most of which were installed within that state, arguably the most significant being a large organ for North Texas State University's concert hall in 1962.[58] Texas architect Joseph Blanton had espoused traditional architectural and tonal conceptions in his *The Organ and Church Design* (1957) and *The Revival of the Organ Case* (1965), thoughts echoed in Paul Bunjes's *The Praetorius Organ*, his dissertation at Eastman from 1966 in which Bunjes, in the words of Lawrence Phelps, "establishes Praetorius as the virtual father of the modern organ through a careful analysis and comparison of Praetorius's *De Organographia* of 1619."[59] Donald Willing, previously head of the organ departments at Trinity University in San Antonio and New England Conservatory of Music, but by 1969 teaching at North Texas State University, likewise championed the cause of the American organ revival, most notably by his collaboration with Otto Hofmann, Dirk Flentrop, and Joseph Blanton to design an organ based on historic principles for

Matthews Memorial Presbyterian Church in Albany, Texas, in 1956.[60]
During the summer of 1971, Anderson had led an organ study tour of
Europe, a for-credit course in the SMU catalog that visited sixty-five
significant organs in the Netherlands, Germany, France, Switzerland,
and Italy, representing Silbermanns, Cavaillé-Colls, and Schnitgers,
from the ancient (Sion, Switzerland) to the rococo (Weingarten) to
the modern (Jürgen Ahrend instruments in Westerhausen and Amster-
dam).[61] Anderson was certainly no historical organ novice prior to
this tour; however, that these visits significantly informed his ideas
about organ tonal design partly explain his subsequent promotion
of mechanical-action organs at SMU. That the national landscape
of organ building had transformed markedly in the decade since the
Aeolian-Skinner had been selected for Caruth Auditorium motivated
Anderson as he took the precipitous step of calling on European organ
builders to submit proposals to construct a modern, mechanical-action
instrument for SMU.

Anderson wrote to Charles Fisk in June 1974, outlining, among
other items, his plan to "construct a new tracker for Caruth, using
about twenty-three ranks of the present Skinner pipes. We are envi-
sioning a four-manual with about sixty stops. Bob [Sipe] is, of course,
unequipped to build this, so I have suggested that he act as tonal architect and finisher, and that he sub-contract the construction of the organ
to someone good."[62] That summer, Sipe canvased European organ
builders—in Anderson's opinion "the best in the world"[63]—with a
subcontracting proposal whereby those builders would work collab-
oratively with him and Anderson to supply pipework and a "keydesk
with electric stopknobs and piston buttons with cables and junctions
for us to attach the combination action" but with voicing and other
relevant matters addressed by Sipe.[64] Alfred Kern himself politely
declined the offer on behalf of his firm.[65] Karl Schuke did not "reject
any cooperation with an oversea organbuilder as a matter of principle," but cautiously noted that "in the past other German builders have
made bad experiences with such cooperations."[66] Metzler und Söhne
of Zürich responded that, "based on past great personal difficulties

with similar arrangements," they would be unable to undertake such a "great" project.[67] Similar disappointing letters arrived from Marcussen and Son in Denmark and Rudolph von Beckerath in Hamburg. Even Casavant declined the collaborative venture, noting "Once bitten, twice shy," and that there were also difficulties relative to Gerhard Brunzema's "firm thinking about oversized trackers. If the concept of this project is reduced substantially in scale, I am sure that we should be willing to talk business."[68] Josef von Glatter-Götz of the Austrian Rieger Orgelbau remarked, "I know of a dozen cooperations between two builders. One built all what is technical and the other all the pipes including specification, scales and voicing. Every one of them was a failure and both builders blamed each other."[69] Forthrightly in his stilted English, Glatter-Götz posits, "Why should a builder such as I who is well equipped with machines, orders and 50 men and who builds whole organs of any size [for] 129 years do the tricky work and leave the joyful work and the fame and praise to someone else?"[70] Nonetheless, Glatter-Götz proffered the suggestion that Sipe move to Germany and work as his employee to "scale, plan, design and construct every detail of the organ, to help to make it, to do the initial voicing etc and then go back to Dallas to install it and your men there could also be Rieger employees."[71] This was no mere sarcasm but represented a serious offer; a subsequent letter from Paul Gunzelmann of Rieger affirmed, with some disbelief, that Glatter-Götz had indeed offered Sipe "the services of the whole company for the duration of the construction of the Caruth organ."[72] The proposition of a local builder collaborating with a larger firm to build a concert hall organ was hardly unprecedented, and Anderson's creative thinking had been sound as far as that went; after all, Jimmy and Nora Williams had subcontracted with Aeolian-Skinner to install many organs through-out Texas and the Southeast, including the Perkins Chapel and Caruth organs, all of which legitimately bore the Aeolian-Skinner nameplate. Following the Caruth installation, Sipe had done much of the work under the aegis of Aeolian-Skinner. Yet these situations differed in that, in this case, the local firm would in essence subcontract with the more established firm, with the final organ receiving the local firm's nameplate—clearly too risky a venture for the European firms to countenance. Nonetheless, the exchange must have enlightened Anderson as to the particular political and economic exigencies driving the European firms, as by November he had abandoned any notion of the Sipe collaboration.[73] The Aeolian-Skinner would remain in Caruth Auditorium for almost two more decades.

Perkins Chapel

Virtually simultaneously with his maneuvering to acquire a new pipe organ for Caruth, Anderson set about to reevaluate the Perkins Chapel organ. The instrument had been subject to almost daily use in its two decades and its deficiencies were becoming apparent. From the outset of his tenure, Anderson had expressed that "the Aeolian-Skinner Co. is concerned about the instrument as am I."[74] Anderson submitted a memo in the spring of 1972 detailing the organ's use: "The only student of mine who uses the Chapel organ is my chapel assistant. He and I are the only ones who practice there. The organ is used for teaching only a few hours a year, when the other teaching instruments are full, due to conflicts like the DSO concerts, or other such unforeseen events."[75] Nonetheless, Anderson then enumerates his practice there at over eight hours a week during busy weeks, four during lighter times, forty-six weeks yearly. His assistant claimed fifteen hours a week of practice, forty-six weeks a year. Anderson then counts five hours a week, thirty-five weeks annually, of services and rehearsals; he considers the seventy-five weddings a year as requiring about 150 hours, and teaching only 30 hours annually, in all totaling 1,653 hours of annual organ usage.[76] During its first decade, the organ had served as the main teaching instrument for Dora Poteet Barclay in addition to its regular use for services and rehearsals, so by the time Anderson had arrived at SMU, the organ was prematurely advanced in its lifespan. While enlargements and improvements during the 1960s kept the organ functioning under such onerous use, Anderson's own evolving aesthetic tastes increasingly diverged from the tonal ethos of

Aeolian-Skinner, whether manifest in Caruth Auditorium or Perkins Chapel. Never one to allow humility to encumber a good organ project, Anderson, in a letter to Charles Fisk in 1974, asserted:

> My primary goal in regard to the Chapel is that there must be a good tracker organ there, because of my OWN work (I practice there) and the influence it has on generations of preachers. I have played for 14 years for just thousands of preachers and University students, all of whom turn into avid organ fans, and this includes the Theology faculty, the most brilliant bunch on campus (along with some lawyers and engineers). So, in this case, I want a Fisk ala Old West in a period case in the back gallery. . . . This is my first proposal; the second is to take out the Skinner and sell it, and build a new Fisk tracker in the front. I would hope for the larger scheme, but would settle for the smaller. The chancel front is perfect for an organ.[77]

Indeed, the idea of a tracker organ for the rear balcony had been floated almost a decade before in a wish list Anderson had sent to Aeolian-Skinner, yet nothing had come of the suggestion.[78] Relative to the new tracker in the front upper chancel, Anderson had drawn up both a conventional, three-manual, circa-forty-three-rank stoplist and one for a larger, four-manual instrument of a decidedly classical bent, at least in terms of nomenclature. This hypothetical organ would have a Hauptwerk, Rückpositiv, Brustwerk, Swell, and Pedal.[79]

During the summer of 1974, Charles Fisk did develop a design for a twenty-seven-stop, three-manual and pedal organ, with a Georgian period case for the balcony (the Récit was comprised solely of the Cornet V), for a total cost of $118,000. Bob Sipe likewise submitted a proposal for the rebuilding of the Perkins Chapel organ in July 1974, in accordance with the stoplist designed by Anderson. Neither project came to fruition, leaving Anderson to content himself with three new keyboards for the Aeolian-Skinner from Laukhuff in 1977.[80] Although the historical record is murky, why these projects never materialized is probably best attributable to difficult political circumstances with SMU administration and general economic malaise at the time. From

Robert Anderson at the Perkins Chapel organ. Robert T. Anderson Papers,
SMU Archives, DeGolyer Library, SMU.

1972 until 1987, "the continuing dynamic and ever dramatic saga of Southern Methodist University would see more presidents and acting presidents—six—than in all the years before, a notable turnover and trauma following three presidents who had each served fifteen years or more."[81] The oil embargo of 1973 had curtailed energy use to such a degree that, among other things, SMU was not permitted to light its own Christmas tree.[82] With a backdrop of rising unemployment, stagflation, and generally slow economic growth, even Anderson had to scale back his creative vision for the organ program to match economic realities.

A Decade of Change

The recession of the mid-1970s compelled university administration to think innovatively about funding. In late 1975 Dean Kermit Hunter sought an endowment of the organ department from philanthropists Charles and Kitty Trigg. Mrs. Trigg had graduated with a bachelor's of music from SMU in 1931, studying organ and piano, so would presumably have been open to such a proposition. His first proposal to them involved a $400,000 "re-do" of the organ program, in this case replacing the Caruth Aeolian-Skinner and moving it to McFarlin to "replace that old rattletrap." In outlining his plea to obtain his goal, Hunter praises the organ department:

> I can tell you in complete frankness, and without fear of contra-
> diction, that we have the best department of pipe organ in the
> United States. One of our students won the Grand Prix de
> Chartres three years ago, and another won it two years ago. . . .
> The idea that a college student from America would win it even
> once is phenomenal and to have won it two years in a row is
> almost unbelievable. One of our students won the Grand Prix du
> Disque for the best pipe organ recording of the year in France. . . .
> And so it goes on.
>   A private university must do what it can do best, and what
> other universities cannot do. No other university in the United
> States has Bob Anderson and Larry Palmer, and that is why we
> are superior.[83]

Hunter then boldly proposed a second, "more important and far reaching," idea: for a $2 million donation the couple could establish the
"Charles and Kitty Trigg Pipe Organ program, [which] would have
its own catalog every year and become a distinctive program at SMU,
but a much more important thing would be the Charles and Kitty
Trigg Music Center, with the entire music program in your names."[84]
Strangely, the second proposal failed to benefit the organ program
beyond the advantages outlined in the first proposal, although the
latter proposal was clearly the one preferred by Hunter. The additional
$3.6 million would endow the music program, providing for scholar-
ships and buttressing weak programs, Hunter reasoning that

> year by year we continue to lose good high school students to
> the University of Texas, to North Texas State, to Texas Tech,
> and also to Eastman and Curtis and Juilliard, simply because we
> cannot furnish them any scholarship aid. Skyline High School
> in Dallas has far better equipment for class piano than we have
> at SMU. Our opera program is almost nonexistent, because
> we cannot afford the people or the equipment. We have almost
> given up teaching violin. Occasionally one of our students will
> do something important, but he or she generally does it several
> years after leaving SMU.[85]

Hunter's forthright-though-dour epistle unsurprisingly failed to
inspire the Triggs to such a magnanimous donation, and they ended
up supporting SMU in other ways.[86] His pessimism, however, does
illustrate the long-term struggle in which SMU had always found
itself. As an institution, it was always several steps behind the Eastern
universities and, if Hunter is to be believed, its School of Music was
even outshone in some respects by a local high school, with other
regional universities eliciting more attraction to music students than
the Meadows School of the Arts. With the entire music school suffering from the economic travails and with each department needing its
own capital improvements, Anderson's pleas to upgrade the organs
through the decade were inevitably destined to remain unheeded.

To paraphrase Hunter's commendation, that the organ department managed to flourish at all through these years can be attributed only to the leadership and skill of Palmer and Anderson.

Politics and Programs at the Meadows School of the Arts

Anderson's contention that an organ studio should consist of fewer students of higher quality not only directly but also delicately countered the general recruitment philosophy of the Meadows School of the Arts; it also unwittingly resulted in a prestigious and an almost unmanageably large studio of organ majors and concentrations. The music division had indeed grown from 187 majors in 1968 to 286 in 1972,[87] and during the autumn of 1973, the organ studio counted 33 undergraduate and graduate majors or concentrations out of a maximum possible enrollment of 40.[88] A Meadows master plan issued in 1973 suggested that the school's infrastructure and faculty could handle 350–370 music students, but this would have to be accomplished on a shrinking budget. Dean Hunter wrote a memo to Provost James Brooks in 1972 complaining about the reduction in the budget for 1972–1973: "Some faculty members have denied themselves raises in order to get equipment for proper teaching. Some have turned down enticing offers, because they have believed in our future. . . . Since 1964 we have steadily grown, year after year, from 225 [arts] majors to more than a thousand, from 7,000 student hours to nearly 30,000."[89] If Anderson would not obtain his two new tracker organs, his faculty colleagues likewise felt themselves to be in comparable positions of want, both in terms of capital renewal and because the school had fallen in arrears with salaries. Hunter issued another imploration to Brooks in January 1975: "While we know that there is a budget crunch and while we recognize the School of the Arts does not generate 200% of its cost as yet, the thing this faculty is most concerned about is the wide discrepancy in salary scales between the Meadows School of the Arts and the University average. . . . We find that a full professor in the arts makes about 17% less than the university average, and associate professor nearly 12% less."[90] Despite these issues, the organ department throughout the 1970s maintained enrollment numbers that, despite a gradual decline from the early 1970s, still normally measured in size third only to the Piano and Voice Departments:[91]

Semester	Undergraduate	Graduate	Total
1977, Fall	6	25	31
1978, Spring	6	22	28
1978, Fall	4	19	23
1979, Spring	4	16	20
1979, Fall	7	20	27
1980, Spring	6	19	25
1980, Fall	8	15	23

The Meadows School of the Arts' liberal admission policy during the early 1970s adversely affected the quality of the students and the teaching by the later 1970s, only confirming Anderson's assertion that an organ studio, and by extension, a school of music, would benefit from "streamlining" and selectivity in admission. Anderson had overtly recommended this in 1976 when he suggested to Division of Music chairman William Hipp that "it would be better to reduce the size and activity of the school in order to achieve this [raise in quality]. Numbers of students do not impress me—only numbers of good students. . . . Excellence begets excellence."[92] During the late 1970s, under the direction of the new dean, Eugene Bonelli, Meadows would implement a Music Task Force aimed at addressing budgetary and quality issues and whose report, issued on November 5, 1980, would directly contradict the progrowth objectives of the master plan from only seven years earlier and instead echo Anderson's own philosophy.

This report from 1980 concluded that faculty were overloaded and overworked, recommended phasing out several less popular majors (such as commercial music), proposed eliminating the widespread practice of graduate students teaching majors, and advocated reducing the piano faculty.[93] The committee thus summarized its findings: "Our recommendations are based on the premise that achieving quality in the Meadows School of the Arts at Southern Methodist University is predicated on serving a limited number of music majors. We propose that the Music Division serve a smaller, more select number of Music Majors with the highest possible quality of pre-professional training."[94] The report, though highly critical of many areas of study, specifically recommended not only the phasing out of certain positions but also the termination of several professors, and lavishes only praise on the organ department, which it classifies as "a program with great strength, [that] needs instruments and scholarships."[95] Dean Bonelli concurred with this evaluation, maintaining that "Drs. Anderson and Palmer have both gained international reputations in their field. This faculty is now maximally utilized. Dr. Anderson carries a full load, primarily in organ performance; Dr. Palmer teaches organ, harpsichord, the Sacred Music Seminar, and is Director of Graduate Studies . . . primary needs are for a new practice harpsichord and two practice organs."[96] Bonelli implicitly recognized the team Anderson and Palmer had become. Although Anderson had always managed to procure publicity for the organ department, Larry Palmer, as eventual head of keyboard studies, had developed a harpsichord program that granted thirty graduate degrees in harpsichord between 1970 and 1986. The university's support of harpsichord studies culminated in 1983 when Gustav Leonhardt was granted an honorary doctorate.[97] Although the decade was fraught with budgetary peril and administrative political hazards, and although the desired new organs were not forthcoming, Anderson and Palmer managed to guide the program to great success both in terms of enrollment and student quality. By some metrics at least, the organ department would see no greater pinnacle of success than it experienced in the 1970s.

Chapter 7

Halcyon Days and New Opportunities

The 1980s commenced with the organ program positioned formidably, poised to produce even more competition laureates and highly coveted church and university musicians. In the autumn of 1981, Dean Eugene Bonelli announced to the faculty and staff of the Meadows School of the Arts that Robert Anderson had been appointed the Meadows Foundation Distinguished Teaching Professor for 1981–1982. According to Bonelli, "Dr. Anderson becomes the first professor in the Meadows School of the Arts to be named to this rotating chair which has been established by the Meadows Foundation to annually honor one faculty member in the school for distinguished teaching."[1] The next year, he was appointed University Distinguished Professor of Organ and Sacred Music, an honor only awarded to faculty who met certain criteria and career accomplishments and that included a yearly salary stipend of $7,000 for professional development. To receive a distinguished professorship, faculty were required to have achieved the rank of full professor, be well recognized with "scholarly credentials" in their field, demonstrate excellence in teaching and "intellectual breadth," not hold an endowed chair, have served SMU for at least six years, and be at least 45 years old.[2] Anderson held the distinguished professorship until his retirement. In a 1986 memorandum, Anderson enumerated the opportunities those funds had afforded him the prior year, notably allowing him to visit the Bodleian library to study Felix Mendelssohn's Bach scores and funding journeys to East Germany for research on historic organs and to perform in Leipzig. Demonstrating the eclectic pedagogical sense that propelled him to appreciate music and organ building styles of diverse eras and locales, he contended that the funds allowed him to "develop expertise in the instruments of various countries and periods—I consider this one of my most vital teaching tools."[3] He used subsequent years' awards also to commission new music.[4] Anderson toured Europe annually from 1977 through the 1980s, performing at seventy-five European churches, cathedrals, and concert halls from 1977 through 1986 alone, such tours often including recording sessions for various national radio stations and presentations at scholarly conferences.[5] In 1962 Anderson had joined Colbert-Laberge Concert Management, which subsequently became Lillian Murtagh Concert Management, which, after her death, became Murtagh-McFarlane Concert Artists. Anderson's friend and local organist Howard Ross managed him professionally starting in 1980, but Anderson eventually accepted management through Phillip Truckenbrod Concert Artists.[6]

In 1984 the Meadows School of the Arts received an endowed professorship for another faculty position in the organ department. It was conceived and funded by Willis Tate and his wife, Joel Estes Tate, who had graduated from the School of Music in the 1930s studying organ with Mrs. Horace Whaling. President Tate, assuming office in 1954, had steadfastly supported musical endeavors throughout his tenure; by the time of his retirement in 1972, he had overseen the development of the Meadows School of the Arts complex, crowned with the Aeolian-Skinner organ in position in 1989, teaching generations of pianists and most significant instrument on campus. His magnanimity extended beyond these highly visible, large-scale gifts, however, and even included the donation of a small organ practice room deep within the labyrinthine corridors of the building. The Tate family donated $500,000 which was matched by the Meadows Foundation, initiating a $1 million endowed chair in the organ department.[7] The revenue yielded from this endowment, however, eventually supported a chair in the Piano Department instead. Concert pianist Tedd Joselson was appointed the first Joel Estes Tate Professor of Music in the autumn of 1986,[8] after whose brief tenure eminent Spanish pianist Joaquín Achúcarro assumed the position in 1989, teaching generations of pianists at SMU while cultivating a worldwide concert career and enhancing the reputation of the Meadows School of the Arts.[9]

A Historic Portuguese Organ Acquired by SMU

Journalist Jani Leuschel began an opinion piece in the December 6, 1984, *Daily Campus*, the university's newspaper, encapsulating the optimism of the year and the fortuitous circumstances which the organ department was relishing, observing that "someone in the organ department must have been saying their prayers. Besides the recent donation of a million-dollar organ chair to honor Joel Estes Tate, the university has added a baroque chamber organ built by Pascoal Caetano in 1762 to the Spanish art collection of the Meadows Museum."[10]

In a March 1975 letter to Susan Tattershall, an organ artisan and restorer at that time working in Spain, Anderson outlined his vision for a historic instrument in the Meadows Museum, in his words "a very beautiful museum of art. . . . It has as central focus a great collection of Spanish painting."[11] According to Anderson, the museum director, William B. Jordan, "an eminent authority on Spanish art . . . is interested in music as a part of the life of the Museum, and we often have concerts there, particularly harpsichord, chamber music, and small choral ensembles."[12] The performance space consisted of a grand staircase and central court of travertine marble, patterned after the transept at Burgos Cathedral. Anderson writes to Tattershall, an

Robert Anderson with a student. Robert T. Anderson Papers,
SMU Archives, DeGolyer Library, SMU.

authority on Iberian organ building, that "I am interested in knowing about the availability of a small, old, Spanish organ for the museum."[13] Not until several years later did such an opportunity arise through the contact of Swiss organist Guy Bovet, who lobbied for SMU to purchase the organ.[14]

Dr. Maarten Vente, by the early 1980s a retired professor of music at the University of Utrecht in the Netherlands, had been seeking a buyer for his eighteenth-century Iberian chamber instrument. A noted organ expert and musicologist in Europe, Dr. Vente had published frequently on historic organ topics, including restorations in which he was involved, not the least of which was his own 1762 Pascoal Caetano Oldovini chamber instrument of one manual and seven registers, originally built for Evora Cathedral in Portugal and removed and restored by him with assistance from Flentrop in 1967. (Apparently Vente's original acquisition of the organ came about after he had assisted Flentrop with the restoration of the cathedral's main organ.[15]) Pascoal Caetano Oldovini, of Italian background, spent most of his career working on organs in South Portugal. According to Vente himself, Caetano "built an organ for Elvas Cathedral (ca. 1765, extant), adapted the famous Hulenkamp organ of Faro Cathedral to Portuguese standards (ca. 1755), restored and adapted the wonderful 1562 Renaissance organ of Evora Cathedral (ca. 1760) and built two other organs for this cathedral: the organ at the Gospel side of the choir with 1½ manuals and the Epistle organ This last one, the Epistle organ of 1762, is in our possession."[16] This little organ had undergone few alterations through the years, a Flentrop representative acknowledging that "nothing of the instrument was changed basicly, all the work could be described as preservation. Most of the work was done to the windchest. As far as possible the original leathering was kept; the stops of the wooden pipes were releathered though, to assure a good tone quality."[17] Mr. Vente additionally clarified that the restoration was minimal, and that "all but three small pipes of the Mixture are original; the foot tread for the bellows is missing, but can easily be replaced."[18] The actual stop knobs are unlabeled, but the stoplist utilizing modern nomenclature works out to the following:

1. Open Diapason 8' from tenor a.
2. Bourdon 8' (the lowest seventeen pipes are permanently on)
3. Principal 4'
4. Fifteenth 2'
5. Mixture II
6. Cymbale II
7. Sesquialtera II

The compass is of forty-five notes, short octave, keys covered with boxwood, the façade pipes of nearly pure tin, and the interior pipes are mostly of metal as well, although the bass of the Bourdon 8' is of wood. The case is of Iberian chestnut with the interior painted red, the entire organ reflecting both Italian and Iberian organ building styles. Susan

Tattershall restored the nightingale stop, which, although present on the instrument in its original iteration, had not been included in the Flentrop renovation.[19]

Dean Bonelli arranged the purchase of the organ for $50,000, the funds having been supplied by the Meadows Foundation of Dallas.[20] Larry Palmer wrote enthusiastically to the faculty of the museum's new acquisition that "it has been a long-standing dream of the SMU organ faculty of having a suitable instrument in the Meadows Museum of Spanish Art, one of the most effective spaces for music in the fine arts complex at Southern Methodist University. . . . Both Anderson and I enthusiastically recommended to Dean Eugene Bonelli that we attempt to acquire this instrument." Palmer continues, "The organ was originally to have been placed in the gallery of the Meadows Museum, but we decided after its arrival here to set it on the right on the main floor, to the right of the grand staircase, thus allowing better access and making it available for use in teaching and concerted chamber music."[21] Indeed, with a polychromatic backdrop of Spanish masterworks by Murillo, Velasquez, Goya, and Picasso, the organ was dedicated in December 1984 by Guy Bovet, visiting professor of organ during Anderson's sabbatical that semester, joined by the Texas Baroque Ensemble and playing music of Coelho, Carreira, Cabezón, Herédia, Frescobaldi, de Arauxo, Scarlatti, Seixas, and Soler.[22] The gentle, windswept sounds of this instrument must have been a revelation to the Dallas ears that were largely unaccustomed to authentic European organs.

Only five years before, Alfred Kern had built a new organ for University Park United Methodist Church nearby, allowing Texans to experience the colorful tonal palette of that Alsatian instrument, which rendered French music authentically.[23] But that was a large church/concert instrument for which the expectations were different, the mild temperament of the Caetano organ being ill-equipped for either modern liturgical or concert use. Bovet claimed "This music is just in another world. You can really hear the music of the time. . . . [It] makes this place come alive."[24] In preparing the concert, he proffered that "the organ was a pleasure to practice upon. 'It's the only good instrument in the school.'"[25] Dean Bonelli, through whose initiative the organ had been acquired, lauded the new acquisition as a "great treasure which will become an important part of the Museum's collection. To our knowledge, this will be the only 18th-century European tracker-action organ owned by an American

The 1762 Pascoal Caetano Oldovini chamber organ. Robert T. Anderson Papers, SMU Archives, DeGolyer Library, SMU.

University. We will ensure the preservation and use of this treasured instrument for future generations."[26] A reviewer in the campus paper praised Bovet's performance: "Playing works from the Renaissance through the early classical period, the internationally renowned organist brought to life the still, immovable beauty of the Spanish paintings that cover the walls of the museum."[27] In a dedication speech that evening, Dr. Vente averred that "we are very grateful that this organ has found a fine destination in ideal surroundings."[28] He expressed hope that the instrument would stimulate research into Iberian music and even the other organs at Evora Cathedral.

The instrument remains arguably the oldest pipe organ in Texas, certainly deserving the accolades proclaiming its inimitability. Larry Palmer championed the instrument tirelessly, featuring it in hundreds of concerts he and his students would perform in the Meadows Museum, both in its original location and, after 2001 when His Royal Highness Juan Carlos and Queen Sophia of Spain dedicated it, in the new museum building on campus, where the organ now resides in an upstairs gallery.[29] Congruent with his early music specialty, Palmer utilized the Oldovini organ to spur his own further research into the builder's other instruments. Palmer subsequently performed in Portugal and offered his own knowledge of SMU's organ to João Paulo Janeiro, a Portuguese organ scholar.[30]

A New Concert Organ for Dallas—and SMU

An organ department of national stature required equivalent instruments of national stature, the lack of which on the SMU campus was readily apparent by the mid-1970s. The Hillgreen, Lane in McFarlin had ceased performing viably in the days of Dora Poteet Barclay. The 1951 Aeolian-Skinner in Perkins Chapel was limited by its size and by the hours per day available for practice in what had become a preaching and worship laboratory for theology students. The Aeolian-Skinner in Caruth Auditorium, although utilized for significant musical events in the life of the community, had fallen short of the expectations Robert Anderson had initially borne for it.

If the organ studio was to be populated by quality students receiving the highest quality education, the university needed to provide instruments that could realize these educational aspirations. The acquisition of the Portuguese organ certainly aided to this end; yet an important concert instrument was still wanting.

The Aeolian-Skinner in Caruth Auditorium had been problematic from a mechanical and tonal level from the beginning. Anderson had requested changes to the stoplist beginning only months after its inauguration, such projects continuing—mostly in the summers—throughout the 1970s. Aeolian-Skinner had acknowledged some of the flaws in No. 1438, from voicing, mechanical, and persistent electrical concerns, to acoustic problems with the auditorium largely beyond their control. Yet the instrument was still significant for Dallas at the time, being the ninth and largest instrument in Dallas from this noteworthy American builder in a city whose musical visions often exceeded its practical grasp. By midcentury, the Pilchers, Esteys, and Hillgreen, Lanes, all of whose organs had proliferated throughout the city in the first half of the century, had been failing and were being replaced with nondescript Möllers (University Park Methodist Church, 1950; Christ the King Catholic, 1947) or Wicks (First Community Church, 1952; Gaston Avenue Baptist, 1950), if they were being replaced at all. Not only had Aeolian-Skinner built the most instruments in Dallas in the postwar period, but their cadre of instruments were also resoundingly musical, sturdy, and appreciated by their institutions.[31] When the Caruth instrument was conceived, Aeolian-Skinner was a natural choice for such an important venue, deserving the national attention it received. One could handily accuse Anderson and Palmer of avaricious visions in their seeming dissatisfaction with the Aeolian-Skinner, as if they simply coveted an upgrade, an organ more in keeping with the design aesthetics of the time. However, this would not be a fair assessment. The meteoric success of the organ department at SMU had led to a flourishing church music and organ culture in Dallas, many of whose churches employed SMU graduates who, like their teachers, bore aspirations for organs conceived along historic tonal designs. By Robert Anderson's 1985 accounting, he had taught 308 students at SMU alone, this list not even considering the numerous students of Larry Palmer, whose tenure at that time was already almost fifteen years.[32] Although certainly not all of these students remained in Dallas, a great number of them did, and new organs were commissioned with increasing frequently through the 1970s and 1980s. The 1979 Alfred Kern instrument at University Park United Methodist represented the grand French tradition—a newly built, European tracker organ with a distinctly French classic voice. Schantz had poised itself as a successor to Aeolian-Skinner's American Classic style, installing large instruments at Park Cities Baptist Church in 1971 and at Lovers Lane United Methodist in 1978. Casavant installed a large instrument at Northpark Presbyterian in 1986. Further, the blossoming organ culture engendered Dallas's own first native builders. Robert Sipe began working on organs at SMU during his high school days, continuing through the 1960s when he built, along with Rodney Yarbrough, the first modern tracker organ in North Texas at St. Stephen Methodist in Mesquite; later in the 1960s he was appointed vice president of Aeolian-Skinner. On his return to Dallas, Sipe established his own workshop, built a large tracker instrument for First Presbyterian (1977) and rebuilt the German-inspired Schlicker at Zion Lutheran (1982).[33] Dallas native Marvin Judy, whose father had been a professor at SMU's Perkins School of Theology,[34] built his Opus 1 in 1971 at Oak Cliff Christian Church. Larry Palmer commissioned Judy to build his home organ in 1984.[35] In 1978 Judy built (as Schudi Organ Company) his Opus 6, a stunning fifty-two-rank organ in the sumptuous acoustics of St. Thomas Aquinas Catholic Church. The French-inspired instrument, voiced by George Gilliam, was envisioned for this Romanesque space and quickly became a haven for concerts,[36] for many years its incumbent being Anderson student Paul Riedo, who also assumed the new Dallas Symphony organist position some years later.[37]

A confluence of at least two circumstances in the early 1980s, related in some ways to the changing organ landscape of North Texas, tangibly led to a new organ project for SMU's Caruth Auditorium.

In the words of *Dallas Morning News* classical music critic Lawson Taitte in 1993,

> Even though 11 organs dot the SMU campus, the school's two organ professors, Robert T. Anderson and Larry G. Palmer, clamored for years to get a major new teaching instrument— to no avail. The turnaround came when Mr. Anderson went on leave a decade ago and Mr. [Guy] Bovet, the prominent Swiss organ virtuoso, substituted as a visiting professor. The outsider, Mr. Bovet, told then-dean of SMU's Meadows School of the Arts Eugene Bonelli that the school could never keep its prestigious position as one of the finest organ programs in the United States unless it got a new instrument. Only then did the ball get rolling.[38]

In fact, Bonelli had always been supportive of the organ department through the years, but the outside evaluation bore a certain urgency the resident organ faculty were unable to muster. Bovet had already been responsible for finding the Caetano organ, his relationship with SMU bolstered during his residency as professor of organ during Anderson's sabbatical during 1984. This afforded him the opportunity to offer his opinions to the administration, encouraging them to explore a new teaching and concert instrument. Bovet is wont to deflect too much personal credit, however. He recalled in 2019, "It was entirely my opinion, and Bob, although he kept a certain affection for the old instrument, understood very well what I was talking about. He knew that at a time when new instruments were built in many places of the US, something had to be done about the organ situation at SMU. We visited Dean Bonelli several times, and he was also very easy to convince and happy to undertake a new project of this importance. We got only help from him."[39] The future of a new concert instrument at SMU was already unwittingly and inextricably being shaped by plans underway for the new Dallas Symphony center, which was to feature a pipe organ as the centerpiece of its hall.

Dallas's new concert hall took shape in the early 1980s when the executive board of the Dallas Symphony, led by local entrepreneur

Stanley Marcus, appointed I. M. Pei as architect[40] and Russell
Johnson's Artec Consultants, Inc., as acousticians. Local billionaire
H. Ross Perot suggested the new complex be named after Morton
H. Meyerson, former president of Electronic Data Systems, chairman
of the board of Perot Systems, and a leader in the symphony hall
development process.[41] By early 1982 Bonelli had been appointed to
assemble the organ design subcommittee for the new hall, drawing
a team of Dallas-based experts to assist in the process. A commit-
tee comprised of local musicians Howard Ross, Jody Lindh, Paul
Lindsley Thomas, and James Livengood, and chaired by Robert
Anderson,[42] began deliberations to select a builder, which, by
April 1982, resulted in proposal requests to C. B. Fisk (Gloucester,
Massachusetts), Rieger Orgelbau (Austria), Klais Orgelbau (West
Germany), Marcussen and Son (Denmark), Orgelbau Th. Kuhn
(Switzerland), and Karl Schuke (West Germany).[43] Schuke was seen
as a safe but bland choice, an assessment somewhat confirmed by
the façade drawing. The committee expressed reservations about
Klais's tonal qualities and thought that Rieger's sound "may not be
what is required in a hall designed for orchestral music."[44] By 1985
C. B. Fisk had been contracted as the builder. Anderson, of course,
had long been partial to Fisk, even during the 1970s having suggested
two Fisk organs for Perkins Chapel. Anderson later recalled that
"we chose the most expensive builder and the smallest design. . . .
But we wanted a good instrument, with a fresh attitude toward the
design."[45] As the 1980s progressed, the development of Fisk, Opus
100, the first modern mechanical organ in an American concert hall,
would likewise progress. Among the traumas that plagued the entire
process was the death of company founder Charles Brenton Fisk in
1983, who had longed to build an instrument for an American concert
hall, but whose reticence to do so had only grown through the years
after dead-end efforts, most notably at Davies Symphony Hall in San
Francisco. Disagreements about the visual design with the I. M. Pei
office famously imperiled the project at times, for which only the
façade was complete by the Meyerson Symphony Center's opening

in 1989.[46] Funding for the organ was supplied by the philanthropy of Amelia Lay Hodges in memory of her husband, Dallas food magnate Herman W. Lay, who had died in 1982.[47] Herman Lay had long connections to SMU, even endowing the university with a chair in marketing.[48] Thus was the Herman W. and Amelia H. Lay Family organ dedicated in September 1992 by Michael Murray and David Higgs.[49]

Robert Anderson's intimate involvement on the organ subcommittee convinced him that SMU needed a Fisk organ too. In December 1984 Anderson wrote to Virginia Lee Fisk that "I talked to Gene Bonelli this evening; he met with the Provost of the University today, and told me that he wishes to negotiate a contract for a new Fisk organ for Caruth Auditorium as soon as possible (soon after the new year)! Isn't that fantastic?"[50] Anderson and Palmer, along with Fisk representatives, developed the stoplist for a new eclectic-style university instrument that spring, Fisk receiving the down payment in June 1985.[51] Anderson recalled the mutual genesis of both Opus 100 and what would be Opus 101: "C. B. Fisk, Inc. is perhaps America's most distinguished organ builder. Fisk was chosen as the builder after an exhaustive investigation for a builder for the Dallas Symphony Hall, which will be also a Fisk organ, Opus 100. The SMU organ will be Op. 101, built in the year following installation of the Dallas Symphony organ. Both contracts were negotiated in 1985—delivery time for the D.S.O. organ was projected 6 years, the S.M.U. organ at 7 years, so we are looking at 1992 as the installation time for the S.M.U. organ."[52] Anderson further specifies that the organs at Stanford University, House of Hope Presbyterian (St. Paul, Minnesota), Harvard University, and North Carolina School of the Arts all inspired the selection of Fisk for these two Dallas instruments. Anderson and Palmer, however, had a larger vision for Caruth Auditorium than simply one new instrument: They wanted two! Anderson wrote to Bonelli in January 1985: "My approach to Caruth is to solicit a design for the front from Fisk, and the design for a small, period instrument for the back gallery of Caruth from Brombaugh. I think that this is the logical approach to take. One organ can't do everything, and it would be superb to have an instrument to play old music in the same place. Guy agrees with this philosophy, as does Larry."[53] Ultimately, Caruth would not receive two instruments, but only one—the new Fisk Anderson had been coveting since the 1970s. (St Luke's Episcopal Church in Dallas would purchase the old Aeolian-Skinner for $110,000, offsetting some of the cost of the Fisk.[54]) The rigorous research and disciplined thought that had been applied before commissioning Fisk to build the organ at the Meyerson would now inform the SMU concert hall project. Although these two major instruments—installed within so close a time—would tax the Fisk shop, duplicate efforts were avoided where they could be, and Dallas would benefit from these two new concert instruments.

Caruth Auditorium's Fisk, Opus 101

The dedication of C. B. Fisk's Opus 101 in Caruth Auditorium on Sunday, September 19, 1993, represented the culmination of nine years of cooperative labor from Robert Anderson, Larry Palmer, various SMU officials, and the Fisk firm, fresh off their recent successful installation of Opus 100 at the Meyerson Symphony Center. The organ was a personal project for Anderson and Palmer, and it seemed appropriate that, rather than rely on an outside musical guest to perform the actual dedication, they should themselves present the instrument to the public for the first time in recital. The excitement was palpable in all musical quarters in the city—from the many SMU graduates in local churches to the AGO stalwarts and organ aficionados to this writer, who was in high school at the time, trying to figure out who would drive him to the event. Yet this event would not go as planned.

Three days prior to the dedication, Robert Anderson underwent heart bypass surgery, a fact unbeknownst to most as they gathered in the auditorium for either of the two recitals that day.[55] What was to have been a program of two parts played by two performers was now the sole purview of Larry Palmer, who played the entire program quite

C. B. Fisk's Opus 101 in Caruth Auditorium.
Photo courtesy of Len Levasseur.

ably, playing his planned works: "Dialogue in C" of Louis Marchand, featuring the full-throated French reeds, and the "Wir Glauben" with double pedal, often attributed to Krebs, featuring, in the words of Susan Ferré writing in the *Diapason*, "beautiful singing principals, gentle reeds (dulcian and trechterregal), and tremulant affecting all, work[ing] to create the illusion of being elsewhere besides in a relatively dry concert hall." Palmer was able to prepare at the last minute the Bach Fantasie in C Minor, BWV 562, which Anderson had programmed to prove that "Opus 101 speaks well the language of JSB." Palmer, who had written the definitive biography of Hugo Distler in 1967, chose to play that composer's Trio Sonata, Opus 18/11, in which "one was reminded why Palmer is considered an expert on the music of Distler" with his "caring yet playful performance." Larry Palmer continued with the "Nocturne" by Germaine Tailleferre, a transcription of a wind quintet not on the original program. The program ended with Franck's Chorale no. 1 in E Major, during which "the audience was treated to the French romantic sounds which exist in this three-manual organ. Remember that Opus 101 does not claim any kin to a Cavaillé-Coll, the full organ sound was thrilling to hear." Before an encore of a Frescobaldi canzona, "heartfelt applause thanked Palmer, who at the last moment had to perform double and triple duty."[56] The headline for the *Dallas Morning News* article offered an accurate abstract of the event: "SMU Organ Makes an Impressive Debut: Inaugural Concert Transcends Absence of a Key Performer." Reviewer John Ardoin continued:

> The second major organ to be dedicated in Dallas within a year was heard publicly for the first time Sunday afternoon at Southern Methodist University. Like the Lay Family Organ in the Meyerson Symphony Center, which was inaugurated in September 1992, the university's new instrument was built by the Charles Fisk Co. of Gloucester, Mass.
>
> The Meyerson organ was Fisk's Opus 100; SMU's organ is its Opus 101. Both are of an imposing scale, importance and physical beauty, though their impact is naturally different because of the space for which each was designed.

What these organs appear to have in common, however, is their versatility to adapt in an extremely clean and rich manner to the wide range of sound that has resulted from 400 years of organ writing and thinking. Fisk has convincingly brought together the best of the past as far as sound goes with the best of today in terms of electronic know-how.[57]

This new organ, then, and most appropriately for a teaching instrument, represented the amalgamation of the best of the past and present in terms of tonal and mechanical design.

Additional programs followed that week that demonstrated the organ in an accompanimental role. On Tuesday was a concert for instruments, choir, and organ, with organists Janet Hunt, Annette Albrecht, and future SMU organ professor Stefan Engels, who accompanied the Meadows Chorale under director Constantina Tsolainou in Britten's *Rejoice in the Lamb*. Ferré's review of this work is as interesting for her noting of Stefan Engels's playing as for her comments on the organ, observing that it was Engels's "experience [that] made possible a quiet, discreet, subtle performance, never louder than the quietest voice, but equally sustaining in the heady crescendi, by his constant use of the Swell pedal, handregistering, and manual changes. This was organ accompanying at its best."[58] Organist Henry McDowell concluded the evening accompanying Vaughan Williams's *Five Mystical Songs*. Marie-Claire Alain, a familiar visitor to the campus over the last decades, on September 24 performed a program (in high heels!) consisting of Bach for the first half, with her brother's *Two Fantasies*, the *Postlude pour l'Office de Complies*, and *Trois Danses* comprising the second half, in which the organ "talked through its nose, growled and roared its heart out."[59] The next day was scheduled a master class for SMU students and a panel discussion "centered on the planning and designs for the sister organs, Opus 100 at the Meyerson and Opus 101 at SMU."[60] Robert Anderson was able to attend many of these dedicatory events, but only as a listener, confined to a wheelchair in the back of the auditorium.

Caruth Auditorium
Southern Methodist University
C. B. Fisk, Opus 101 (1993)[61]

GREAT

16 Prestant
8 Octave
8 Spillpfeife
8 Flûte harmonique
8 Violoncelle
4 Octave
4 Open Flute
2⅔ Twelfth
2 Fifteenth
1⅗ Seventeenth
Progressive Mixture
Full Mixture V–VII
16 Trommeten
8 Trommeten
8 Trompette
4 Clairon

SWELL

16 Bourdon
8 Flûte traversière
8 Viole de gambe
8 Voix céleste
4 Principal
4 Flûte octaviante
2 Octavin
Mixture
Cornet III
16 Basson

PEDAL

32 Untersatz (ext. Sw.)
16 Contrebasse
16 Prestant (Gt.)
16 Bourdon (Sw.)
8 Octave
8 Spillpfeife (Gt.)
8 Violoncelle (Gt.)
4 Superoctave
Mixture IV
32 Posaune (ext. Gt.)
16 Bombarde
16 Trommeten (Gt.)
8 Trommeten (Gt.)
8 Trompette (Gt.)
4 Clairon (Gt.)

COUPLERS

Great to Pedal
Positive to Pedal
Swell to Pedal 8, 4
Swell to Great
Positive to Great
Swell to Positive
Octaves Graves on Great

COMBINATIONS

Six Swell divisionals
Six Positive divisionals

8 Trompette

8 Hautbois

8 Voix humaine

4 Clairon

POSITIVE

8 Principal

8 Gedackt

8 Quintadena

4 Octave

4 Rohrflöte

2⅔ Nazard

2 Doublet

2 Quarte de Nazard

1⅗ Tierce

Sharp IV

16 Dulcian

8 Trechterregal

8 Cromorne

Six Great divisionals

Six Pedal divisionals

(toe studs only)

Twenty general pistons duplicated
on toe studs

REVERSIBLES

Great to Pedal

Swell to Pedal

Positive to Pedal

32 Untersatz (toe stud)

32 Posaune (toe stud)

MECHANICALS

Swell Pedal, Crescendo Pedal

ACCESSORIES

Tremulant for entire organ

Great Ventil

Wind Stabilizer

Octaves Graves

Crescendo Off

Sforzando I and II

Solid State control system

Kowalyshyn Servopneumatic Lever

Pedal is flat and parallel.

This seventy-three-rank, fifty-voice, 3,681-pipe instrument was designed as an eclectic teaching instrument, offering a number of unique tonal and engineering features. A coupling assist device proprietary to Fisk and invented by Fisk voicer Stephen Paul Kowalyshyn in 1990, aids in intermanual coupling. Fisk explains of this unique device that "it is somewhat similar to the Barker Lever; but unlike the Barker Lever, the KSPL [Kowalyshyn Servopneumatic Lever] is a true servo: it faithfully follows the speed and travel of organists' fingers. Sixty-one of these KSPL levers, mounted in a pressurized plenum, labor almost transparently to greatly multiply the power of the organist's touch. When another division is coupled to the Great, the KSPL does all of the hard work of coupling, while the organist maintains the feel and control of playing the Great action alone."[62]

Anderson praised the instrument:

It has long been our desire at SMU to have a magnificent mechanical action organ of eclectic design. We chose Fisk because of their obvious commitment to quality workmanship and their fresh approach, spearheaded by the philosophy of the late Charles Fisk and realized in his design for the Meyerson organ, Op. 100. We quickly realized that this was the way to go—from concept to fruition minor design features have changed; the result far surpasses my expectations. The action is excellent; the organ is comfortable to play. The individual voices have a distinct character which places them in a league with the best instruments of any period. The character of the sound adapts itself with east to an 18th century Plenum or Plein jeu as well as to the symphonic needs of the 19th and 20th repertoire. The Pedal organ has a stunning gravity. The Full Swell is versatile and gripping because of the Mixture and the 16' Bourdon; the enclosure is tight. The Crescendo Pedal shows the smooth build-up of the ensemble. The reed colors are rich and varied. The organ has a full complement of playing aids making complex registrations or use of the instrument by many students, faculty or guest artists possible without encumbrance.[63]

A Progressive Mixture on the Great draws only the lower pitches of the Full Mixture, which is a traditional, German, eighteenth-century chorus mixture. "The Progressive Mixture does not break back but adds lower pitches in the treble. This makes an appropriate effect for 19th-century music."[64] An Octaves Grave functions as a suboctave coupler, lending gravitas to the Great division. A wind stabilizer

"engages winkers for performance of 19th and 20th century repertoire,"[65] while the balanced swell pedal activates a three-sided swell
box, which allows for an unusual range of dynamic subtlety. The organ
boasts a battery of fiery French reeds that attain their fullest character
in the lower registers, while the Germanic-style reeds bloom in the
upper octaves. In tonal philosophy the Fisk offered what Anderson
had really wanted since before the Aeolian-Skinner: an organ that was
eclectic but could play relatively authentically baroque and romantic
French and Germanic music, the latter of which his own studies had
predisposed him to favor. Yet in its ability to render music of these
schools satisfactorily, the instrument likewise can perform modern
music. In a way this reflected both Anderson's and Palmer's own musical development. Both had received significant musical formation in
German-speaking lands, yet both were purveyors of new music, regularly commissioning new works for organ and harpsichord. Southern
Methodist University now had a concert organ to integrate these
professors' visions.

Throughout the autumn of 1993, major performers were brought
in to showcase the organ, and the roster of artists recalled the 1920s
and 1930s, when performers such as Courboin, Schreiner, Karg-Elert,
Poister, and the other leading musicians of the day all made stops at
the organ in McFarlin Auditorium. Certainly since the first days of his
tenure at SMU, Anderson had ensured that major luminaries played,
and the likes of Alain, the Duruflés, and Tagliavini had all been fixtures
of the organ department for decades, but now there were no apologies
to be made. That initial dedicatory season continued on September 30,
with Michael Farris performing Buxtehude, Schumann, Mendelssohn,
and Pärt's still relatively new "Annum per Annum," and concluding
with Dupré's Prelude and Fugue in G Minor, Opus 7/3.[66] Farris had
studied with Anderson and was at that time teaching at the University of Illinois, Urbana-Champaign, although shortly thereafter he
would be appointed to the Eastman School of Music faculty before his
untimely death in 1999.[67] On October 18, 1993, SMU alum and professor of organ and sacred music at Northwestern University Wolfgang

Rübsam returned to play a concert of Bach, Widor, and Reger, while 31-year-old Olivier Latry from Notre Dame Cathedral performed two weeks later a program that included much French music, including of Boëly, Vierne, Duruflé, Guillou, and an improvisation. Swiss organist Guy Bovet, who suggested a new concert instrument to the dean in 1984, performed in November a concert of Francisco Correa de Arauxo, Juan Cabanilles, Bach, Albert Alain, Frank Martin, and two of Bovet's own pieces. His participation in the dedication series provided a proper bookend to the organ project, and Lawson Taitte claimed that "Mr. Bovet's virtuosity and musicality honored the instrument as much as the occasion honored him."[68] Larry Palmer wrote at the opening of this first season:

> It is with great pleasure that we celebrate the completion of Fisk Opus 101 by welcoming back to SMU as organ recitalists a number of our distinguished former students. . . . Our deepest gratitude is due the supportive Dean Eugene Bonelli, who found funding for the organ; to the Meadows Foundation, for its ongoing support which allows this School of the Arts to move upward to new levels of excellence, and to the dedicated artists of the Fisk Organ Company, sensitive craftspeople who construct, with utmost integrity, instruments of such superb musical character, creations beautiful both to eye and ear.[69]

Anderson had had to wait for over thirty years into his tenure at SMU, and Palmer over twenty, before they were able to see the realization of their dreams for a suitable concert instrument for their teaching studios.

Dallas's, and SMU's, position as an important southern terminus of organ building and teaching is presciently observed in Charles Brenton Fisk's 1972 letter to Robert Anderson, in which he thanks Anderson for hosting him on his "recent sojourn in Texas. What I saw and felt during those twenty-four hours has broadened my understanding, and leaves me no longer having to imagine a lot of things I have heard about for so long. SMU is a great place. I like your method of teaching; I like the atmosphere. No wonder old Bob S[ipe] sounds homesick when he gets on the subject!"[70] Through Anderson's guidance, Charles Fisk had seen the latent potential in the organ culture of North Texas, and through Fisk's work, Anderson was able to envision his ideal concert organs, which ultimately were manifest in Fisk's Opus 100 and 101, those instruments serving as a focus for a much more comprehensive organ culture. Even Lawson Taitte observed in a piece published the morning of the Caruth dedication that "some of the hottest tickets in Dallas these days are organ recitals," then citing the Meyerson instrument and one other, noting that "these are only the tip of the iceberg of the fine organs in the Dallas area, most of which were built during the last 20 years." Taitte posed the question then: "Why has Dallas become an international center for the art of the organ? Observers of the organ scene agree that the answer is surprisingly simple. 'It's the groundwork and the vision of Bob Anderson,' Mr. [Paul] Riedo says. 'He's dedicated his life to the organ, and as a teacher over the last 30 years he has produced generations of fine organists.' Many of Mr. Anderson's former students, such as Mr. Riedo, play important roles in the Dallas musical community."[71] Anderson's health problems would begin to slow him down over the next few years, but not until he had shepherded the Dallas organ community to new heights.

A New Era of Dallas Organs

In what was certainly a result of good planning and probably also a bit of serendipitous fortune, 1,800 members of the AGO gathered in Dallas during the summer of 1994 to partake of the rich organ palette the city could now offer.[72] Dallas had hosted the AGO national convention last in 1972, during which time Anderson had ensured that SMU would be the center of activity. Now, however, rather a victim of his own success, the city boasted so many more concert organs, not the least of which was the Meyerson, that SMU was less of a focal point. Local AGO steering committee member Ellen Hart explained that "Dallas is still a place where people go to church and churches still build organs. . . . The Meyerson made people here aware of what goes into building an organ."[73] The university still hosted events, including both Anderson and Rübsam performing at Caruth Auditorium, presenting the instrument to a new, and possibly more discerning, public. Dallas summoned premiere musicians, ensembles, and lecturers from around the world to enliven the city, including Jean Guillou, Carole Terry, Hans Fagius, Luigi Tagliavini, Christoph Wolff, William Bolcom, Paul Hillier, the Texas Baroque Ensemble, and Musica Antiqua Köln.[74] Conrad Susa's opera *The Wise Women*—akin to a medieval mystery play and scored only for guitar, flute, harp, percussion, and organ—was commissioned for the occasion.[75]

The Meyerson organ, even before its completion, had evoked the notion of an international organ competition to draw attention to Dallas as a center of organ culture—of which Anderson, SMU, and Fisk would be on the forefront. Dallas's own nervous paranoia in the early twentieth century that it was somehow inferior to the sophisticated cities on the East Coast had motivated city leaders to bring great musicians to town, oftentimes playing at SMU's McFarlin Auditorium; this fixation continued to shade and to inform decisions in the city even to more recent decades. Thus it was that columnist Wayne Lee Gay wrote in April 1997 in the *Fort Worth Star-Telegram*, "After years of jealously watching Fort Worth's Van Cliburn International Piano Competition, Dallas hopes to move into the front rank of the competition world this week with the first Dallas International Organ Competition. 'The Cliburn sets the standard,' says George Schrader, the former Dallas city manager who heads the board of advisers of the competition. It opens today at Caruth Auditorium on the Southern Methodist University campus."[76] Anderson would serve as chairman of the jury for the First Triennial Dallas International Organ Competition, joined by colleagues Marie-Claire Alain from France, Hans Fagius from Sweden, Tsuguo Hirono from Japan, Ludger Lohmann from Germany, Martin Haselböck from Austria, and Gillian Weir from England.[77] Twelve contestants, all under 30, were drawn from forty-three players auditioned in the United States, Germany, and Japan to compete in a semifinal round at Caruth Auditorium. Six participants would then move on to the final rounds at the Meyerson.

Anderson expressed his hopes for the enduring legacy of this competition: "Already Dallas is famous in the organ world because of the Fisk at the Meyerson, and as the contest grows, there will be more and more perks added to the first prize, including, we hope, a recording contract."[78] While the Cliburn competition was managed by its own foundation with a $3 million budget, this fledgling organ competition would have to get by on a shoestring budget of $500,000, about $100,000 of which was provided by the Dallas Symphony Association, the remaining being underwritten by Ward Lay, son of Herman and Amelia Lay, the donors of the Fisk, Opus 100.[79] Adding to the prestige of the competition was the involvement of the Dallas Symphony Orchestra, with whom the finalists would play a commissioned work, in the case of the 1997 competition, William Bolcom's "Humoreske for Organ and Orchestra." Eugene Bonelli, who by this time had left SMU to become president of the Dallas Symphony, tirelessly promoted the organ at the symphony, just as he had championed the organ department at SMU. Bonelli was keen to promote the event as "the only organ competition in which the finalists perform with a major symphony orchestra."[80] Was the Dallas competition actually intended to rival the venerable Cliburn competition? If prize money is any indication, yes. The 1997 competition awarded $25,000 to first place, $15,000 to second place, and $5,000 to third, with $5,000 awarded to the audience favorite. (The Cliburn offered prizes of $25,000, $20,000 and $15,000, respectively.[81]) Eugene Bonelli boasted, "Our prizes will be the largest of any competition in the world."[82] Indeed, there were few actual international organ competitions at the time, so this competition would raise Dallas to the levels of Calgary, St Alban's, and Chartres, arguably the only competitions that were of similar scope and budget.

The Dallas International Organ Competition produced three first place laureates during its three successful iterations. Although utilizing a blind jury system, all three winners were from North Texas. Stewart Wayne Foster, then a student at Denton's University of North Texas, won in 1997; James Diaz, organist and choirmaster at the nearby St. Michael and All Angels Episcopal Church, triumphed in 2000; and Bradley Hunter Welch, then organist at Dallas's Highland Park Presbyterian Church, received the honor in 2003, before the competition withered in the face of political and economic exigencies beyond its control.[83] Although Anderson had chaired the first two juries, John Scott served as jury chairman for the final competition.[84]

Robert Anderson's Retirement

Eugene Bonelli joined the Dallas Symphony as president in 1994, leaving a lasting legacy of support for the arts, music, and the organ department in particular at SMU. Anderson and Palmer could not have asked for a more supportive administration, and it is unlikely the Caruth organ project could have been completed under prior deans, particularly those less interested in music than Bonelli. Carole Brandt, the new dean, was trained in drama and theatre, and her leadership would reflect those priorities.[85] By his own admission, Anderson's health had been declining for years, now a matter of public record after his absence at the organ dedication. In 1995 he received the Heart Patient of the Month award, for which he enthusiastically prepared a public speech in which enumerated the healthy changes he had made in his life since his heart surgery. He woefully admits to having a family history of heart disease, along with cancer and diabetes, his litany of health problems likewise exacerbated by poor choices prior to his lifestyle change: "I had smoked since the age of 16, not much, about 1–2 cigarettes a day. I had been treated for high blood pressure since 1978. I enjoyed and cooked rich foods. . . . My cholesterol level had been high, but it was being treated successfully. My weight was 150, about as high as it had ever been. All of this, of course, adds to impending tragedy." Anderson admitted stress as an aggravating factor for his condition, adding, "When one is a professional person such as I am, stress factors are constantly hovering. I have spent years going to meetings for many different organizations, chairing many of them. I am a goal-oriented person and this leads to stress. People have said, 'Bob never leaves 'till tomorrow what he can do today.' Somehow one squeezes it all in, and people notice this. . . I am trying to change this pattern. I spend more time at leisure—reading, going to concerts or films, spending time with friends."[86] Ironically, his well-crafted, erudite speech to this audience (he continues in great detail by suggesting proper exercise amounts and offering healthy menu alternatives) probably involved hours of preparation and multiple rewrites, all likely contributing to the stress of which he so sternly warned his listeners. Yet he probably enjoyed this stress and certainly had learned to thrive in it.

He had two minor strokes in 1991 that affected his left side, and thus his playing, and in 1992 he was diagnosed with Parkinson's disease, but he was always hopeful it could be treated to extend his useful years. He vowed that "I won't give in to the effects which constantly get in the way of most things that I do."[87] Parkinson's disease is particularly insidious for an organist who depends on fine motor movements and coordination to ply his craft, and Anderson realized his career was fast coming to a close. He requested and was granted early retirement from SMU as of June 1996, assuming the title of University Distinguished Professor of Music emeritus.[88] He resigned from Phillip Truckenbrod's management that same summer, citing the "effects of Parkinson's disease which is slowing me down considerably." Waxing pensively at his retirement, he continued, "I look back on a marvelous career as a teacher and player, working with Lilian, Buddy and you. You all have been most kind to me and I am most thankful for it."[89] He had been teaching five organ students at the time of his retirement, whom he continued to mentor on an adjunct basis until each student had finished their programs, and was retained by the university additionally to teach another semester of Organ Survey class in order to complete this writer's coursework, who was thus his last undergraduate student.[90] Larry Palmer succeeded Anderson as head of the organ department.

Chairing the juries of the Dallas International Organ Competitions of 1997 and 2000 would consume Robert Anderson's final years in Dallas, although by the final competition in 2003, he had moved to Hawaii where his brother, Ron, lived, eventually moving into assisted living. Robert Theodore Anderson died on May 29, 2009, survived by brother Ron Anderson and sister Dorothy Faller.[91]

Anderson's Legacy

As word of his death reached the organ world, remembrances flooded in. Gerre Hancock said, "Robert Anderson, always a visionary and a leader, added immensely to the history of the study of the organ. . . . His dedication to the art of organ-building and organ-teaching will ever be a model."[92] Meadows School of the Arts dean Carole Brandt claimed he was a "Meadows crown jewel in a University where it honored the School as its crown jewel." Marilyn Mason, chairman of the organ department at the University of Michigan, lauded him as "one of the greatest organ teachers of this generation," while Eileen Guenther, president of the AGO, asserted that he "was an amazing performer, and one of the most ardent supporters of the organ and its music that I have ever encountered." His colleague Dr. Kenneth Hart, professor of sacred music emeritus at SMU, remembered him as "a faithful and encouraging friend and a consummate musician and churchman. . . . A high percentage of the finest organs in the region are due to his influence."[93]

Carlton Young, teacher, hymnal editor, composer, conductor, and former colleague at SMU, eulogized Anderson at his memorial service on Tuesday, September 22, 2009, most appropriately held in Perkins Chapel, the space in which "Bob's pedagogy, performing, and accompanying skills, and repertory were first joined." Young recalled:

Bob thought musically, as a composer thinks, within the music. Bob could re-create composers' musical ideas, criticize, compare, select, and juxtaposition them in his head, sing and/or play them. This gift and acquired skills informed Bob's approach to phrasing, articulation, tempo, and registration, which always proceeded from the music, not superimposed o centered performance practices n the music.

It is obvious Bob would have had a successful academic and performing career wherever he might have located. Our good fortune is that it happened on this campus and in this city, the epicenter of Bob's career as distinguished teacher, exciting and imaginative performer, and gifted tonal architect.[94]

Anderson would undoubtedly claim that his most important legacy is his generations of students, populating universities and churches throughout the world, many of whom compose and perform regularly, as he did. A student who experienced his Organ Survey or Organ Literature courses learned the mechanics behind the music, how articulation and musical matters affected organ building, and vice versa. In lessons Anderson sought to present the music in such a way that the student could understand the composer's intentions in the same way that Anderson could—not always an easy task for student or teacher. This writer experienced Anderson as an undergraduate student, and he surely adjusted his pedagogical style for graduates, but an important component of lessons—if one did not play a piece perfectly the first time—was repeating back a phrase he first played or sang, exactly mimicking his careful slurring or whatever aspect of articulation or rubato he was trying to communicate. Anderson would give a student the tools to make informed and individual musical decisions, but the wise student knew to save the individual interpretations for times when he was out of earshot! Anderson's formative years with Walcha were certainly evident in his pedagogical approach to the end. Carlton Young observed:

> By listening to Walcha firsthand and in recordings, (parenthetically, Walcha learned Bach's vast organ works by hearing them), Bob acquired Walcha's articulation, phrasing and registration skills which allow the multiple lines in Bach's preludes, fugues and trio sonatas to unfold, thus enabling the listener to aurally experience the composer's architecture, tonal and harmonic

colorings, and dramatic gestures. And in works based on biblical texts or chorales, the listener more clearly understands Bach's tonal exegesis. Bob brought these performance skills and listener-centered performance practices to the preparation and performance of other works in his expansive organ repertory, and his students and colleagues introduced these qualities into other performing media, particularly choral music.[95]

Anderson's interpretation of a piece had been reached after much personal deliberation and score study (he always recommended score study away from the keyboard), so by the time a student was beginning a piece, Anderson's interpretation would have already solidified into a fairly narrow interpretive spectrum, and he was always up to the task to communicate to his students why this way was to be preferred. (Although his own interpretations or stylistic assumptions would certainly change through the decades.) His approach was holistic—hand position, body position, ear training, all related to performance. Dr. Carolyn Shuster Fournier, French-American musicologist and organist, recalled that "he underlined the importance of a calm and relaxed body position while playing Bach's First Trio Sonata for organ in E-Flat Major." Erik Goldstrom, his chapel assistant from 1987 to 1989 assessed him as an "amazing pedagogue, he could simply destroy you at a lesson but then always build you back up and leave you with a sense of encouragement. He, more than anyone else, freed my playing and helped me find my musicianship." As with many teachers, he could certainly be abrasive during lessons and could grow frustrated with a recalcitrant student who failed to make progress as fast as he would have liked. Robert Poovey said, "He was utterly and completely devoted to his students. He was honest . . . brutally so at times. He was totally and completely dedicated to excellence. He insisted on it and he got it." Dr. Christopher Anderson, associate professor of sacred music at SMU (no relation), and a student from 1988 to 1991 remembered that

I played for him once all 11 of Brahms' late chorale preludes. . . . For me at that time, there was a "right" way to approach the music, and I was certain I had found it. Bob made extensive comments and suggestions—more than a naïve and overly confident student wanted to hear. I will never forget the moment when I was leaving Caruth Auditorium after that lesson: Bob was sitting about halfway back in the middle of the hall, and he called to me to say that I would be surprised to find how differently I played this music in twenty years. This was the wisdom of a master teacher who knew the influence of life experience upon music making, that one's humanity cannot be separated from one's musicianship.[96]

Every student of "RTA," as he was affectionately known, could recount legions of their own stories. His influence on his students transferred, then, not only to their playing but also to the ideas of organ design. Hence, many fine instruments have been built under their auspices that directly reveal Anderson's thoughtful approach.

As a consultant, Anderson was involved with the building of dozens of organs, the most important being Fisk, Opus 100, at the Meyerson Symphony Center: "Widely acclaimed as one of the finest in the world, the Meyerson organ has helped spark a spreading interest in organs in symphony halls. Revolutionary in both design and sound, it has become a point of reference in the design of subsequent concert hall instruments."[97] In fact, Seattle's Benaroya Hall installed a Fisk in 2000.[98] According to Manuel Rosales, builder of the organ at Los Angeles's Disney Hall, "The Meyerson was the first serious opportunity to prove that it really could work and that the audience could get excited about having an organ." Lynn Dobson, builder of the organ at Philadelphia's Kimmel Center, observed of Fisk, Opus 100, that "it has become a standard to measure from. . . . Certainly the conversations in Philadelphia often go to the Meyerson, and everyone on our design team has been to Dallas."[99] At long last, Dallas, then, had become a haven for musical culture in general and a thriving center of organ activity specifically from which those on the East Coast could glean inspiration.

Chapter 8

An Enduring Legacy

The tale of organ studies at SMU neither began nor ended in the life and work of Robert Theodore Anderson. As crucial as he was to the success of the organ program at its height, Bertha Stevens Cassidy had, in her own meticulous and modest way, fashioned an organ culture that wove itself integrally into the fabric of university life. A formidable technician herself, the constraints of the era were not particularly conducive to building her own concert career, and SMU was largely a training center for the church organist. In Dora Poteet Barclay SMU would finally have an organ professor whose performing experience could infuse an aspiration for professional performance outside of Sunday morning. Robert Anderson, of course, was able to guide the organ program to become a benchmark for organ training around the nation, teaching concert organists and shaping fine church organists, both of whom could now avail themselves of scholarship and theological training heretofore unavailable. The extent of Anderson's accomplishments would have been unlikely without his "standing on the shoulders of giants" in the form of his predecessors, and they would certainly have been curtailed had his efforts not been assisted by other faculty and staff serving alongside him. He frequently spoke of his debt to Eugene Bonelli for his efforts on behalf of the organ program, culminating in the installation of Fisk, Opus 101, in Caruth Auditorium in 1993, but others involved in the program need to be placed in their proper historical context, not altogether the easiest task, given Anderson's larger-than-life persona.

Harpsichord Studies at SMU

When Larry Palmer arrived at SMU in the fall of 1970, he was already a seasoned professor, having taught at two universities in Virginia after graduating with his DMA from Eastman. Prior to his acceptance of the position of associate professor of harpsichord and organ at SMU, Marilyn Mason had urged him against such a prospect, suggesting that he "would be quite unhappy working with the head of the organ department, Robert Anderson," given that Palmer had been "so independent and successful in Norfolk."[1] Perhaps part of her reticence was that she had another colleague in mind for the position; yet they certainly both realized the challenging circumstances into which Palmer would be stepping, as he would be assuming the harpsichord studio from James Tallis, a beloved young professor who had died of a brain tumor after barely a year at SMU. Harpsichord and early music scholarship and performance were emerging disciplines, and Tallis had had little chance to establish the program. Palmer would need to carefully shape the program after its traumatic inception, all under the presumptive gaze of a legendary organ professor. Palmer remembers these early days and his relationship with Anderson: "I did not have the difficult time with Robert Anderson that Mason had envisioned. We had a mutual respect for each other, and my forty-five years on the faculty of the Meadows School were mostly happy ones."[2] Palmer was already recognized as a harpsichord and early music scholar, having been appointed harpsichord contributing editor of the *Diapason* in 1969, and doubtlessly Anderson respected Palmer and knew he could bring teaching excellence to the organ program.

Some of Palmer's first—and longest-lasting—contributions to the university's music culture were his annual faculty recitals on the harpsichord and organ, beginning in November 1970, in which he played music of Bach and Rochberg in Caruth Auditorium.[3] Palmer's scholarship and performance experience on harpsichord resulted in a great burgeoning of that program at SMU; with harpsichord and organ study so integrally related, this only benefited the organ program. Palmer recalled these early days: "Among the early successes in Dallas were the interactions with the soon-to-be stellar harpsichord builder Richard Kingston. I introduced him to my beautiful two-manual harpsichord, commissioned from William Dowd in 1968 and delivered shortly after the dawn of 1969; it was Bill's penultimate instrument to have foot pedals for changing the stops. This harpsichord served as a major influence for Richard's instruments. He also benefited from several of the many harpsichord students that swarmed to SMU in those early years, several of whom took part-time jobs at Richard's Dallas shop."[4] Palmer brought Isolde Ahlgrimm, professor of harpsichord at the Music Academy in Vienna and his own mentor, to SMU during the autumn of 1979 as a visiting professor, teaching Palmer's harpsichord majors while he was on sabbatical.[5]

Palmer had likewise studied with the eminent Dutch organist, harpsichordist, and conductor Gustav Leonhardt at the Haarlem Summer Academies of 1964 and 1967, continuing correspondence with him through the years and eventually nominating him for an honorary doctorate from SMU, conferred on him in 1983. According to Palmer:

Leonhardt's visit to SMU occurred in the form of a recital and masterclass during the festivities when SMU bestowed on him his first honorary doctorate. As part of my twelve years on the SMU faculty senate I had the opportunity to suggest that GL was a most worthy recipient. The senators and university president agreed, so one of the proudest moments of my life was reading the citation that I had written for the bestowal of the honor at Commencement. And thus it was that Leonhardt henceforward always addressed his missives to his "Doktor-Vater," perhaps the first time in history that a student was father to the teacher?[6]

Palmer adds, "While he received other doctorates during his career, including one from Harvard in 1991, the doctorate from SMU was the one he always cherished the most."[7] Palmer's infectious enthusiasm for his chosen instrument resulted, in the mid-1980s, in a harpsichord studio at SMU that trained eight to fourteen students at a time.[8]

Palmer's 1989 book *Harpsichord in America: A Twentieth-Century Revival* "concerns the major figures whose activities revitalized the all but forgotten harpsichord," which Palmer manages to make "come alive to both the general reader and the musical specialist."[9] An avid promoter of ensemble performances, he established Music in the Meadows Museum in 1982—concerts capitalizing on the acoustics and the aesthetic surroundings of the former museum lobby, often utilizing the Caetano organ,[10] while his Limited Editions concerts at his home would often feature guest musicians, any of his collection of historic keyboard instruments, or the seven-stop Schudi pipe organ, whether in early music or in new music that Palmer intentionally commissioned throughout his career. The fifty works he commissioned or were written for him span the breadth of his own eclectic musical interests, from Oberlin classmate Calvin Hampton's "Consonance for Larry" (1957) for organ,[11] to Gerald Near's *Concerto for Harpsichord* (1980) and *Triptych for Harpsichord* (1983), to Vincent Persichetti's *Sixth Harpsichord Sonata*, (1977),[12] to Herbert Howells's *Dallas Canticles* (1975), written for SATB choir and organ. Palmer's thirteen full-length recordings include an album of the music of Hugo Distler, harpsichord and organ solo literature, and the first recording of the 1993 C. B. Fisk organ in Caruth Auditorium at SMU.

As a church organist, Palmer served St. Luke's Episcopal Church in Dallas (1971–1980), St. Andrew's Episcopal Church in Grand Prairie (1980–1985), and St. Luke's Lutheran, Richardson (1985–1990), while as a concert organist he performed throughout the United States and Europe. Active in the AGO, he was elected dean of the Dallas Chapter in 1977. Larry Palmer established SMU's satellite campus of Fort Burgwin, near Taos, New Mexico, as a center

for harpsichord studies, for many summers organizing a conference and workshop centered around the harpsichord and its music,
bringing students of the instrument to meet composers and performers, among them Neal Roberts, Tony Brazier, Jane Clark, Stephen
Dodgson, Susan Ferré, and Charles Lang.[13] Richard Kingston, the
harpsichord builder who had come to know Palmer when they both
arrived in Texas in 1970, was a frequent collaborator. The idyllic and
secluded historic fort, with its new classroom buildings and casi-
tas for lodging, provided a serene location to focus on harpsichord
music, undistracted by the cares of daily life.

Larry Palmer's decision to relocate to Dallas in 1970 was perhaps
fortuitous. Certainly he recognized the cultural potential of the city,
and, in retrospect, Palmer himself was the center of much of this flourishing musical activity. His student Jan Worden Lackey evaluated the
particular zeitgeist so characteristic of the time:

> There was much new in the music world in Dallas in the 1970s
> and much of it revolved around the harpsichord. A young profes-
> sor had come to SMU to lead its new degree program. Soon
> after his arrival a young man who, at that time had completed
> only one instrument, opened a professional harpsichord-build-
> ing shop. The faculty member was Larry Palmer; the builder,
> Richard Kingston. We three, together with some others, founded
> and served on the board of directors of the Dallas Harpsichord
> Society.
>
> The city was ready for historic keyboards and early music.
> There was a lot of publicity for our events. The *Dallas Morning
> News* printed concert notices, reviews, and feature articles, as
> did other local publications, for there was considerable inter-
> est in these concerts, lectures, instruction possibilities, and
> instruments.[14]

One of Larry Palmer's students from the mid-1990s, Dr. Sean Vogt
(MM, organ performance, 1999; MM, choral conducting, 1999), evaluated his relationship with Palmer as being one more of mentorship
rather than simply of a teacher to a student:

Serialists are prisoners of the figure twelve,
while I feel greater freedom with the figure seven.
Igor Stravinsky (Paris, May 1952)

It may seem odd to introduce serialism as a headlining quote for reflection on my time with Larry Palmer, but my quiet observation during and after my time at SMU reflects this—as an analogy. Serialists maximized the full extent of every number available in Western music. RTA, likewise, loved knowing every possible piece of music and told me, and many others with whom I've spoken, that "I play everything." He did. His students also played massive and impressive amounts of literature. Contrary to this, I found LP to care more about the music-making, spending time exploring the musical options. The teaching was the same with organ and harpsichord with the only variation being certain techniques specific to each instrument.

The best questions, at least to me, are asked by those who have a command of the material. The Socratic method was a staple of LP's teaching. His questions often took me to the library or to a CD (or two or three) which I of course listened to but also used because of their concentrated liner notes. One of many Socratic moments was when we were discussing Schmücke dich, O liebe Seele, BWV 654. At this lesson, we discussed multiple dance types; upon arriving at a sarabande he then, in turn, used that as a means to encourage me to decide how best to bring out the sarabande's characteristic beat two—which means beat one must have a certain articulation. This didn't require an articulation in the score or a suggestion to look at the Little & Jenne book, which I owned and knew. The joy was exploring the music in the moment with a series of questions that led to a strong musical option. Every lesson was like this. I learned to think and explore musically (as historian and theorist) and this translated to playing that reflected strong musical insight and understanding.

If it was possible for RTA to have his students play everything, I think he would have. LP always cared first and foremost about insightful musicality. Innately, I knew this to be true. But it wasn't until I met someone at a musical event only several years ago who, upon learning I studied with LP, said, "Oh . . . all of his students play so musically." I probably learned 7/12ths of the music of RTA's students. In so doing, because of LP, I found a freedom of musical options that I continue to explore with confidence to this day.

Far from being competitors, then, both Palmer and Anderson brought their own unique teaching styles, experiences, and personalities to the organ department, together tendering potential students an environment that could personalities and preferred career paths.

Personalities in SMU Organ and Sacred Music

When Lloyd Pfautsch assumed the mantle of the director of the MSM program in the 1958, he was faced with a veritable tabula rasa relative to graduate sacred music study. The School of Music looked upon the theology musicians as less adept technically, while the theology students held an impression of the music students as being mere performers incapable of advanced academic thought. Pfautsch had to work against both prevailing prejudices and the inherent grain of truth that may have lain at the foundation of such opinions. He, and subsequent directors of the MSM program, knew they had to have the best instructors, whether in a full- or part-time capacity. Robert Anderson, of course, was the earliest and most prominent hires of Pfautsch.

In 1964 Lloyd Pfautsch was appointed associate dean at the School of the Arts, where he continued as director of choral activities and where, in developing one of the first MM degrees in choral conducting, he advanced choral conducting pedagogy by video recording student conductors for later critique, which today is standard practice.[15] His career trajectory necessitated relinquishing directorship of the MSM program, which Carlton Young assumed in 1964. In 1968 Jane Marshall, an SMU alumna and English professor, earned her MSM, subsequently teaching conducting, music theory, and choral arranging at the music school while directing the Church Music Summer School at Perkins from 1975 to 2010.[16] Carlton Young said of this prolific composer of two hundred anthems, including the venerable "My Eternal King" and "Awake, My Heart," the latter of which was awarded the 1957 anthem prize from the AGO, that he considers her "the most sensitive and text-oriented hymn tune composer of the late 20th century. She was that good."[17] One of Pfautsch's and Marshall's students, Natalie Sleeth, an organist and composer whose husband taught homiletics at Perkins, was catapulted to fame after publication of her "Jazz Gloria," which premiered at the annual Christmas worship service in Perkins Chapel. Sleeth published over two hundred works in her career, from anthems to Sunday School songs, some of which have been appropriated in the congregational corpus of numerous denominations; one might dare say that the ubiquitous "Seek Ye First" is one of her most treasured congregational hymns in some churches.[18] Young—appointed director of the Master of Arts Program in Church Music Education at Scarritt College in Nashville, Tennessee, in 1975—would be replaced by Wesleyan scholar and hymnologist Roger Deschner. A graduate of the University of Texas at Austin (1949), Union Theological Seminary (1952), and Yale University (1955), the Fellowship of Worship Artists still honors his life and work through the Roger Deschner Award presented at their biannual gatherings.[19]

Upon Deschner's retirement in 1987, Kenneth Hart came to SMU to direct the sacred music graduate program. Raised in Ottumwa, Iowa, he held an undergraduate degree from Grinnel College, where he won the Steiner Prize in Composition and the Hill Prize in Performance. He earned an MSM from Union Theological Seminary and a DMA from the Cincinnati College–Conservatory of Music, also serving as an officer in the US Air Force. He performed solo organ recitals throughout the United States, England, and New Zealand, and his choirs won prizes both domestically and internationally, including at the St. Moritz Choral Festival and the Collegiate Choral Festival in Mexico City. He served churches in Iowa, Boston, New York, Cincinnati, Lincoln, and Dallas.[20] Hart's pedigree as a conductor, organist, and scholar continued the tradition Pfautsch had started; Hart and Pfautsch, in fact, became friends, Hart eventually writing Pfautsch's biography, *A Day for Dancing: The Life and Music of Lloyd Pfautsch*, published by the University of North Texas Press (2014).

Ken Hart, along with his wife, Ellen, was a musical force in the Dallas community for decades. Kenneth Hart died on December 27, 2022.

Hart's tenure arguably coincided with a time of fundamental change in attitudes toward sacred music, in which the liturgical expectations for the organist/choirmaster job description were evolving in some quarters to incorporate global music, additional instruments, and ensembles, and in which the organist's leading of congregational hymnody is challenged by new worship expressions. An organist of noted repute himself, Hart's support of traditional church music in Perkins Chapel services exemplified the winsome manner in which sacred music could be communicated to an increasingly skeptical ecclesiastical culture. In the fall of 1992, Hart was joined in the sacred music program by C. Michael Hawn, a graduate of Wheaton College and Southern Baptist Theological Seminary in Louisville. A fellow and former president of the Hymn Society of the United States and Canada, Hawn's appointment represented the new perspectives that the MSM program sought to address. A student of global music and ethnomusicology, Hawn is a hymnological scholar of importance, having published hundreds of articles and several books on topics in church music, and is American editor for the UK-based *Canterbury Dictionary of Hymnology*. Hawn had been a consistent supporter of the organ in university life, allowing students to experience models of church music in which global music could coexist with traditional church music in a mutually beneficial manner. Hawn, a University Distinguished Professor of Sacred Music, in retirement initiated and served as the director of the Doctor of Parish Ministry program at Perkins School of Theology.

Kenneth Hart's retirement in 2005 represented an opportunity to change philosophical directions in the Sacred Music Department, had the prevailing desire been so; yet, fortunately, Dr. Hart was replaced with another organist/scholar in Christopher Anderson. Anderson holds a bachelor's degree from Transylvania University, an MM and MSM from SMU, where he studied organ with Robert Anderson, and a PhD in performance practices from Duke University, with additional studies at the Staatliche Hochschule für Musik in Stuttgart. Having taught at the University of North Dakota, Grand Forks, Anderson came to SMU in 2006. A "scholar and organist whose work has centered on early musical modernism, modern German history and philosophy, [and] the organ's position in Western culture," Anderson specializes in the music of the German Romantics, Max Reger especially, his *Max Reger and Karl Straube: Perspectives on an Organ Performing Tradition* (2003) having received the Max Miller Book Award from the AGO via the Boston University School of Theology. He has edited the *Selected Writings of Max Reger* (2006) and *Twentieth-Century Organ Music* (2012), a festschrift in honor of his mentor, Robert T. Anderson.[21]

In 2015 Larry Palmer retired as professor of music emeritus, concluding a forty-five-year teaching career at SMU. The Meadows School of the Arts, however, was poised to benefit from SMU's ambitious program to create one hundred endowed chairs university-wide, honoring the centennial of the university's founding.[22] Sarah and Ross Perot Jr. bestowed the Leah Fullinwider Centennial Chair in Music Performance in honor of Sarah's mother, and thus the organ program would continue under the auspices of a new, German-born concert organist, Stefan Engels, appointed to the Fullinwider Chair in 2014. Having studied organ, piano, harpsichord, choral conducting, and church music at the universities of Aachen, Cologne, and Düsseldorf, he studied in the United States with Wolfgang Rübsam and Robert Anderson, with whom he earned an Artist Certificate Diploma. Having won the Concerto Gold Medal at the 1998 Calgary International Organ Competition, his career since then had consisted of performing professionally through Karen McFarlane Artists, chairing the organ department at Westminster Choir College from 1999 to 2005, and, immediately prior to his return to SMU, teaching as a professor at the University of Music and Performing Arts "Felix Mendelssohn Bartholdy" in Leipzig from 2005 to 2015. Among his personal interests is the music of Sigfrid Karg-Elert, in service of whose music Engels founded the Leipzig Karg-Elert Festival. Engels's recordings of Karg-Elert's complete organ works included much music that had been heretofore unrecorded.[23] The cyclic nature of history is most evident here, as Bertha Stevens Cassidy in the late 1920s had found inspiration from her brief studies with Karg-Elert in Leipzig,

Stefan Engels, the Leah Fullinwider Centennial Chair in Music Performance.
Courtesy of Stefan Engels.

championing his music in Dallas upon her return, and even inviting him
to perform a recital at SMU in 1932. Karg-Elert, alternately in and out
of fashion throughout the decades, has once again found an advocate on
the SMU campus.

Engels's arrival in 2014 also occasioned SMU alumnus Wolfgang
Rübsam to donate his 1974 two-manual, six-rank, Rudolf Janke organ
to the organ department in honor of his teacher, Robert Anderson.
The Buzard Organ Company dismantled, cleaned, delivered, and
installed the organ in one of the basement practice rooms at the Meadows
School of the Arts. Engels remarked that "this inspiring instrument
will now serve future generations of organ students at Meadows."[24]

Practice Organ
Southern Methodist University
Rudolph Janke (1972)
Relocated in 2014 by John-Paul Buzard[25]

Manual I   **Manual II**

8 Rohrflöte   8 Spitzgedakt

4 Prinzipal   4 Gedakt

                                          2 Quintadena

Pedal

16 Subbaß   **Couplers**

                                          II-I

                                          II-P

                                          I-P

                                          Tremulant (hitchdown)

Growth in the organ studio required the addition of Scott Dettra as an adjunct associate professor of organ in 2019. Dettra, who concertizes internationally and holds degrees from Westminster Choir College, had been director of music at Church of the Incarnation in Dallas, before which he was at Washington National Cathedral. Michael Hawn retired as director of the MSM program in 2017, with Dr. Marcell Steuernagel appointed as assistant professor of church music and director of the MSM program. A native of Brazil, Steuernagel continues Hawn's advocacy for global and cross-cultural music. Holding a PhD in church music from Baylor University, Steuernagel's extensive and eclectic musical background includes having presented lectures and having held teaching and church positions throughout the United States, Europe, and South America.

The Janke practice organ. Courtesy of Dr. Jason Alden.

Perkins Chapel Organ Renovation

By the late 1990s, Perkins Chapel had been used daily for university functions, as a teaching lab for seminary students, for rehearsals and concerts, and for memorial services and weddings. University administration had early realized the financial and public relations benefit of renting the chapel on the weekends for weddings, and Saturdays had been reserved for the wedding business since the first month after the chapel opened. Yet the Georgian-inspired, Mark Lemmon–designed chapel, while a fixture of university and community life, needed an aesthetic and liturgical transformation. By the mid-1990s a committee had been engaged to recommend a direction for a chapel renovation. Comprised of representatives from SMU worship communities, the sacred music faculty and university organist, and faculty from the Perkins School of Theology, as well as the associate vice president of the university, the committee was chaired by Perkins worship faculty member Marjorie Procter-Smith and advised by Susan J. White, professor of worship at Westcott House, Cambridge. Evaluating the chapel from manifold perspectives, the committee acknowledged that "the vast majority of the worship services which take place at Perkins Chapel include one or more forms of music—organ or other keyboard, congregational singing, solo vocal, choral, and/or instrumental performance. In addition, Perkins Chapel provides a setting for teaching, performance, and rehearsal/practice within the various components of the degree programs in Church music at Perkins School of Theology. As a place for both choral and instrumental (including organ) music performance Perkins Chapel has few rivals in a space of its size."[26] Ultimately, the chapel would close from 1997 until late 1999 for a complete renovation that involved formulating a more flexible chancel space, including the addition of a lower chancel extending into the nave, upgrading the sound and lighting systems, replacing the dated floors with modern hardwood, repurposing transept rooms, and upgrading some structural components. Coinciding with an SMU capital campaign launched in 1995, the family of Joe and Lois Perkins, original benefactors of the chapel, continued their financial support through Charles and Elizabeth Perkins Prothro and C. Vincent and Caren Prothro of Dallas and the Perkins-Prothro Foundation.[27]

To address organ renovation, however, the situation required the initiative of Dr. Kenneth Hart, director of the MSM program, with the help of adjunct organ professor George Baker. Baker was an Anderson student whose career had taken him from music to medicine and back to music again. A Dallas native, Baker's father had been chaplain at SMU in the 1940s, and Baker himself had been baptized in Perkins Chapel only a few months after its dedication. After earning a bachelor's degree from SMU in music, he left for France to study with Marie-Claire Alain, Pierre Cochereau, Jean Langlais, and André Marchal, having been awarded the Prix de Virtuosité under Langlais. Baker continued his studies in the United States, obtaining a master's degree in theory and composition from the University of Miami and a DMA from the University of Michigan, after which he taught at the Catholic University of America in Washington, DC.[28] By the age of 30, he had amassed first prizes from the AGO Competition (1970), the Grand Prix de Chartres (1974), and the International Improvisation Competition (1979), also finding time to record the complete organ works of Bach in 1979, the first by an American. Baker's subsequent recordings include the complete organ works of Vierne and Milhaud. By the early 1980s, however, Baker felt that he "had climbed Mount Everest in my specialty," and, seeking new challenges, entered medical school at age 32. In his fourth year of medical school, Baker elected to specialize in dermatology, noting that "perhaps it has to do with external beauty, wanting people to look their best, feel their best."[29] After an internship at Parkland Hospital in Dallas and a residency in Oregon, Baker returned to Texas to practice in Austin. Returning to Dallas in 1996, Baker resumed his connection with SMU, this time enrolling in the MBA program and working part-time in the dermatology clinic at SMU. Robert Anderson's relinquishing of his full-time teaching duties this same year afforded Baker the opportunity to step into organ teaching duties at SMU, where he taught organ improvisation on an adjunct basis, served as organist for university worship, and was positioned to guide the organ renovation in Perkins Chapel.

The funding secured for the chapel renovation did not include provision for the organ modernization, in response to which Baker recorded a CD in 1997 entitled *Riches to Rags*, featuring music of Bach and Joplin recorded on two organs in France, as well as at Perkins Chapel itself, to raise money for the anticipated $400,000 project.[30] The Horace Cabe Foundation of Gurdon, Arkansas, whose president, Charles Cabe, had graduated from SMU in 1965, eventually provided the remainder of the funding for the organ renovation project, which Marvin Judy of Schudi Organ Company in Dallas was engaged to complete. Judy's father, Marvin Judy Sr., had been a professor at Perkins at Perkins School of Theology during the 1960s when Baker's father had been chaplain and a professor there, and perhaps it was serendipity that their respective sons were mutually involved in the organ renovation. With Baker as tonal designer and Judy effecting the process, the renovated organ would find itself enlarged with an expanded specification:

Perkins Chapel
Southern Methodist University
Schudi/Dupont (2000)
Rebuild of Aeolian-Skinner, Opus 1167 (1950/1963)[31]

GREAT
32 Bourdon (digital)
16 Montre (new)
16 Bourdon
8 Montre (ext.)
8 Bourdon
8 Diapason
8 Flûte Harmonique (new)
8 Bourdon
8 Flûte (new)
4 Prestant
4 Flûte ouverte (new)
2⅔ Quinte (new)
2 Doublette
Cornet III (new)
Fourniture IV (new)
16 Bombarde (37 new pipes)
8 Trompette (ext, 12 new pipes)
4 Clairon (ext, 12 new pipes)
Chimes (digital)
Harp (digital)
Celesta (digital)
Zimbelstern (digital)

SWELL (enclosed)
16 Bourdon (formerly in Ped.)
8 Diapason
8 Bourdon
8 Salicional
8 Voix Celeste

CHOIR (enclosed)
16 Quintaten (former Gt)
8 Flûte (Gt)
8 Cor de Nuit
8 Viola de Gambe
8 Unda Maris
4 Prestant (new)
4 Flute
2⅔ Nasard (added in 1972)
2 Doublette
1⅗ Tierce (new)
1 Piccolo
Cymbal III (new)
8 Cromorne (new)
16 Trompette (new)
8 Trompette (ext.)
4 Trompette (ext.)
Trompette Royale
Tremblant

PEDAL
32 Montre (digital)
32 Flûte Ouverte (digital)
32 Soubasse (digital)
32 Flûte Douce (digital)
16 Contrebasse
16 Montre (Gt.)
16 Bourdon (Sw.)
16 Bourdon doux
10⅔ Quinte (Resultant)

5⅓ Gross Nasard
   (ext. 2⅔, 12 new pipes)
  4 Prestant
  4 Flûte Octaviante
3⅕ Gross Tierce (ext., 12 new
   pipes)
2⅔ Nasard (new)
1⅗ Tierce (new)
   Plein Jeu III (new)
16 Basson
  8 Trompette
  4 Clairon (ext.)
  8 Hautbois
  8 Clarinette (formerly on
   the Choir)
  8 Voix Humaine (new)
   Tremblant

COUPLERS
Swell to Great 16,8, 4
Choir to Great 16, 8, 4
Great to Pedal 8
Swell to Pedal 8, 4
Choir to Pedal 8, 4
Choir to Choir 16, 4
Swell to Choir 16, 8, 4
Swell to Swell 16, Unison Off, 4

MECHANICALS
Swell and Choir Expression Pedals
Crescendo Pedal

  8 Octave
  8 Flûte (Gt.)
  8 Bourdon
  4 Octave
  4 Flûte (Gt.)
64 Bombarde (digital)
32 Contre Bombarde (new)
32 Contre Trombone (digital)
32 Contre Basson (digital)
16 Grande Bombarde (new)
16 Bombarde (Gt.)
  8 Trompette (Gt.)
  4 Clairon (Gt.)

COMBINATION PISTONS
Great: 6
Swell: 6
Choir: 6
Pedal: 6 (four as thumb
   pistons, two as hitch levers)
General Pistons: 24
General Cancel
Memory bank pistons A–H
Walker Control System

REVERSIBLES
Great/Choir Transfer
All four 32s on thumb pistons
   and pedal hitch levers,
Swell to Great
Swell to Pedal
Great to Pedal
Choir to Pedal
Next/Previous pistons under
   each manual
Tutti

*In addition to the 1950 core of the instrument, several stops were
added or altered in 1963, at which time also the mixtures were
extended in pitch and in the number of ranks. Certain stop nomenclature was also altered. Under the direction of and to the designs
of George Baker, Marvin Judy of Schudi Organ Company in Dallas
completely rebuilt the organ from 1997 to 2000, not only significantly adding to the number of pipe ranks but also incorporating
Walker digital resources. The console was rebuilt and modernized,
with new keyboards of mastodon tusk ebony and ivory installed.
Jean-François Dupont of Caen, France, voiced much of the organ.*

The French accent of the new organ was enhanced by the voicing work
of Jean-François Dupont, a Caen-based organ builder who maintained,
among other significant instruments, the Cavaillé-Coll organ at Saint-
Ouen de Rouen. Kenneth Hart and George Baker modeled the tonal
design somewhat after Messiaen's stoplist at La Trinité. Manuel Rosales
helped design the Cromorne in the expressive Choir. This stop was
appropriate for French classic literature when paired with a cornet on
another manual; that it was enclosed aided in its utility in Romantic and
other styles of music. Rosales also assisted with the new 32' Bombarde
unit and an en chamade that was added to the rear gallery a few months
after installation. A Grand Cornet on the Swell was made possible by
the 5⅓' and the 3⅕' stops, gaining power in the treble as the *anches*
decreased. A nearly complete 16'-8'-4' reed battery on each manual
allowed for an authentic French Grand Jeu. The Voix humaine on the
Swell was well-suited for French Romantic literature, as was the Flûte
harmonique on the Great, both new additions to the original specification. The original Unda Maris and parent rank were revoiced but kept on
the Choir, still allowing that quintessential Aeolian-Skinner string sound
to remain. Marvin Judy discovered that the Trompette in the Swell, an
original 1951 rank, had come from Aeolian-Skinner, Opus 909 (1933),
at All Saints Episcopal Church in Worcester, Massachusetts, possibly
removed from that organ during a renovation in the early 1940s.[32]

The Pedal was filled out through a judicious use of borrowing,
although one might argue that the provision of electronic 32s was
beyond the scope of an organ designed for a chapel of fewer than three
hundred seats. Indeed, from the console even a mild full organ could

seem oppressive due to the chambers' speaking into the fairly narrow upper chancel, but the instrument's ensemble gained cohesiveness as the sound permeated the room. Nonetheless, it was a large instrument for a small space, a fact made only more noticeable with the installation of the Trompette en chamade on the back wall a few years later. Although the instrument may have spoken with a French accent, particularly in the reeds and mutations, the silvery, shimmery strings and the velvety smoothness of the principals and flutes allowed the instrument to function eclectically in an American church environment. George Baker recalls: "All of us worked hundreds if not thousands of hours on the project. Jean-François and I were tuning the organ at 2:00 am on the day of Stephen Cleobury's dedicatory concert. . . . When Notre-Dame de Paris organist Philippe Lefèbvre came to see and play the organ, he exclaimed: 'Ah! It's a little Notre-Dame!' When French organist Pierre Pincemaille came to record, he said that he would 'love to play on that organ every Sunday.' These comments made all the blood, sweat and tears worth it! I gained a whole new respect for organ builders during that project!"

The organ was first presented to the public on April 3, 2000, in a dedicatory recital by Stephen Cleobury of King's College, Cambridge, featuring mostly juxtaposed English and French music:

Sonata in G	Edward Elgar
Allegro maestoso	
Psalm Prelude, "Lo, the poor . . ."	Herbert Howells
Choral No. 3 in A Minor	César Franck
Kyrie (*Messe pour les paroisses*)	François Couperin
Plein chant du premier Kyrie, en taille	
Fugue sur les jeux d'anches	
Récit de Cromorne	
Dialogue sur la Trompette et le Cromorne	
Plein chant (du dernier Couplet)	
Ut, re, mi, fa, sol, la	William Byrd
Prelude and Fugue on a Theme of Vittoria	Benjamin Britten

Suite, Opus 5   Maurice Duruflé
   Sicilienne
La Nativité du Seigneur   Olivier Messiaen[33]
   Dieu parmi nous

Philippe Lefebvre, one of the organists of Notre Dame Cathedral in Paris, continued the dedication series the next month, the reviewer observing: "The refurbished instrument gets the timbres right: the brassy clangor, the tangy mutations, the plush, purring foundations. And with four 32-foot pedal registers, three of them very effective electronic simulations, the thunder should cure the most intractable case of constipation. But in what is, after all, a rather modest space, I kept wishing the instrument were about 15 percent quieter. Its pressurized effect wearies the ear, and the Voix humaine stop is way too loud. And can't the loud whoosh of the chapel's air conditioning be tamed?"[34]

This writer console-assisted both Cleobury and Lefebvre at their respective concerts. Cleobury's program was one of typical English restraint and, while highly musical, tread no new ground. He avoided the larger reeds and the full organ sounds, preferring to highlight the expressive, subtle capabilities of the instrument. Lefebvre, however, expressed no such reservations, playing the organ as he might have at Notre Dame, complete with its 32′ manual flue. The organ's new specification and voicing allowed and even suggested this type of playing, Lefebvre availing himself of the entire instrument. Paired together, the inaugural concerts demonstrated nearly every stop and thousands of the seemingly limitless combinations possible from its tonal palette. The solution to the organ's "pressurized effect" was simply to avoid long jaunts of full organ.

Kenneth Hart arranged the music for the chapel rededication, featuring a brass ensemble accompanied by the Sipe gallery organ, which formerly had served as a practice organ at Meadows but which had been rebuilt and installed in the chapel's loft in 1997. The organ dedication service for the School of Theology several months later featured Hart playing the new organ and this writer playing the Sipe gallery organ in a duet by Samuel Sebastian Wesley.

Southern Methodist University
Perkins Chapel Gallery
Robert L. Sipe and Associates
(Built as a practice organ in 1967, installed in Perkins Chapel in 1997)[35]

Manual I	Manual II
8 Gedeckt	8 Holz Gedeckt
4 Principal	4 Spillflöte
Mixture II-III	2 Gemshorn
	Sesquialtera II
Pedal (unit)	
16 Bourdon	**Couplers**
8 Bourdon	I-Pedal
4 Bourdon	II-Pedal
	II-I

The historic chancel organ would end its almost seventy-year tenure as the result of a disastrous steam leak in January 2018. This writer was the last to play it on a Friday night after wedding rehearsals; shortly thereafter, a valve in the steam room underneath the chancel malfunctioned, and the chapel filled with steam overnight. By morning the edifice had become waterlogged, with plaster falling from the ceiling and the organ soaked, many of the Aeolian-Skinner leathers having become irretrievably glued into the open position, and many of the wooden pipes soaking up water and coming unglued. Fortunately, steam failed to damage the secondary pipe organ in the gallery, located as it is on the other side of the chapel from the steam room. This little organ, while limited in capability, and arguably a much better practice instrument than an exhilarating service instrument, has been able to fulfill day-to-day liturgical duties.

The loss of this historic instrument gave the organ and sacred music faculty, now led by Stefan Engels and Christopher Anderson, an opportunity to reassess the organ needs for the chapel. Although a fine concert instrument, such as a mechanical action, centrally located Fisk in the chancel, had been considered as far back as the 1970s by Robert Anderson, that solution failed to address some of the modern requirements of a chapel that required a liturgical instrument of the utmost flexibility. Given the other musical ensembles and religious groups hosted by the chapel, combined with the limited floor space in the chancel, a freestanding tracker instrument seemed impractical. A new organ would have to be housed in the existing chambers. This writer remembers talking with Stefan Engels about what type of instrument would serve not only university worship functions but also the practical concerns of providing music for weddings. His concern, too, was one of pedagogy: What type of instrument would not only complement the other organs on campus but also fill a unique void in the local organ community? What type of organ did North Texas lack? Given the dynamic organ culture of the area, the question was not simple to answer. The area now had organs from all the major builders, and from many minor ones. American builders predominate, but the Canadian firms have made inroads, and several European builders are represented with major instruments dating back to the 1970s. From historic chamber organs and concert hall organs to symphonic organs and all manner of neobaroque fashions, North Texas is fortunate to have such an assortment of pipe organs. However, the area is deficient in historic instruments, lacking examples of fine, early twentieth-century instruments. It seemed that, all things being equal, SMU needed a classic E. M. Skinner organ. Given the right specimen, it would have been conceived for Protestant music not unlike much of that produced in the chapel. It would have a wide tonal palette to satisfy musical needs for weddings. As a teaching instrument, it would complement the Fisk in Caruth and suit some repertoire

more appropriately, particularly Romantic music of the early twentieth century.

   Later that year, through the help of Jason Alden, who services
most of the major organs in Dallas and maintains the instruments
at SMU, and with the advice of Jonathan Ambrosino, the university purchased the 1927 E. M. Skinner, No. 563, housed in the
former Fourth Presbyterian Church in New York City. This organ
will bring with it a history, here elucidated by Jason Alden and
Stefan Engels:

> The period 1924–32 is further regarded as the zenith of
> the firm's work in that period, mechanically and artisti-
> cally. In 1925, Fourth Presbyterian Church of New York
> City contracted with Skinner for its No. 563. Due to Skin-
> ner's backlog, the organ was not built and installed until
> 1927. The organ, with its three manuals and 37 ranks, was
> designed specifically for Fourth Presbyterian. The bulk of the
> instrument was erected in a freestanding case in the church's
> rear balcony. Two ranks, forming an "Echo" section, were
> installed in a room to the left of the chancel area, to create
> mysterious, distant effects. (Coincidentally, the New York
> organ is almost identical in size to the original Perkins Chapel
> Aeolian-Skinner.) In 1953, Fourth Presbyterian sold their
> building to Annunciation Greek Orthodox Church. Because
> the pipe organ is not an integral part of Orthodox worship,
> the then 26-year-old Skinner essentially went into a mode of
> slumbering storage. Because it was not used, there was no
> need to tune or service it, thus no intrusion from organ tech-
> nicians or others. The instrument is a pristine example of a
> company in its prime.[36]

Thus the organ was removed from the church in the summer of 2019
to a storage facility in Norwood, Massachusetts, awaiting refurbish-
ment. The remnants of Perkins Chapel's damaged Aeolian-Skinner
were sold to Our Redeemer Lutheran Church in Dallas, only a few
miles north of the campus.

Perkins Chapel
Southern Methodist University
E. M. Skinner, No. 563 (1927)
Relocated, restored, and installed in 2023
Agreement and Specification: March 16, 1927[37]

GREAT (enclosed)
16 Bourdon
8 Diapason
8 Second Diapason
8 Claribel Flute
4 Octave
4 Flute
2 Fifteenth
8 Tuba (in Choir)
8 French Horn
Chimes

SWELL (enclosed)
16 Bourdon
8 Diapason
8 Rohr Flute
8 Salicional
8 Voix Celeste
8 Flauto Dolce
8 Flute Celeste
8 Aeoline
4 Octave
4 Flute Triangulaire
Mixture IV
16 Waldhorn
8 Cornopean
8 Oboe d'Amore

ECHO (enclosed)
8 Chimney Flute
8 Vox Humana
Tremolo
Chimes

PEDAL (unenclosed)
32 Resultant
16 Major Bass
16 Bourdon
16 Echo Bourdon (Sw.)
8 Octave
8 Gedeckt
8 Still Gedeckt (Sw.)
4 Flute
16 Trombone
16 Waldhorn (Sw.)
8 Tromba
Chimes

COUPLERS
Swell to Pedal 8, 4
Great to Pedal 8
Choir to Pedal 8
Swell to Choir 8
Great to Great 4
Swell to Swell 16, 4

8 Vox Humana
   Tremolo

CHOIR (enclosed)
   8 Concert Flute
   8 Gamba
   8 Dulciana
   4 Flute
   2⅔ Nasard
   2 Harmonic Piccolo
   8 Clarinet
      Tremolo
   8 Harp (t.c.)
   4 Celesta

Swell to Great 16, 8, 4

COMBINATION PISTONS
Swell: 6
Great: 6
Choir: 4
Pedal: 5
General: 4
General Cancel
Choir to Great 16, 8, 4
Choir to Choir 16, 4

MECHANICALS
Swell and Choir expression
   pedals
Crescendo pedal
Sforzando pedal (reversible
   pedal and piston)

REVERSIBLES
Echo On/Off
Great On/Off
Both On
Release

This instrument was originally installed in Fourth Presbyterian Church in New York City in 1927. The facility was acquired by the Greek Orthodox Church of the Annunciation during the 1950s, at which time the organ was made redundant. It was purchased in situ by SMU in 2018.

E. M. Skinner had little representation in Texas even at its height, and this instrument will fill a need in the local organ world. A three-manual instrument, Opus 694 had been installed in First Presbyterian Church

E. M. Skinner, Opus 563, as it stood for decades at the former Third Presbyterian Church in Manhattan, New York. Courtesy of Dr. Jason Alden.

in Dallas in 1928; Skinner had built instruments for the Plaza Hotel in San Antonio and the Third Church of Christ, Scientist, in Houston, also both in 1928, but none are extant.[38] Bertha Stevens Cassidy, the first organ professor of SMU, likely would have known and coveted a Skinner organ for the new McFarlin Memorial Auditorium in 1926, but, whether because of the backlog at Skinner or the high price tag, had to settle (in her case, enthusiastically) for two undistinguished Hillgreen, Lane instruments. It would take nearly a century for a grand symphonic Skinner organ to find its way to the SMU campus.

The Legacy of SMU Organs and Organists

The narrative of organs and organists at Southern Methodist University cannot be considered in isolation from larger cultural trends. Most music schools saw unprecedented numbers of organ majors in the postwar decades, mirroring the professional demand for graduates' services. Fulbright scholarships in abundance offered the possibility for study with legendary European organists. SMU saw its largest enrollment of organ majors during the 1960s, but by the turn of the century, enrollment had dipped precipitously low. Haig Mardirosian, in his *The Organ on Campus*, analyzed numbers supplied by the National Association of Schools of Music (NASM) to ascertain that, of universities offering music degrees, only "a little more than 12 percent list any degree in organ in their catalogs."[39] He further enumerates the decline in organ majors from 2014 through 2017 in which, at least at NASM institutions, undergraduate enrollments dropped by 24 percent while doctoral enrollments decreased 19 percent, although enrollment in master's degrees did increase by 7 percent.[40] Unfortunately, a pessimism borne out by statistics reflects a reality that many university organ programs stand at the precipice of shuttering. Once a bastion of church music led by Peter Lutkin, Northwestern University's discontinuing of its organ program in the early 2000s demonstrated that even iconic organ departments are susceptible to the same budgetary pressures and administrative shortsightedness as any academic program.[41] If not every administrator realizes that, in the words of Mardirosian, "a robust music department enhances and diversifies the curriculum in the liberal arts and in the professional tracks [and that] it brings vibrancy to the campus community," how much less will they be able to perceive the value of the organ or sacred music major?[42] The 2013 closing of the Sacred Music Department at Luther Seminary in Minneapolis, "considered a premier training ground for those seeking rigorous integration of both musical and theological theory," provoked shock and outrage from the community, one graduate lamenting that it is "the end of an important era."[43] The closing of the organ department at the Hartt School of Music in 2015 was also indicative of the direction of organ study in some institutions.[44] Southern Baptist Theological Seminary's 2019 dismantling of the traditional course of study for church music and organ performance in favor of ubiquitous general "worship" studies is possibly one result of the "worship wars" that still flare up from time to time. The precarious situation of Westminster Choir College should evidence that even historic and reputable music programs—in this case, an entire music school—are not safe from the chopping block. Organ studies at the university level must survive, then, by thriving.

One need look no further than the contributions of hundreds of students to discern SMU's reputation as a hallowed training ground for performing organists and sacred musicians. These musicians leave no more tangible legacy than the organs they cause to be built and leave behind for successive generations. As Scott Cantrell wrote: "The explosion of evangelical megachurches and the withering of many mainstream Protestant congregations [doesn't] bode well for centuries' worth of classical church music, or for its signature instrument, the pipe organ. In Dallas, though, plenty of mainstream churches, even in the central city, are prospering. With large and vital congregations, they're building new buildings and, yes, installing big new and refurbished pipe organs, many with price tags over $1 million. They're even redoing sanctuaries to provide better acoustics for music from Gregorian chant to John Rutter."[45]

For better or for worse, Dallas remains unburdened with the historic baggage associated with East Coast organ installations. The region's relative prosperity and active civic-corporate partnerships all but ensured that organs would be replaced on a regular basis, sometimes with each successive organist conceiving a new organ. Thus, the city had to create its own church music and organ culture, and in both cases the principal actors were compelled by the desire to establish a haven of civility on the prairies. Since the seventies new instruments have been installed in local churches, universities, and homes, originating in the workshops of Bedient, Casavant, Dobson, Fisk, Goulding and Wood, Daniel Jaeckel, Rudolf Janke, Juget-Sinclair, Keates, Alfred Kern, Gabriel Kney, Létourneau, Longmore, Nichols & Simpson, Richards, Fowkes & Company, Rieger, Rosales, Reuter, Schantz, Schoenstein, Visser-Rowland, Wicks, and Karl Wilhelm. Local builders Dan Garland, Marvin Judy, Ross King, Roy Redman, and Robert Sipe all have produced meticulous, historically informed instruments, all thoughtfully considered for their space and liturgical use.

Whether they studied with Bertha Stevens Cassidy, Dora Poteet Barclay, Robert Anderson, Larry Palmer, Stefan Engels, or any of the assisting adjuncts through the decades, Southern Methodist University organ alumni have held positions in churches and universities throughout the world, often concertizing, composing, writing, and teaching in order to cultivate their careers.

SMU organists were at the forefront of efforts as Dallas toiled for that perceived sophistication of East Coast cities. Whether it was bringing those important musical luminaries who performed in McFarlin Auditorium during those interwar years, introducing culture and sophistication to a city struggling to find its identity, increasing the numbers of organ students winning competitions, or establishing creditable parish music ministries where there had been none before, the organists of SMU actively lent their abilities to the efforts, and the city of Dallas owes much of its present cultural success to these generations of musicians.

Glossary

AAGO: The diploma Associate of the American Guild of Organists is the second most advanced of the top three certifications the American Guild of Organists offers. It is granted upon successful completion of keyboard and written exams.

AGO: The American Guild of Organists, an association of musicians founded in 1896, aims to support the work of academic, church, and concert organists. Membership was originally only open to those who passed the requisite tests, although now it is open to anyone. The official periodical is the *American Organist* magazine.

Brustwerk (German): In traditional *Werkprinzip* organ design, this division was located directly below the main division (*Hauptwerk*) and was located directly in front and slightly above the player (*Brust* = chest, *Werk* = division) and contained some light stops, perhaps a couple of solo reeds, and maybe a high-pitch mixture.

Choir: This refers to a secondary manual on a three-manual organ. It can be enclosed in a swell box and contains lighter sounds, some of which are most useful for accompanying a choir. In American tradition, it is typically the bottom manual.

Chorale: Generally, this term is the same as "hymn," but within the German nomenclature. They are strophic, sacred poetic texts set to music. Much organ music, Germanic or not, is inspired by chorale tunes.

cipher: This technical term refers to a pipe when it plays by itself, usually caused when the palette is stuck open, because of either an object (often simply dust) or a mechanical problem.

Clavierübung: Often referred to as the Clavier-Übung III or German Organ Mass, Johann Sebastian Bach published these works in 1739. Considered to be one of Bach's most significant works, most of the movements are based on chorale tunes, their arrangement inspired by Martin Luther's *Small Catechism*.

Echo: A division of an organ that is often located at a distance from the main organ. It could be located in the ceiling, along the wall

261

opposite of the main organ, or even in a basement, its tone wafting through chutes to the main level. Often it contained the softest stops. This division was popular in early twentieth-century organs.

FAGO: The highest level of exam certification of the American Guild of Organists, earning the fellow certificate implies complete master of the theoretical and practical mechanics of the church music profession.

flue: A type of organ pipe/stop whose sound is produced through channeling air through a narrow passageway at the foot of a pipe, exiting through the mouth of the pipe. This is the most common type of organ pipe, from which most stops are derived. Its sound production differs from pipes of the reed variety.

Gastarbeiter (German: guest worker): These temporary or migrant workers to West Germany from the mid-1950s to the mid-1970s were invited to settle on a short-term basis to relieve national labor shortages. A large number of such workers came from Turkey.

Great: In organ terminology this is the main keyboard (manual) of the instrument, containing the most prominent, powerful stops. It is also known as the *Grande Orgue* in French or the *Hauptwerk* in German.

Hauptwerk (German: main division): This is the terminology for the primary manual of the German organ.

legato: This musical term refers to smooth, connected playing. In organ technique this is usually accomplished by finger substitution.

manual: Keyboards on the organ are properly called manuals to distinguish them from the pedals, which are also a keyboard but played by the feet.

microdots: A means of steganographically passing messages surreptitiously via the printing of tiny dots, which could at times only be seen through a microscope. It was often a means of communicating between zones in Berlin after the building of the wall.

Mixture: This organ stop involves three or more ranks playing a single note. These high-pitched stops correspond with the harmonics of the particular note, reinforcing the fundamental pitch when used properly. In the late nineteenth and early twentieth centuries, mixture stops were used less. Their return to the organ's stoplist in the mid twentieth century is a result of a renewed appreciation and understanding of historic organ building practices.

oeuvre (French): The collected works of a composer.

Orgelbewegung (German: Organ Revival): With its origins in Germany in the 1930s, the Organ Reform Movement sought to reinvigorate scholarship relative to organ design and building, informed largely by instruments of the baroque era. This movement emphasized historic building techniques but also corresponded to renewed interest in performance practice and early music.

Orgelbüchlein (German: Little Organ Book): Written by Johann Sebastian Bach between 1708 and 1717, these forty-six short chorale prelude settings demonstrate different musical means of treating a melody. They have typically been staples of the organ student's repertoire, even to the present day.

Pedal: On the organ the Pedal division is the "keyboard" played by the feet. Generally, it will play the bass in a four-part composition.

Positiv (Positif): Sometimes interchangeable with *Choir* because it is often on the first manual, this division on the organ reflects more historical awareness of German performance practice. Short for *Rückpositiv*, the Positiv historically was found on the balcony railing, to the organist's back (Rück.) Unlike the *Choir*, which generally contains accompanimental sounds and can be enclosed, the Positiv generally contains bright stops of higher pitch.

Praktische Orgelschule (German: Practical Organ Course): Written between 1819 and 1821, Johann Christian Heinrich Rinck composed these exercises to methodically teach the fundamentals of organ playing. As a didactic organ method, it was unique for its time and was used well into the twentieth century.

Rank: A set of organ pipes of the same tone quality. An organist combines ranks based on pitch, volume, and timbre to create a "registration." Sometimes used synonymously with stops, technically multiple stops can be derived from a single rank. (See *Unification*.)

Récit (French): See *Swell*.

reed: A reed pipe produces sound as air is channeled through a thin piece of metal (the reed) that then vibrates, creating a sound at a particular pitch. The construction is similar to any orchestral reed instrument, such as the oboe or clarinet. Unlike the orchestral trumpet, the organ trumpet is considered a reed stop since its sound is produced with a reed.

Solo: Generally the fourth manual on an American organ. As suggested by the name, this division contains solo stops such as the orchestrally imitative clarinets, oboes, French horns, strings, and trumpets. The Solo was a popular division during the heyday of the orchestral transcription.

stop: A stop is a particular sound at a particular pitch, controlled by a rocker switch or a stop knob at the command of the organist. The organist combines stops to create a certain registration. Multiple stops can be derived from a single rank.

Swell: In American organ manual arrangement, the Swell is generally the third manual, and is so called because it is contained within a swell box, a shuttered chamber whose shades the organist can open or close with a foot lever, thus effecting a swelling of loud and soft. In French this manual is called the Récit.

tracker: In organ building the tracker refers to the mechanical linkage between the key and the pipe. In shorthand parlance the term means any mechanical action organ. This type of organ was largely replaced by electric or electropneumatic action in the early twentieth century. The *Orgelbewegung* renewed interest in historic, tracker organ building.

transcription: A transcription is an arrangement from one instrument to another. In the late nineteenth and early twentieth centuries, transcriptions were popular among both organists and audiences, and performers could be found playing Wagner overtures, Beethoven symphonies, and Chopin piano works on the organ. The *Orgelbewegung* sought to revive interest in music written originally for organ, thus have transcriptions fallen out of favor during the second half of the twentieth century.

unification: This term refers to the division of a single pipe rank into multiple ranks, common in some electric action organs and a staple of theatre organ registration. Through a process of wiring, an organ builder could take a standard 8′ stop and create another stop at 4′ pitch. Thus, the pipe playing middle C at 8′ pitch plays the C above when it is wired at 4'. Nearly any desired pitch can be extracted from a single rank. However, this means of garnering stops results in tuning and voicing challenges. Thus, the *Orgelbewegung* aimed to reign in the excesses of unification and return to mechanical action, which rendered unification virtually impossible.

Werkprinzip (German: Principle of Works): This term developed in the twentieth-century's *Orgelbewegung* to designate a type of historical organ building in which the different organ divisions related to each other both visually and aurally. The *Brustwerk* is situated in front of the organist, the *Hauptwerk* forms the visual center of the organ, the *Recit* or *Oberwerk* may crown the organ case at the top, the *Rückpositiv* is located centrally on the balcony railing, and the pedal may be divided in towers on either side. This type of organ design is also predicated upon a certain relationship of 8' Prinzipals to each other between divisions.

Endnotes

Foreword

1. Alexis de Tocqueville, "In What Spirit the Americans Cultivate the Arts," in *Democracy in America*, trans. and ed. by Harvey C. Mansfield and Delba Winthrop (Chicago and London: University of Chicago Press, 2000), 439.

Chapter 1

1. Paul H. Santa Cruz, "Biographical Note," *Robert S. Hyer Papers, 1899–2001: A Guide to the Collection*, revised by Joan Gosnell, 2010, accessed June 21, 2023, https://txarchives.org/smu/finding_aids/00072.xml.
2. John 8:32 as paraphrased in Charles Wesley, *Hymns for Children* (Bristol: Farley, 1763), 35–36.
3. Darwin Payne, *One Hundred Years on the Hilltop: The Centennial History of Southern Methodist University* (Dallas: SMU Press, 2016), 2.
4. Payne, *One Hundred Years*, 1.
5. Payne, *One Hundred Years*, 2.
6. Payne, *One Hundred Years*, 3.
7. Boaz to Hyer, March 7, 1910, in Payne, *One Hundred Years*, 13.
8. Mary Martha Thomas Hosford, *Southern Methodist University: Founding and Early Years* (Dallas: SMU Press, 1974), 29–30.
9. "Call Mass Meeting to Get University," *Dallas Morning News*, May 18, 1910, p. 5; "Has Higher Value than Mere Dollars," *Dallas Morning News*, April 23, 1911, p. 16.
10. Marshall Terry, *From High on the Hilltop: Marshall Terry's History of SMU* (Dallas: Three Forks, 2008), 15.
11. Mary Martha Thomas, "Southern Methodist University: The First Twenty-Five Years, 1915–1940." (PhD diss., University of Michigan, 1971), 32.
12. *Texas Almanac: City Population History from 1850–2000*, Texas Almanac Online, accessed December 13, 2016, http://texasalmanac.com/sites/default/files/images/CityPopHist%20web.pdf.

13. Hosford, *Southern Methodist University*, 30.

14. "Symphony Orchestra," *Dallas Morning News*, May 10, 1895.

15. "A Musical Treat," *Dallas Morning News*, July 7, 1897, p. 5.

16. "Dallas Symphony Club," *Dallas Morning News*, January 31, 1901, p. 2.

17. "Music Notes," *Dallas Morning News*, August 27, 1899, p. 24.

18. "Hook & Hastings (1902)," *Organ Historical Society (OHS) Pipe Organ Database*, accessed December 2021, https://pipeorgandatabase.com/organ/3126.

19. "Organ Recital at Trinity Church," *Dallas Morning News*, July 5, 1905, p. 12.

20. "Pipe Organ Recital," *Dallas Morning News*, July 16, 1905, p. 6.

21. "Install Pipe Organ," *Dallas Morning News*, June 19, 1907, p. 5.

22. "To Dedicate Edifice," *Dallas Morning News*, August 25, 1907, p. 7.

23. "Dedicate New Organ at St. Mary's Chapel," *Dallas Morning News*, April 11, 1910, p. 8.

24. "Eddy Gives First Concert Tonight," *Dallas Morning News*, June 10, 1913, p. 5. The Hook & Hastings, No. 2310, at the Scottish Rite Cathedral was likely the largest in the city at the time, with some fifty-three ranks and a well-appointed console with player mechanism. See the *OHS Pipe Organ Database*, accessed January 31, 2017, https://pipeorgandatabase.com/organ/15956.

25. Hosford, *Southern Methodist University*, 51.

26. Payne, *One Hundred Years*, 8; and Ray Hyer Brown, *Robert Stewart Hyer: The Man I Knew* (Salado, TX: Anson Jones, 1957), 135.

27. B. T. Pettit to Estey Organ Company, March 22, 1913; this letter, and all subsequent correspondence to and from Mr. Pettit, comes from Mr. John Carnahan of the Brattleboro Historical Society, Brattleboro, VT (hereafter cited as Brattleboro). Also, here and below, original syntax and spelling have been preserved in letters as they reveal much about the writer and the era.

28. "Mrs. J. H. Cassidy to Conclude Long Connection with S.M.U," *Dallas Morning News*, June 3, 1934.

29. "Westminster Church Pipe Organ Recital," *Dallas Morning News*, March 17, 1912.

30. "Salesman's Order Form," Estey Organ, May 23, 1913, Brattleboro.

31. "Bertha Stevens Cassidy," accessed June 21, 2023, https://www.findagrave.com/memorial/71234435/bertha-cassidy.
32. Columbia Baptist Church website (accessed December 8, 2016), http://columbia-baptist.org/?page_id=19. Or "Rev. Stevens Urged to Reconsider His Columbia Charge," *Cincinnati Enquirer,* March 5, 1899, p. 16.
33. "Mrs. J. H. Cassidy to Conclude Long Connection with S.M.U.," *Dallas Morning News,* June 3, 1934, p. 10; "Eventful Career Fills Life of Busy Dallas Organist," *Dallas Morning News,* August 3, 1938, p. 2.
34. Thomas Scott Burnham, "Texas Section," *American Organist,* no. 2 (January 1919): 176.
35. "Reengaged as Organist for Temple Emmanuel," *Jewish Monitor* (Dallas), September 5, 1919, p. 5.
36. "Mrs. Cassidy, Organist, Music Director, Dies," *Dallas Morning News,* June 28, 1959, p. 16.
37. "J. H. Cassidy, Printing Firm President, Dies," *Dallas Morning News,* August 4, 1941, p. 4.
38. "Clamor of the Bells," *Dallas Morning News,* April 3, 1904, p. 24.
39. "Choirs Give Song Recital," *Dallas Morning News,* March 28, 1907, p. 4.
40. Benjamin Thomas Pettit (1865–1931) was the Southwestern representative for Estey Organ Company and also a member of First Methodist Church in Dallas. "Early Texas Resident Dies in Local Hospital," *Dallas Morning News,* November 13, 1936, p. 7.
41. Pettit to Estey Organ, March 22, 1913, Brattleboro.
42. Pettit to Estey Organ, March 22, 1913, Brattleboro.
43. JGE to Pettit, March 31, 1913, Brattleboro. The initials "JGE" presumably stand for Jacob Gray Estey.
44. Pettit to Estey Organ, May 23, 1913, Brattleboro.
45. Pettit to Estey Organ, May 23, 1913, Brattleboro.
46. Pettit to Estey Organ, July 11, 1913, Brattleboro.
47. Pettit to Estey Organ, September 8, 1913, Brattleboro.
48. Pettit to Estey Organ, September 11, 1913, Brattleboro.
49. Pettit to Estey Organ, September 17, 1913, Brattleboro.
50. "Associate Pastor Commences," *Dallas Morning News,* June 8, 1913.

51. "Shop Order," Estey Organ, October 1, 1913, Brattleboro.

52. Pettit to Estey Organ, October 23, 1913, Brattleboro.

53. Pettit to Estey Organ, November 1, 1913, Brattleboro.

54. Pettit to Estey Organ, November 3, 1913, Brattleboro.

55. Estey Shop Order #1165, October 1, 1913, Brattleboro.

56. Brown, *Robert Stewart Hyer*, 143.

57. Notebook for Dr. Hyer's Faculty Selection, SMU 1991.0016, series 1, box 4, folder 3, Dorothy Amann Papers, Southern Methodist University Archives (SMU Archives), DeGolyer Library (DeGolyer), Southern Methodist University, Dallas, TX (SMU).

58. Payne, *One Hundred Years*, 8.

59. Payne, *One Hundred Years*, 9.

60. *The Rotunda* (Dallas: SMU Press [?], 1916), 181.

61. A. H. Henning, *The Story of Southern Methodist University, 1910–1930*, vol. 1 (unpublished manuscript, n.d. [1930s?]), 411.

62. Thomas, "Southern Methodist University," 123.

63. Thomas, "Southern Methodist University," 123.

64. Payne, *One Hundred Years*, 43.

65. Henning, *Story of Southern Methodist University*, 394.

66. Scott D. Feldhausen, "A History of the University of Kansas Organ Program," (DMA thesis, University of Kansas, 1999). This entire dissertation affirms that, in terms of the arrangement of the organ program within the school and the structure of pay for the music teachers, KU and SMU operated similarly at the time.

67. *Bulletin of Southern Methodist University: Annual Catalogue 1915–16 and Announcements 1916–1917* (Dallas: SMU, 1915), 90.

68. Thomas, "Southern Methodist University," 90.

69. *The Rotunda* (Dallas: SMU Press, 1917), 182.

70. *The Rotunda*, (Dallas: SMU Press, 1919), 145.

71. *Rotunda* (1917), 183.

72. *The Rotunda*, (Dallas: SMU Press, 1924), 253.

73. *Bulletin of SMU: 1915–16*, 131.

74. *Bulletin of Southern Methodist University: Annual Catalogue with Registration for 1918–1919* (Dallas: SMU, 1919), 156.

75. *Bulletin of SMU: 1915–16*, 18.

76. Thomas, "Southern Methodist University," 143.

77. "Presents Organ and Voice Pupils Tuesday," *Semi-Weekly Campus*, April 4, 1923.

78. *Bulletin of SMU: 1915–16*, 99.

79. George Elbridge Whiting, *First Studies for the Organ: 24 Pieces consisting of preludes, postludes, pastorals and chorals varied intended for beginners in pedal obligato playing and especially adapted for church use*, 2 vols. (Boston: Arthur Schmidt, 1879.)

80. Dudley Buck, *Eighteen Studies in Pedal Phrasing*, Op. 28, 2 vols. (New York: G. Schirmer, 1868).

81. Christian Heinrich Rinck, *Practical Organ School*, ed. William Best (London: Novello, n.d.)

82. "Directory of School of Music and School of Theology," *Campus*, October 1, 1919.

83. Clarence Dickinson, *The Technique and Art of Organ Playing* (New York: H. W. Gray, 1922).

84. Edward Shippen Barnes, *School of Organ Playing*, Op. 31 (Boston: Boston Music Company, 1921).

85. *Bulletin of SMU: 1915–16*, 99.

86. Henning, *Story of Southern Methodist University*, 123.

87. Frank Reedy to Rev. S. H. Hay of First Methodist Church, September 25, 1916, SMU 2000.0347, series 1, box 1, folder 2, Meadows School of the Arts Records, SMU Archives, DeGolyer, SMU (hereafter cited as Meadows Records).

88. Henning, *Story of Southern Methodist University*, 412.

89. "University Concert Opens Musical Season," *Dallas Morning News*, September 15, 1915, p. 6.

90. "SMU Faculty Gives First Public Recital," *SMU Times*, October 30, 1915. The official news periodical of SMU would go through several iterations and publishing schedules during the first several decades. *SMU Times*, *Semi-Weekly Campus*, and the *Campus* were all titles for the same publication before settling on the *Daily Campus*.

91. "Scottish Rite Masons Preparing for Reunion," *Dallas Morning News*, October 31, 1909, p. 22.

92. "Musical Organizations Preparing for Successful Season," *Campus*, October 28, 1919.

93. "Monthly Musical Held at Gaston Avenue Church," *Dallas Morning News*, February 28, 1919.

94. Thomas Scott Burnham, "News and Notes," *American Organist*, no. 5 (January 1922): 411.
95. "Music Students Give Recitals Last Night," *Semi-Weekly Campus*, February 28, 1923.
96. "Pupil Presented in Organ Recital," *Semi-Weekly Campus*, May 16, 1923.
97. *Bulletin of SMU: 1915–16*, 99.
98. "Music Club to Give Pipe Organ Program," *Semi-Weekly Campus*, February 2, 1924.
99. "Hook & Hastings (Opus 1599, 1894)," *OHS Pipe Organ Database*, accessed June 21, 2023, https://pipeorgandatabase. com/organ/15954.
100. "Large Audience Present at Scottish Rite Cathedral," *Dallas Morning News*, February 4, 1918, p. 4.
101. "More than Thousand Hear Organ Recital," *Dallas Morning News*, March 8, 1915, p. 14.
102. Burnham, "Texas Section," 176.
103. Clifford Demarest, "A Message from the Warden," *American Organist*, no. 1 (June 1918): 327.
104. *Bulletin of Southern Methodist University: Annual Catalogue 1917–1918 with Announcements 1918–1919* (Dallas: SMU, 1917), 125.
105. "Musical Club Has Been Organized Here," *Semi-Weekly Campus*, February 2, 1924.
106. The official name of this company was Hillgreen, Lane & Co., although it was colloquially and properly referred to as Hillgreen, Lane, which is the convention that will be used here forward.
107. Mrs. J. H. Cassidy to Estey Organ, October 6 , 1924.
108. Pettit to Estey Organ, October 30, 1924, Brattleboro.
109. Estey Organ to Cassidy, October 30, 1924.

Chapter 2

1. *Bulletin of SMU: 1917–1918*, 152.
2. *Southern Methodist University: Annual Catalogue with Registration for 1925–1926* (Dallas: SMU, 1926).
3. Thomas, "Southern Methodist University," 143.
4. "Fund for Auditorium Given S. M. U.," *Dallas Morning News*, February 7, 1924, p. 1.

5. "Organ Recital at McFarlin Church," *Dallas Morning News*, December 9, 1924, p. 9.

6. "Organ Recital at McFarlin Church."

7. "S.M.U. to Open Auditorium at Four-Day Fete," *Dallas Morning News*, March 5, 1926, p. 13.

8. "S.M.U. to Open Auditorium at Four-Day Fete," p. 4.

9. "Attendance Big at M'Farlin Services," *Semi-Weekly Campus*, April 8, 1926, p. 4.

10. "Auditorium at S.M.U. Will be Center of Culture of Future, Dr. Bizzell Says," *Dallas Morning News*, March 26, 1926, p. 15.

11. "Courboin to Give Organ Programs," *Semi-Weekly Campus*, March 24, 1926, p. 1.

12. "Courboin to Give Organ Programs."

13. "Auditorium at S.M.U. Will be Center of Culture of Future, Dr. Bizzell Says," *Dallas Morning News*, March 26, 1926, p. 15.

14. "S.M.U. to Open Auditorium at Four-Day Fete."

15. "4-Day Program to Dedicate $700,000 McFarlin Auditorium at S.M.U.," *Dallas Morning News*, March 21, 1926, p. 14.

16. Elbert Haling, "Over the Air," *Semi-Weekly Campus*, April 6, 1929, p. 2.

17. The Juilliard School installed Hillgreen, Lane, Op. 781, in 1924, as found in the OHS database, accessed June 21, 2023, https://pipeorgandatabase.com/organ/35478. Carnegie Hall installed Hillgreen, Lane, Op. 456, in 1916, accessed June 21, 2023, https://pipeorgandatabase.com/organ/24551.

18. Rollin Smith, "Hillgreen, Lane & Co.," *Tracker* 16, no. 1 (Winter 2017): 30–37.

19. Smith, "Hillgreen, Lane & Co." See also "Cincinnati Chapter of the American Guild of Organists," accessed March 19, 2020, http://www.cincinnatiago.org/.

20. "Death Takes Former Organist and Leader in Musical Circles," *Dallas Morning News*, April 14, 1934, p. 8. Watkin was somewhat of an opera and even organ impresario, active in Dallas music and church music circles starting in the 1880s.

21. "Activities of Guild Members," *New Music Review and Church Music Review* (May 1920): 200, 222.

22. "Courboin to Give Organ Programs."

23. Frances Arnold Ellis and Skipper Steely, *First Church of Paris* (Paris, TX: First Methodist Church, 1985), 160.

24. Bynum Petty, email to the author, December 2016.
25. "Eventful Career Fills Life of Busy Dallas Organist," *Dallas Morning News*, August 3, 1938, p. 2.
26. The contract for both organs is held by the OHS Library and Archives, https://organhistoricalsociety.org/archives/about-the-archives/.
27. The specifications and descriptions of these organs are in the OHS Library and Archives.
28. "Move Music School into Auditorium," *Semi-Weekly Campus*, April 14, 1926, p. 1.
29. Contract, OHS Library and Archives.
30. Contract, OHS Library and Archives.
31. "Presents First of Organ Recital Series," *Semi-Weekly Campus*, February 19, 1927, p. 3.
32. "Mrs. Chapman Gives Recital," *Semi-Weekly Campus*, April 6, 1928, p. 4.
33. "Music Notes-Studio Gossip," *Dallas Morning News*, April 23, 1928, 4.
34. Notice, *Semi-Weekly Campus*, April 4, 1928, p. 4.
35. "Organist Gives S.M.U. Program," *Dallas Morning News*, March 23, 1927, p. 8.
36. Palmer Christian program of February 27, 1927, SMU 2000.0347, series 1, box 1, folder 4, Meadows Records.
37. Payne, *One Hundred Years*, 2ff.
38. "Seth Ward, TX," Texas State Historical Association Online, accessed December 31, 2016, https://tshaonline.org/handbook/online/articles/kbs20.
39. "Church Services," *Houston Post*, December 19, 1908, p. 7.
40. "Church Music Today," *Houston Post*, January 31, 1909, p. 33.
41. "Houston Social Events," *Galveston Daily News*, March 5, 1911, p. 33.
42. "Mrs. Whaling Dies Here; Ex-Teacher," *Dallas Morning News*, December 1, 1951, p. 4.
43. "Girl 16 Years Old Becomes Church Organist," *Dallas Morning News*, April 2, 1922, p. 4.
44. "Scottish Rite to Open Reunion," *Dallas Morning News*, May 6, 1923, p. 10.
45. "Organist Guild to Hear Concert and Music Talk," *Dallas Morning News*, October 11, 1931, p. 6.

46. "In Musical Circles," *Corsicana Daily Sun*, December 7, 1927, p. 14.

47. In a January 25, 2017, interview with the author, William Teague, a student of Dora Poteet Barclay in the late 1930s, recalled having met Cassidy socially during his student days, noting her energy and enthusiasm.

48. "Dallas Organist to Play Sunday at Church Dedication," *Corpus Christi Times*, April 12, 1940, p. 13.

49. "Financial Supplement to Report of Dean of Music," SMU 2000.0347, series 1, box 1, folder 5, Meadows Records.

50. Henning, *Story of Southern Methodist University*, 395.

51. "Install Third Practice Organ," *Semi-Weekly Campus*, October 12, 1929, p. 1.

52. "S.M.U. Organ Pupils to Display Talents," *Dallas Morning News*, December 9, 1928, p. 5.

53. "Mrs. Whaling to Give S.M.U. Organ Recital," *Dallas Morning News*, October 9, 1932, p. 4.

54. "Nevin's 'Sketches' on S.M.U. Organ Program," *Dallas Morning News*, October 16, 1932, p. 15.

55. *SMU Annual Catalogue, 1925–1926*, 185.

56. *Southern Methodist University: Annual Catalogue with Registration for 1927–1928* (Dallas: SMU, 1927), 91.

57. "Cassidys Will Coach Abroad This Summer," *Dallas Morning News*, May 15, 1927, p. 6.

58. Bertha Cassidy, "Dallas Musicians Hear Organs in Liverpool and Cambridge, England, and Tell Hosts of Music Life Here," *Dallas Morning News*, July 17, 1927, p. 5.

59. Jürgen Schaarwächter, "Rootham, Cyril," *Grove Music Online*, *Oxford Music Online*, Oxford University Press, accessed December 27, 2016, http://www.oxfordmusiconline.com.proxy. libraries.smu.edu/subscriber/article/grove/music/23807.

60. "Cyril Bradley Rootham," *Musical Times* 79, no. 1142 (April 1938): 307–8.

61. Bertha Cassidy, "Dallas Organists Spend Day with Dr. Karg-Elert, Regarded as Foremost Writer of Organ Music," *Dallas Morning News*, July 24, 1927, p. 6.

62. Cassidy, "Dallas Organists Spend Day with Dr. Karg-Elert," p. 6.

63. Letter of July 15, 1927, in Sigfrid Karg-Elert, *Your Ever Grateful, Devoted Friend: Sigfrid Karg-Elert's Letters to Godfrey*

Sceats, 1922–1931, ed. Godfrey Sceats and Harold Fabrikant (Caufield, Australia: Fabrikant, 2000), 13. "Ich beasbsichtige ernstlich nach meiner Rückkehr englischen Sprach-Unterricht zu nehmen und zwar bei einem Dolmetscher, der bei den paar Lektionen, die ich Mrs. und Miss Cassidy aus Texas zu geben hatte, unsere Unterhaltung übersetze, (hast du Töne? Die Damen zahlen pro Stunde 50 Dollar!!!! Ja, ja, Amerika das Land der Dollars)."

64. "Measuring Worth," accessed June 22, 2023, https://www.measuringworth.com/, and "Historical Dollar to Marks Conversion Page," accessed June 20, 2022, http://www.history.ucsb.edu/faculty/marcuse/projects/currency.htm#infcalc.

65. Mrs. J. H. Cassidy, "Germans Hiss French Music," *Dallas Morning News*, August 7, 1927, p. 5.

66. "The Festspielhaus Visited by Dallasites," *Dallas Morning News*, July 31, 1927, p. 5.

67. "Mrs. Cassidy to Open New Organ in Bryan," *Dallas Morning News*, May 6, 1928, p. 5.

68. "Organists to Gather Here for Meeting," *Dallas Morning News*, May 13, 1928, p. 6.

69. "Thanksgiving Music Featured in Church Services Sunday," *Dallas Morning News*, November 25, 1928, p. 5.

70. "Music Notes; Studio Gossip," *Dallas Morning News*, February 26, 1929, p. 12.

71. "Hubbells Will Hold Meeting on Wednesday," *Dallas Morning News*, April 5, 1930, p. 10.

72. "Reception to Honor Dean of Texas Organists," *Fort Worth Star-Telegram*, May 12, 1931, p. 12.

73. "Bonelli First Recitalist of Active Month," *Dallas Morning News*, January 10, 1932, p. 11.

74. From the letters ca. February 15–18, 1932, in *Everyone Is Amazed: Sigfrid and Katharina Karg-Elert's Letters from North America January to March, 1932*, trans. Harold Fabrikant (Caufield, Victoria, Australia: Fabrikant, 2001), 22e and g. "Hier in Dallas sieht es gut aus: Kakteen auf der Strasse, bluehende Pflanzen um die Haeuser, kein Schnee, wie jetzt zuletzt immer, und auch kein Matsch. Cassidys sind naturlich liebe Menschen. Sie haben ein feines Haus—mit Orgel naturlich; einige Deutsche waren mit an der Hahn, und weil das "Adolphus" (unser Hotel) zu teuer und zu weit ist, hat uns seine liebe Koenigsbergerin in

ihr Haus gebeten." The woman from Koenigsberg was Anna Lisbeth Todd, piano professor at SMU and wife of Harold Hart Todd. She had been born in Prussia.

75. "Karg-Elert Changes Local Program upon Arrival Here," *Dallas Morning News*, February 19, 1932, p. 11.

76. Stewart Sabin, "Concerts," *Democrat and Chronicle* (Rochester, NY), March 14, 1932, p. 15. This program given in Rochester is slightly altered too. In fact, Karg-Elert tailored each program to fit the instrument at hand, but the frequency with which this was done suggests that the instruments he encountered were not exactly what he had expected.

77. John Rosenfield Jr., "Famous Organist of Leipzig Heard in Recital Here," *Dallas Morning News*, February 20, 1932, p. 10.

78. Harvey Gaul, "Karg-Elert Plays Organ," *Pittsburgh Post-Gazette*, February 2, 1932, p. 16.

79. "Mrs. J. H. Cassidy to Quit S.M.U. in June," *Dallas Morning News*, October 12, 1933, p. 3.

80. "Mrs. J. H. Cassidy to Conclude Long Connection with S.M.U.," *Dallas Morning News*, June 3, 1934, p. 10.

81. "Cassidy to Conclude Long Connection with S.M.U."

82. "Mrs. J. H. Cassidy to Dedicate Organ at Church Sunday," *Dallas Morning News*, June 30, 1935.

83. "Mrs. J. H. Cassidy to Play in Palestine," *Dallas Morning News*, July 12, 1935, p. 2. Mention of the organ's electrification and rededication is found in Jack Selden's *Seven Score and Ten: One Hundred Fifty Years of the Presbyterian Church in Palestine, Tex.* (Palestine, TX: Clacton Press, 1999), 176.

84. "Mrs. Cassidy Returns, Resume Music Duties," *Dallas Morning News*, September 11, 1936, p. 3.

85. "Mrs. Cassidy in Organ Program at McFarlin," *Dallas Morning News*, October 31, 1936, p. 10.

86. "Eventful Career Fills Life of Busy Dallas Organist," *Dallas Morning News*, August 3, 1938, p. 2.

87. Paul R. Powell, "Robert H. Coleman," *Canterbury Dictionary of Hymnology*, Canterbury Press, accessed February 1, 2017, http://www.hymnology.co.uk.proxy.libraries.smu.edu/r/robert-h-coleman.

88. Robert Coleman, ed., *Coleman's Male Choir* (Dallas: Robert H. Coleman, 1928), #8.

89. "Baptist Circle to Give Tea," *Dallas Morning News*, October 11, 1936, p. 5.

90. This is suggested by United States Census records for the James Harvey Cassidy family for 1910, 1920, 1930, and 1940, each of which lists additional, nonfamily young women living in the household; https://www.archives.gov/research/census/online-resources.

91. "J. H. Cassidy, Printing Firm President, Dies," *Dallas Morning News*, August 4, 1941, p. 4.

92. "Clubs-Studios," *Dallas Morning News*, April 27, 1947, p. 14.

93. "Church Organist to Retire after Years of Service," *Dallas Morning News*, June 5, 1945, p. 10.

94. W. A. Criswell, "In Appreciation for Mrs. J. H. Cassidy," *Baptist Reminder* (Dallas), June 17, 1945, p. 1.

95. "Organists Guild Host at Dinner for Mrs. Cassidy," *Dallas Morning News*, May 18, 1948, p. 11.

96. "Miss Cassidy, Organist, Dies," *Dallas Morning News*, October 31, 1950, p. 9. Her death certificate from the Texas Department of Health indicates cancer as the cause of death.

97. "Latin Major Named SMU Girl of Year," *Dallas Morning News*, May 1, 1952, p. 14.

98. "Mary A. Hill Is Bride of Harlan Hall," *Dallas Morning News*, June 4, 1956, p. 3.

99. "Honors Day," *SMU Campus*, May 4, 1956, p. 5.

100. "Organ Recital," *Dallas Morning News*, May 10, 1957, p. 10.

101. "Barclay Student in Recital Here," *Dallas Morning News*, January 31, 1959, p. 7.

102. "Over 300 SMU Students Receive Scholar Titles," *Dallas Morning News*, April 15, 1959, p. 3.

103. "Certificate of Death, Bertha Stevens Cassidy," Dallas County, TX, June 29, 1959.

104. "Will A. Watkin Death Removes Man Notable in Promotion of Pipe Organ Music for Dallas," *Dallas Morning News*, April 15, 1934, p. 1.

Chapter 3

1. There seems to have been no birth announcement, and her date of birth on her tombstone is listed as being 1905. However, all obituaries listed her as being 57 at time of death, indicating the earlier year. See also "Dora Emily Poteet Barclay," accessed

June 25, 2023, https://www.findagrave.com/memorial/11423891/dora-emily-barclay.

2. "Superintendent Sims Has Made the Following Assignments of Teachers for the Public Schools of Cameron for the Coming School Year," *Cameron Herald*, July 19, 1906, p. 5.

3. "Letters," *Cameron Herald*, April 2, 1914, p. 12. The antiquated term *normal school* simply refers to a school to train teachers, later mostly known as teacher colleges.

4. "Milam County Summer Normal Begins Monday," *Cameron Herald*, June 11, 1914, p. 1.

5. "Milam County Summer Normal Begins Monday."

6. "Dallas Organist to Study in New York," *Cameron Herald*, July 26, 1923, p. 4.

7. "Talented Waco Girl Makes Enviable Record as Pipe Organist for Church," *Waco News-Tribune*, July 11, 1920, p. 1. The Poteet family had moved to Beaumont for a brief time, which apparently had provided the opportunity to study with Professor Kirkpatrick.

8. "Talented Waco Girl."

9. Lorenz Maycher, *Conversations with William Teague* (Kilgore, TX: East Texas Pipe Organ Festival, 2013), 6. Dr. Teague reiterated this in a phone interview with the author, January 25, 2017. That she studied with Wiesemann (pronounced "Wise-man") is affirmed in a March 1995 interview by Henry Evans of former student Russell Brydon.

10. "Baylor University School of Music," *Waco News-Tribune*, November 30, 1928, p. 9.

11. "Sidelights and Highlights," *Corsicana Daily Sun*, October 30, 1951, p. 4. Dr. Wiesemann engaged in numerous musical activities; in addition to his experience as a practical church musician, he composed, accompanied silent films, taught privately, and would eventually teach at Texas State Women's College (now TWU) in Denton, Texas, before moving to New Jersey the last decade of his life.

12. "Sidelights and Highlights."

13. "Music Contest to be Held Thursday," *Dallas Morning News*, January 30, 1922, p. 7. Dora Poteet is listed as a student at Bryan, which would have been Bryan Street High School, later renamed Crozier Technical High School.

14. "Recitals to Be Given by Music Students at S.M.U.," *Dallas Morning News*, May 23, 1921, p. 14.

15. "Girl 16 Years Old Becomes Church Organist," *Dallas Morning News*, April 2, 1922, p. 4. For the record on the Hook & Hastings at First Methodist Church, Dallas, see "Hook & Hastings (Opus 1599, 1894)," *OHS Pipe Organ Database*, accessed June 22, 2023, https://pipeorgandatabase.org/organ/15954.

16. "Lasslet Speaks before Y.M.C.A. Sunday Meeting," *Dallas Morning News*, June 13, 1921, p. 6; and "Chinese Boy Chosen Mayor of Y.M.C.A. Summer School," *Dallas Morning News*, June 28, 1922, p. 6.

17. *The Rotunda* (Dallas: Southern Methodist University, 1923), 238.

18. T. Scott Burnham, ed., notice, *American Organist* 5 (January 1922), 256.

19. Henning, *Story of Southern Methodist University*, 412.

20. "Dallas Organist to Study in New York." Biggs is called "Diggs" in this article.

21. Michael Johnston, "Richard Keys Biggs," accessed January 23, 2017, http://michaelsmusicservice.com/blog/wp-content/uploads/2014/02/Biggs.bio_.jpg.

22. "Musical Club Has Been Organized Here," *Semi-Weekly Campus*, February 2, 1924, p. 2.

23. "Graduating Recital," program, May 12, 1925, SMU 2000.0347, series 1, box 1, folder 3, Meadows Records.

24. The correspondence relative to this incident can be located in box 1, folder 4, Meadows Records.

25. Garland Cullum, "Local Organist Started on Musical Career at Early Age," *Dallas Morning News*, July 7, 1938, p. 2.

26. "Assistant Instructor Music Department," *Dallas Morning News*, July 14, 1925, p. 13.

27. The annual catalog from the 1923–24 academic year shows 149 students in the music school, 124 the following year, and back down to 141 during the 1925–26 school year.

28. "Financial Supplement to Report of Dean of Music," (1926), SMU 2000.0347, series 1, box 1, folder 4, Meadows Records.

29. "Financial Supplement to Report of Dean of Music," series 1, box 1, folder 4, Meadows Records. It should be noted that this document is imprecise as to what "collections" entails, being ambiguous as to whether these amounts represent take-home pay

or simply gross amounts collected by the university from which the faculty would receive a portion.

30. "Y. W. Choral Club Organizes for Season," *Dallas Morning News*, October 4, 1925, p. 6.

31. "Dora Poteet," *Dallas Morning News*, October 13, 1929, p. 9. This is merely a business card advertisement, listing her as organist of the Scottish Rite Cathedral. Most likely Cassidy, Whaling, and Poteet rotated service duties at the cathedral, few of which would likely interfere with their Sunday morning church duties.

32. "Former Cameron Girl to Study Music in New York Studio," *Cameron Herald*, August 25, 1927, p. 11.

33. "Two Organists for Instrument in New Theater," *Democrat and Chronicle* (Rochester, NY), August 30, 1922, p. 20.

34. "Soloists for Radio City Broadcast," *Brooklyn Daily Eagle*, December 25, 1932, p. 56.

35. Ellouise W. Skinner, *Sacred Music at Union Theological Seminary, 1836–1953: An Informal History* (New York: privately printed, 1953), 66.

36. "Former Cameron Girl to Study Music in New York Studio," *Cameron Herald*, August 25, 1927, p. 11.

37. "Dora Poteet Returns after Summer's Study," *Dallas Morning News*, October 2, 1927, p. 5.

38. "Notes," *Cameron Herald*, October 13, 1927, p. 5.

39. FWR, "Reviews and New Music," *Musical Courier*, no. 85 (July 6, 1922): 65.

40. "Second S.M.U. Organ Recital to Be Given Sunday at McFarlin," *Dallas Morning News*, April 8, 1928, p. 7; Burnham, notice, 406.

41. "First Cecilian Twilight Concert Sunday Afternoon," *Dallas Morning News*, November 18, 1928, p. 6.

42. Burnham, 406.

43. "Pipe Organ at Adolphus Hotel," *Corsicana Daily Sun*, September 12, 1928, p. 7.

44. "Second S.M.U. Organ Recital."

45. "Dora Poteet," *Dallas Morning News*, March 1, 1933, p. 8.

46. "Organ Pupils Will Play at McFarlin," *Dallas Morning News*, December 10, 1930, p. 10.

47. "Dora Poteet."

48. "Dora Poteet Recital," *Dallas Morning News* February 5, 1933, p. 8.

49. "Poteet-Markham," *Dallas Morning News*, April 1, 1934, p. 11.

50. "Dora Poteet to Give Mendelssohn Recital," *Dallas Morning News*, November 21, 1934, p. 2.

51. "Three of S.M.U. Music Teachers Recital Artists," *Dallas Morning News*, February 26, 1935, p. 3.

52. *Bulletin of Southern Methodist University* (Dallas: SMU, 1937), 192.

53. "This Pianist Keeps Balance between Teaching and Playing," *Dallas Morning News*, July 5, 1938, p. 2. Although this 1938 article states that the duo piano partnership was formed "five years ago" and was active for two years, thus ostensibly from 1933 to 1935, the newspaper records indicate the broadcasts occurred regularly between 1930 and 1932.

54. "Dora Poteet Elected Associate of Guild," *Dallas Morning News*, June 15, 1934, p. 14.

55. "Leading Organists Hear Dora Poteet in N.Y.," *Dallas Morning News*, July 31, 1935, p. 4. This article also states that she "spent time studying theory with Frank Wright, in preparation for examination for fellowship in the guild." There are no records currently at AGO headquarters that indicate she actually took the FAGO exam.

56. "Miss Poteet to Leave for Guild Convention," *Dallas Morning News*, June 17, 1936, p. 5.

57. "S.M.U. Organist Plays on Program for Guild," *Dallas Morning News*, July 14, 1936, p. 10.

58. Program from Wednesday, June 24, 1936, courtesy American Guild of Organists Archives, New York, NY.

59. "S.M.U. Organ Staff to Begin Recitals," *Dallas Morning News*, October 12, 1934, p. 3.

60. "City Campaign to Pay S.M.U. Debt Resumed," *Dallas Morning News*, January 19, 1937, p. 12. The circumstances of Mrs. Whaling's midyear resignation are a mystery, although it was likely a result of her husband's reappointment. This article, chronicling the January meeting of the board of trustees, seems to suggest that both Mrs. Whaling's retirement and Miss Poteet's promotion were unexpected.

61. It is possible that the connection to Dupré, or the suggestion to study with him, was made by d'Antaffly. D'Antaffly's "Sportive Fauns" is dedicated to Dupré.

62. "Dallas Organist Plans to Study in Europe this Summer," *Corsicana Daily Sun*, May 12, 1937, p. 7.

63. Léonie Rosenstiel, *Nadia Boulanger: A Life in Music* (New York: W. W. Norton, 1982), 280.

64. "Dallas Organist Plans to Study in Europe in Summer."

65. Brydon, interview.

66. Dr. Barbara Marquart, interview by the author, January 19, 2017.

67. Howard "Buddy" Ross, interview by Evans, March 20, 1995.

68. That she was Dupré's "favorite" pupil, or that she performed exceedingly well for him, is common knowledge among all of her former students and appears in most of her official biographies post-1937.

69. Walter Davis, interview by the author, January 23, 2017.

70. Brydon, interview .

71. William Barclay, program notes, *Dora Poteet Barclay Memorial Organ Recital Issue*, Dallas/Fort Worth Chapters of the American Guild of Organists, 1962, LP record.

72. Brydon, interview. This is the only mention of her original intent to study in some fashion with Vierne. Her other students had not heard this.

73. "Dallas Organist Plans to Study in Europe in Summer."

74. "Miss Dora Poteet Returns from Europe," *Cameron Herald*, September 30, 1937, p. 4.

75. "Dora Poteet Organ Concert at McFarlin," *Dallas Morning News*, January 18, 1938, p. 11.

76. Elizabeth Crocker, "Entire Concert Given on Organ By Dora Poteet," *Dallas Morning News*, January 19, 1938, p. 11.

77. Brydon, interview.

78. Cullum, "Local Organist."

79. "Faculty of the School of Music," memo dated January 7, 1940, series 1, box 2, folder 3, Meadows Records.

80. "Poteet Concert Tuesday Night," *Dallas Morning News*, April 25, 1939, p. 8.

81. *Bulletin of SMU*, 1937, p. 184. This rate put her about midrange in the wage scale for music teachers, of whom the highest paid was Dean van Katwijk, who received $171 for two lessons per week, per semester, per student. The lowest paid was Mr. Berry, who received $54 under the same circumstances.

82. 1940 United States census, Dallas County, April 29, 1940.

83. *American Guild of Organists Dallas Chapter Handbook* (Dallas: self-published, 2007), 70.

84. "Fine Arts Teachers to Open New Season," *Dallas Morning News*, August 25, 1940, p. 4.

85. "Dora Poteet Returns From Eastern Tour," *Dallas Morning News*, April 5, 1940, p. 15.

86. "Enthusiasm Greets Organ Recital of Miss Dora Poteet," *Dallas Morning News*, January 18, 1941, p. 11.

87. "Dora Poteet to Leave for Concert Series," *Dallas Morning News*, March 12, 1941, p. 10.

88. "Dora Poteet Off on Concert Tour," *Dallas Morning News*, March 2, 1942, p. 6.

89. "Dora Poteet Plays," *Dallas Morning News*, August 21, 1943, p. 6.

90. "Appearance Set for New Organists," *Dallas Morning News*, August 26, 1944, p. 10.

91. *Bulletin of Southern Methodist University, 1945–1946* (Dallas: SMU, 1945), 26.

92. "Dallas Organist Is Chosen to Open National Festival," *Dallas Morning News*, April 11, 1947, p. 9.

93. "William Barclay, Dora Poteet Wed," *Dallas Morning News*, February 17, 1948, p. 13.

94. Michael Pullin, "Barclay, William Archibald," *Handbook of Texas Online*, accessed January 27, 2017, http://www.tshaonline.org/handbook/online/articles/fbabr.

95. Walter Davis's comment of ca. May 1998 to Peggy Bie on her blog, "Comments and Anecdotal Recollections from Dora Barclay's Friends, Colleagues, and Students at SMU," accessed January 27, 2017. http://www.oocities.org/~peggybie/Students.html.

96. "Horowitz Lists 'Petrouchka,'" *Dallas Morning News*, February 25, 1932, p. 10.

97. Advertisement, *Dallas Morning News*, November 21, 1936, p. 13.

98. Palmer Christian program of February 27, 1927, SMU 2000.0347, series 1, box 2, folder 1, Meadows Records.

99. "Civic Music Association Presents Rubinstein Tuesday," *Dallas Morning News*, March 7, 1939, p. 12.

100. "Lehmann and Melchior in Delightful Recital," *Dallas Morning News*, November 17, 1940, p. 16.
101. Christian program, series 1, box 1, folder 4, Meadows Records.
102. E. Clyde Whitlock, "Music and Musicians," *Fort Worth Star-Telegram*, December 1, 1935, p. 18.
103. "Organ Recital By Harold Friedell" (concert program), folder 2, Meadows Records.
104. "Virgil Fox Presented in Organ Recital," *Dallas Morning News*, February 8, 1942, p. 10.
105. "Enthusiastic House Greets Power Biggs," *Dallas Morning News*, November 14, 1943, p. 15.
106. "Schreiner Plays Recital Sponsored by Organist Guild," *Dallas Morning News*, March 8, 1943, p. 4.
107. "Dupré Popularizes the Organ Recital," *Dallas Morning News*, November 21, 1948, p. 16.
108. Marquart, interview.
109. Maycher, *Conversations with William Teague*, 7. David Craighead's recital, under the auspices of the AGO, was actually hosted by the nearby Highland Park Presbyterian Church on its Kimball organ; "Piano, Organ, Choir Music in Concerts," *Dallas Morning News*, November 20, 1949, p. 4.
110. Elbert Haling, "Over the Air," *Semi-Weekly Campus*, April 6, 1929, p. 2.
111. Davis, interview. Cleaning keys before playing an organ is a tradition in some French circles, so Barclay's horror was probably a bit of an overreaction.
112. Brydon, interview .
113. Davis, interview.
114. Donald McDonald, interview by the author, October 25, 2016.
115. Marcel Dupré's program, Tuesday, December 7, 1948, SMU 2000.0347, series 1, box 2, folder 4, Meadows Records.
116. Rual Askew, "French Organist Exhibits His Renowned Virtuosity," *Dallas Morning News*, December 8, 1948, p. 8.
117. Askew, "French Organist."

Chapter 4

1. Howard Grimes, *A History of the Perkins School of Theology*, ed. Roger Loyd (Dallas: SMU Press, 1993), 67.

2. Grimes, *History of the Perkins School of Theology*, 67.

3. "Theology Quadrangle for SMU," *Dallas Morning News* October 28, 1948, p. 26.

4. "SMU Ready for Building Quadrangle," *Dallas Morning News*, October 28, 1948, p. 1.

5. Pati Haworth, "A Legacy of Love: Four Generations of Organ Philanthropy," *American Organist*, no. 46 (July 2012): 28.

6. Leila Peyton, letter to Eugene Hawk, June 15, 1946, series 1, box 11, folder 20, Eugene B. Hawk Papers, Bridwell Library, Perkins School of Theology, SMU (hereafter cited as Hawk Papers).

7. Hawk to Peyton, December 27, 1945, series 1, box 11, folder 20, Hawk Papers.

8. Early organ description. Although this document refers to the collaboration between Barclay and Harrison, and such cooperation seems likely and reasonable, there is nothing in the archival record to document the nature of this collaboration.

9. Contract between SMU (Umphrey Lee) and Aeolian-Skinner (G. Donald Harrison), August 18, 1948, courtesy of Bynum Petty and the Organ Historical Society.

10. Christopher Long, "Lemmon, Mark," *Handbook of Texas Online*, accessed February 14, 2017, http://www.tshaonline.org/handbook/online/articles/fle64.

11. Hawk to Mark Lemmon, November 16, 1949, series 1, box 9, folder 40, Hawk Papers.

12. Hawk to G. Donald Harrison, November 10, 1949, series 1, box 9, folder 40, Hawk Papers.

13. Hawk to Harrison, November 10, 1949, series 1, box 9, folder 40, Hawk Papers.

14. Joseph Whiteford to Hawk, October 4, 1950, series 1, box 9, folder 40, Hawk Papers. Whiteford here objects to Lemmon's engineer, "who has been consulted and, therefore, feel it necessary to write and say that we cannot guarantee the organ if his recommendations are followed." Robert B. Newman of Bolt, Beranek and Newman, Consultants in Acoustics, letter to Whiteford, October 21, 1950, series 1, box 9, folder 40, Hawk Papers.

15. Hawk to Whiteford, October 12, 1950, series 1, box 9, folder 40, Hawk Papers .

16. Hawk to Umphrey Lee, October 30, 1950, series 1, box 9, folder 40, Hawk Papers .
17. Lemmon to Harrison, May 17, 1950, series 1, box 9, folder 40, Hawk Papers .
18. Whiteford to Lemmon, August 18, 1950, series 1, box 9, folder 40, Hawk Papers .
19. These pipes are in the possession of the author and have been identified as zinc by organ builders. Email with Roy Redman (February 2017) confirms that these are the original façade pipes installed prior to any renovation.
20. Lorenz Maycher, "The Williams Family of New Orleans: A Life Installing Aeolian-Skinner Organs," *Diapason* 97, no. 5, pp. 24–29.
21. Maycher, "Williams Family."
22. Hawk to Harrison, June 20, 1950, series 1, box 9, folder 40, Hawk Papers.
23. Hawk to Harrison, August 29, 1950, series 1, box 9, folder 40, Hawk Papers .
24. Harrison to Hawk, September 6, 1950, series 1, box 9, folder 40, Hawk Papers .
25. Steward M. Doss, "S. M. U. Dedicates Perkins School," *Dallas Morning News*, February 9, 1951, p. 1.
26. Hawk to Mrs. George L. Peyton, March 13, 1951, series 1, box 11, folder 20, Hawk Papers.
27. Hawk to Peyton, March 13, 1951, series 1, box 11, folder 20, Hawk Papers.
28. Hawk to Peyton, April 18, 1951, series 1, box 11, folder 20, Hawk Papers.
29. "Perkins Chapel Organ Dedication Program," May 11, 1951, series 2, box 5, file 17, Perkins School of Theology Records, SMU Archives, DeGolyer Library, SMU.
30. An undated recording from the East Texas Pipe Organ Festival features Dora Poteet Barclay playing BWV 541 at Perkins Chapel, although this recording was not necessarily made at the dedication.
31. Contract, OHS Library and Archives.
32. Obituary for Micky Cates Abbot, *Dallas Morning News*, May 2016, http://www.legacy.com/obituaries/dallasmorningnews/obituary.aspx?pid=180191413.

33. Walter Davis, interview by the author, January 23, 2017.

34. John Rosenfield, "The Passing Show," *Dallas Morning News*, July 18, 1953, p. 6. The auditorium also served as a primary venue for the Dallas Symphony Orchestra, certainly constraining the use of that hall for organ purposes even further. A renovation during this time bricked up the windows, allowing more flexibility for theatre productions but darkening the room considerably.

35. "Recitalists Named by Organist Guild," *Dallas Morning News*, July 26, 1951, p. 8.

36. "Dallas Organist to Give Recital," *Dallas Morning News*, February 23, 1952, p. 4.

37. "Andriessen Work on Webber Recital for Organ Guild," *Dallas Morning News*, March 12, 1952, p. 4.

38. "Musicologist Asks Higher Standards," *Dallas Morning News*, April 29, 1952, p. 9.

39. "E. A. Kraft to Conclude Organ Series," *Dallas Morning News*, March 8, 1953, p. 12.

40. Frank Gagnard, "Dallas Newcomer Brings Organ Series to Finale," *Dallas Morning News*, March 9, 1955, p. 15.

41. "Miss Mason in Debut for Organ Guild," *Dallas Morning News*, February 26, 1956, p. 4.

42. "Noted Organist to Give Recital," *Dallas Morning News*, November 1, 1956, p. 22. The Arlington model carillon consisted of amplified tubes that approximated bell tones. After this dedication, there is no more mention in the media of carillon recitals (or even just bell playing) at Perkins Chapel, probably an indication of this instrument's lack of success.

43. Spencer Mastick, "Teague Recital Proves Versatility of Organ," *Fresno (CA) Bee*, November 16, 1964, p. 3.

44. "Organ Guild to Hold Conclave Meetings Here, Fort Worth," *Dallas Morning News*, December 24, 1952, p. 4.

45. Dr. William Teague, interview by the author, February 18, 2017. Dr. Teague recalls suffering from a cut on his finger, which he had managed to glue together earlier that day. The makeshift solution having come undone early in the recital, he recalls having bled on the organ console and having to wipe it clean between each piece!

46. Frank Gagnard, "Fine Artists By Organist," *Dallas Morning News*, January 20, 1954, p. 6.

47. Dr. Barbara Marquart, interview by the author, January 19, 2017.

48. Dr. Donald McDonald, interview by the author, October 25, 2016.

49. Howard "Buddy" Ross, interview by Henry Evans, March 20, 1995.

50. Davis, interview.

51. Teague, interview.

52. Peggy Bie, "Comments and Anecdotal Recollections from Dora Barclay's Friends, Colleagues, and Students at SMU," accessed January 27, 2017. http://www.oocities.org/~peggybie/Students.html.

53. Davis, interview.

54. Russell Brydon, interview by Evans, March 1995.

55. Brydon, interview.

56. Brydon, interview.

57. Teague, interview.

58. Davis, interview.

59. Brydon, interview.

60. E. Clyde Whitlock, obituary / jacket notes, *Dora Poteet Barclay Memorial Organ Recital Issue.*

61. Maycher, *Conversations with William Teague*, 7.

62. Davis, interview.

63. Defining what constitutes a comprehensive repertoire and what does not is problematic, explaining why most students considered she had a limited repertoire, with a couple students disagreeing. From a survey of her concert programs from the 1930s through the 1950s, her Bach seemed to be most limited. There is virtually no pre-baroque music, which is not unusual for the era. Messiaen appears only at her recital at Park Cities Baptist Church. She was an exponent of Dupré because of her personal connection, but otherwise her programs elicit little concern for living composers, early composers, or music beyond the generally accepted canon of the era.

64. Ross, interview.

65. Marquart, interview.

66. Davis, interview.

67. Marquart, interview.

68. Davis, interview.

69. Davis recalls being assigned the Gleason, while Marquart never used it.

70. Marquart, interview.

71. "Church Will Honor Halls with Sunday Reception," *Odessa (TX) American*, March 28, 1969, p. 8.

72. Undated recording of Dora Poteet Barclay playing at Perkins Chapel, courtesy of East Texas Pipe Organ Festival.

73. Teague, interview.

74. Barclay's live recording at TCU on January 28, 1957, courtesy of East Texas Pipe Organ Festival.

75. Brydon, interview.

76. "Music Clubs and Studios," *Dallas Morning News*, June 20, 1954, p. 5.

77. Peggy Bie, "My Life Story," accessed February, 2017, http://www.oocities.org/~peggybie/index.html#anchor39829.

78. "Peggy C. Bie," *Time Note*, accessed February 25, 2017, https://nekropole.info/en/Peggy-C-Bie#person.

79. "University Names Theory Professor for Music School," *Dallas Morning News*, August 31, 1949, p. 13.

80. "Ellsworth to Play Dedication Recital," *Dallas Morning News*, November 26, 1950, p. 4.

81. "New Electronic Organ Largest Heard in Auditorium to Date," *Dallas Morning News*, December 11, 1950, p. 6.

82. "SMU Will Offer New Music Major," *Dallas Morning News*, July 21, 1951, p. 5. This degree evidenced the scholarly attention sacred music was now receiving in academia, heralding the subsequent hiring of Lloyd Pfautsch and Robert Anderson in a few years to establish the master of sacred music degree.

83. Timothy Binkley, "Historical Note to the Fred Gealy Papers," accessed June 22, 2023, https://www.smu.edu/Bridwell/Collections/SpecialCollectionsandArchives/~/media/Site/Bridwell/Archives/BA10507.pdf.

84. Fred Gealy, letter to Stella Ousley, April 10, 1944, series 1, box 1851a, folder 4, Fred D. Gealy Papers, Bridwell Library, Perkins School of Theology, Southern Methodist University, (hereafter cited as Gealy Papers).

85. "M. P. Möller (Opus 8107, 1950," *OHS Pipe Organ Database*, accessed June 22, 2023, https://pipeorgandatabase.org/organ/34936.

86. Binkley, "Historical Note."
87. Davis, interview.
88. Gordon Young, letter to Gealy, November 4, 1949, series 1, box 1851B, folder 1, Gealy Papers. Gordon Young was not only M. P. Möller's Texas representative but also had that autumn just accepted the position as head of the organ department at Texas Christian University in Fort Worth.
89. "SMU Music School Prepares for Active Season Program," *Dallas Morning News*, September 21, 1952, p. 4.
90. "SMU Given Organ by G. P. Cullums," *Dallas Morning News*, January 4, 1953, p. 10.
91. "M. P. Möller (Opus 8546, 1953," *OHS Pipe Organ Database*, accessed June 22, 2023, https://pipeorgandatabase.org/organ/35972.
92. "Moeller Organs Honor Teacher," *Dallas Morning News*, July 30, 1956, p. 17.
93. "Local Artist to Present Organ Recital," *Dallas Morning News*, February 2, 1958, p. 3.
94. "Reuter Organ Co. (Opus 1179, 1956)," *OHS Pipe Organ Database*, accessed June 22, 2023, https://pipeorgandatabase.org/organ/20995.
95. Marquart, interview.
96. Marquart, interview.
97. Maycher, *Conversations with William Teague*, 42.
98. Brydon, interview.
99. Maycher, *Conversations with William Teague*, 42–43.
100. "Mrs. Barclay Rites Set; SMU Organ Professor," *Dallas Morning News*, March 23, 1961, p. 5.
101. Teague, interview.
102. Whitlock, notes, *Dora Poteet Barclay Memorial Organ Recital Issue*.
103. "Organ Guilds Set Up Fund in Honor of Dora Barclay," *Dallas Morning News*, May 20, 1962, p. 2.
104. Whitlock, notes, *Dora Poteet Barclay Memorial Organ Recital Issue*.
105. "The Artists of the Organ and the Organ of the Artists," published by M. P. Moller, 1956, as quoted by Peggy Bie, "Dora Poteet Barclay, Outstanding Organist and Teacher."

106. Barclay, program notes, *Dora Poteet Barclay Memorial Organ Recital Issue*. Barclay mentions that Dora used the term "beloved maître" to refer to Marcel Dupré.

107. Whitlock, notes, *Dora Poteet Barclay Memorial Organ Recital Issue*.

108. Unknown editorial from the *Fort Worth Star-Telegram* remembered by Teague, interview.

Chapter 5

1. Franklin Delano Roosevelt, "Fireside Chat on the Purposes and Foundations of the Recovery Program," July 24, 1933; First Carbon Files; Speeches of President Franklin D. Roosevelt, 1933–1945; Papers as President, President's Personal File, 1933–1945; Franklin D. Roosevelt Library, Hyde Park, NY; https://catalog.archives.gov/id/197304.

2. Kenneth T. Jackson, *Crabgrass Frontier: The Suburbanization of the United States* (New York: Oxford University Press, 1985), 206.

3. William Read and Jan L. Youtie *Telecommunications Strategy for Economic Development* (Westport, CT: Praeger, 1996), 39ff.

4. *Texas Almanac: City Population History from 1850–2000*, Texas Almanac Online, accessed April 15, 2017, http://texasalmanac.com/sites/default/files/images/CityPopHist%20web.pdf.

5. "Methodist Church, 1939–1968," Association of Religion Data Archives, accessed June 22, 2023, https://www.thearda.com/us-religion/group-profiles/groups?D=525.

6. Grimes, *History of the Perkins School of Theology*, 75, 128.

7. "SMU Will Offer New Music Major," *Dallas Morning News*, July 21, 1951, p. 5.

8. Fred Gealy, letter to Rev. Emmett C. Barrow, October 7, 1953, series 1, box 1850B, Gealy Papers.

9. Carlton Young, email with the author, March 31, 2017.

10. Nita Akin, letter to Merrimon Cuninggim, May 19, 1955, box 26, file 9, Merrimon Cuninggim Papers, Bridwell Library, SMU (hereafter cited as Cuninggim Papers).

11. Cuninggim to Akin, May 20, 1955, Cuninggim Papers .

12. Introduction to the "Report on the Consultation on Church Music, Southern Methodist University, November 28–29, 1955," box 19, file 43, Cuninggim Papers.

13. "Roster of Participants," November 28–29, 1955, box 19, file 43, Cuninggim Papers.

14. The definitive biography of Lloyd Pfautsch, wherein his background is thoroughly covered, is Kenneth Hart's *A Day for Dancing: The Life and Music of Lloyd Pfautsch* (Denton: University of North Texas Press, 2014).

15. *Southern Methodist University Bulletin 1961–62* (Dallas: SMU, 1961), 86; and *Southern Methodist University Bulletin 1962–63* (Dallas: SMU, 1962), 87.

16. Young, email with the author, April 4, 2017.

17. Dorothy Faller, email with the author, October 2016 and April 2017.

18. Albert Goldberg, "French Organist Draws Capacity Crowd," *Chicago Sunday Tribune*, July 7, 1946, p. 3.

19. "2 to Replace Marriott at U. of C. Chapel," *Chicago Daily Tribune*, July 12, 1953, p. 185.

20. Concert programs for these spring events are found in series 1, box 1, folder 8, Robert T. Anderson Papers, SMU Archives, DeGolyer, SMU (hereafter cited as RTAP); "We Must Now Say Goodbye" is in the same collection, series 5, box 43x, folder 6. For biographical information compiled by Anderson himself, see series 1, box 1, folder 1.

21. Obituary: "Lillian Mecherle McCord," *Pantagraph* (Bloomington, IL), November 6, 1994, p. 46.

22. "Mrs. McCord Gets Emeritus Status," *Pantagraph* (Bloomington), February 9, 1972, p. 2.

23. "Two Wesleyan Students Plan Saybrook Recital," *Pantagraph* (Bloomington), May 17, 1952, p. 5. The unusual nature of the pairing is underscored by the fact that both teacher and pupil are called "students" in the headline.

24. "Five at IWU Get Music Scholarships," *Pantagraph* (Bloomington), May 20, 1952, p. 3.

25. "Robert Anderson to Play Recital," *Pantagraph* (Bloomington), January 6, 1954, p. 9.

26. "Mr. Anderson Elected Head of Phi Mu Alpha," *Pantagraph* (Bloomington), May 9, 1954, p. 24.

27. "Anderson to Give IWU Recital," *Pantagraph* (Bloomington), January 14, 1955, p. 3.

28. Lillian McCord, letter to Anderson, February 22, 1987, series 1, box 1, folder 9, RTAP.

29. "Bass Baritone, Organist to Give Tuesday Recital," *Pantagraph* (Bloomington), January 9, 1955, p. 2.

30. "Frank Bohnhurst," birth and death dates accessible on https://findagrave.com/.

31. See RTAP for a complete list of his compositions. His earliest works, dating from 1950, are a Minuet, "Theme and Variations in G minor," "Bouree in D Major," and Scherzo, all written in classical style for piano. Another composition from 1950, "Midwinter," is an accompanied vocal solo.

32. See series 5, RTAP.

33. Hart, *Day for Dancing*, 59.

34. "Biographical Highlights," series 1, box 1, folder 1, RTAP.

35. Anderson's compositions are all collected in series 5, boxes 43X and 47X, RTAP.

36. Robert Anderson, "Rejoice, the Lord is King," (Carol Stream, IL: Hope, 1983).

37. The pieces noted here can be considered his first "serious" forays into composition, as they come from an undated but probably circa 1956, handwritten list of his own compositions. Presumably, this list includes only the works he considers worthy of public performance.

38. Seth Bingham, letter to Anderson, January 29, 1964, series 2, box 3, folder 33, RTAP.

39. Obituary written by Dorothy Faller, Scott Cantrell, and George Baker, 2009, series 1, box 1, folder 38, RTAP.

40. "Biographical Highlights," series 1, box 1, folder 1, RTAP.

41. "Robert Anderson, To Give Organ Recital at IWU," *Pantagraph* (Bloomington), August 22, 1957, p. 3.

42. For Fleischer's biographical particulars, his student days with Straube, and later publishing concerns, see Ames Anderson, et al., *Perspectives on Organ Playing and Musical Interpretation: Pedagogical, Historical, and Instrumental Studies; A Festschrift*

for Heinrich Fleischer at 90 (New Ulm, Minn.: Graphic Arts, Martin Luther College, 2003).

43. "Helmut Walcha (1907-1991) [Student] Remembrances," Pipedreams, accessed March 28, 2017, http://pipedreams. publicradio.org/articles/biographies/walcha_helmut.shtml.

44. Robert Anderson, "Remembrances of Walcha," series 3, box 4, folder 9, RTAP.

45. Peter Hofmann, "Professor Kurt Thomas–Komponist und Chorleiter," accessed April 18, 2017, http://www.kurtthomas. de/?l=92. There exists little information on this organ, except as recalled here by Hofman, who sang in the choir at the Dreikönigskirche during the 1950s. ("Nachdem die 1949 eingeweihte Orgel von Förster & Nikolaus künstlerischen Ansprüchen nicht mehr genügte, beschloss der Magistrat von Frankfurt Walcha eine neue Orgel zu bauen. Dies hervorragende Werk der Firma Schuke / Berlin wurde 1961 eingeweiht und steht heute noch.") Horst Bruchner states further that Walcha was discontent with the turgid sound of the F & N organ, which, although it had survived the war, was voiced according to romantic principles. Thus, on this fiftieth birthday in 1957, the city of Frankfurt secured the purchase of a new instrument, which Walcha would design as a "Bach Organ"; Donald McDonald and Horst Buchner, emails with the author, April 26, 2017. Undated photographic negatives from Anderson's years with Walcha suggest that at least the façade of the new organ was already complete by 1959.

46. Hofmann, "Professor Kurt Thomas."

47. "Helmut Walcha," Pipedreams.

48. Anderson, letter to his parents, February 19, 1959, series 2, box 2, folder 3, RTAP.

49. Anderson, "Career Highlights," series 1, box 1, folder 1, RTAP.

50. "SMU Organist Joins Local Meet Recitalists," *Shreveport (LA) Times*, June 2, 1963, p. 84. Margaret Dickinson (email with the author, April 17, 2017), whose husband, Melvin, was Anderson's roommate in Frankfurt for one year, also recalled little of his tour, other than it was not common for students to play concerts as Anderson did, and that on the tour "he played [the] Buxtehude E minor prelude and fugue because he lost his copy and

borrowed my volume and marked it up in colors of the rainbow so you could hardly see the notes!"

51. "Organist to Perform Fri. at Calvary," *Clarion-Ledger* (Jackson, MS), April 16, 1964, p. 2. It is not clear whether there were multiple tours or just one, or during which year they occurred, although most of the sources suggest one tour during the spring of 1959. George Klump (email with the author, April 14, 2017) states, "As I recall, that tour was not all that extensive. He indicated to me that he wasn't all that pleased about it."

52. Hugh Porter, letter to Anderson, March 26, 1959, series 2, box 2, folder 40, RTAP.

53. "Biographical Highlights," series 1, box 1, folder 1, RTAP.

54. Lloyd Pfautsch, letter to Anderson, c. late 1959, series 2, box 3, folder 13, RTAP. From the series of letters from Pfautsch to Anderson (only that side of the conversation has been preserved), the historical background of Anderson's visits to Dallas, his concerns, and his job prospect at the University of Chicago can fairly easily be reconstructed.

55. Pfautsch to Anderson, c. late 1959, RTAP.

56. "Dallas-Fort Worth International Airport," Texas State Historical Association, accessed April 2, 2017, https://www.tshaonline.org/handbook/online/articles/epd01.

57. "Services Held for Dr. Jacobs," *SMU Campus*, December 9, 1959, p. 1.

58. Pfautsch to Anderson, December 13, 1959, series 2, box 3, folder 13, RTAP.

59. Hart, *Day for Dancing*, 105.

60. Pfautsch to Anderson, December 13, 1959, RTAP.

61. Richard D. Hoffland, chairman of the Sacred Music Department, Millikin University, letter to Anderson, February 26, 1960, series 2, box 3, folder 36, RTAP.

62. Although Anderson's letter of acceptance to SMU does not survive, his decision was communicated to the administration by May 2, 1960, when Pfautsch writes Anderson a long letter of welcome offering to assist finding housing; series 2, box 3, folder 13, RTAP.

63. Anderson, letter to Eugene Bonelli, May 29, 1969, series 1, box 1, folder 13, RTAP.

64. Pfautsch to Anderson, May 2, 1960, series 2, box 3, folder 13, RTAP.

65. Pfautsch to Anderson, June 7, 1960, series 2, box 3, folder 13, RTAP.

66. Payne, *One Hundred Years*, 176.

67. Payne, *One Hundred Years*, 192.

68. Proposed Stoplist for New SMU Chapel, series 3, box 4, folder 11, RTAP. This seventy-two-stop, 105-rank, mechanical action organ with electric stop action would have a Hauptwerk, Rückpositiv, Brustwerk, Swell, and Pedal divisions. Anderson failed to elucidate on how he proposed building such a sizable instrument in such a small space!

69. Arthur Poister, letter to Anderson, April 21, 1960, series 2, box 3, folder 40, RTAP.

70. Payne, *One Hundred Years*, 193.

71. "Faculty Addition of 29 Brings Teachers to 228," *SMU Campus*, September 23, 1955, p. 8.

72. "Harrell to Join School of Music," *SMU Campus*, February 17, 1956, p. 1.

73. "Master of Music in Piano Performance and Pedagogy @ SMU," SMU Piano Pedagogy Department, accessed January 4, 2023, https://www.smupianopedagogy.org/our-philosophy.

74. "McFarlins Give $250,000 to SMU," *Dallas Morning News*, April 2, 1961, p. 1.

75. Robert Sipe, email with the author, January 25, 2017.

76. "SMU Fine Arts Center Receives $4,000,000," *SMU Campus*, August 29, 1962, p. 1.

77. "Algur Hurtle Meadows," Texas State Historical Association, accessed April 5, 2017, https://tshaonline.org/handbook/online/articles/fmezk.

78. "Forbes Music Building Begins Era," *SMU Campus*, April 23, 1965, p. 2.

79. "Biographical Note," *Willis M. Tate Papers, 1939–1989: A Guide to the Collection*, accessed June 22, 2023, https://txarchives.org/smu/finding_aids/00084.xml. Technically, he would serve uninterrupted until 1971, when he was appointed chancellor, but he briefly resumed the presidency again four years later after the resignation of his successor, Paul Hardin.

80. "Studio Notes," *Dallas Morning News*, May 18, 1932, p. 8.

81. Olin Chism, "Million-Dollar Chair Honors SMU's Joel Estes Tate," *Dallas Times Herald*, December 2, 1984, C-9.

82. "The Woman's Angle," *Dallas Morning News*, May 13, 1954, p. 1.

83. "Metro Report," *Dallas Morning News*, December 7, 1984, p. 28A. The Tate's $500,000 donation would be matched by a grant of the same amount from the Meadows Foundation. According to Barbara Marquart, Mrs. Tate had desired to take organ lessons with Anderson but his schedule already full, so she was passed on to Marquart.

84. Klump, email with the author, April 11, 2017.

85. Roy Redman, email with the author, April 11, 2017.

86. John Hooker, email with the author, April 11, 2017. For information on the General Theological Seminary organ, see the *New York City Organ Project*, Accessed April 17, 2017, http://nycago. org/Organs/NYC/html/GenTheoSem.html.

87. Sterling Wheeler, letter to John Tyrrell, June 13, 1962, series 4, box 6, folder 35, RTAP.

88. Thomas V. Potter, letter to Anderson, March 2, 1962, series 4, box 6, folder 35, RTAP.

89. "Specification of an Organ Prepared for Southern Methodist University Fine Arts Center Recital Hall," March 14, 1962, series 4, box 6, folder 35, RTAP.

90. Joseph Whiteford, letter to Anderson, March 30, 1962, series 4, box 6, folder 35, RTAP.

91. Contract with annotations from Robert Anderson, March 14, 1962, series 4, box 6, folder 35, RTAP.

92. "Specification of an Organ," March 14, 1962, series 4, box 6, folder 35, RTAP.

93. Anderson, "Complete Specification with Additions to Contract. Including Correct Nomenclature," July 9, 1962, series 4, box 6, folder 35, RTAP.

94. Willis Tate, letter to John Tyrrell, August 1, 1962, series 4, box 6, folder 35, RTAP.

95. Anderson, letter to Mark Miller, March 6, 1963, series 4, box 6, folder 35, RTAP.

96. Anderson, letter to John Hansen, April 7, 1964, series 4, box 6, folder 35, RTAP.

97. Anderson to Whiteford, May 10, 1964, series 4, box 6, folder 35, RTAP.

98. Anderson to Whiteford, May 10, 1964, series 4, box 6, folder 35, RTAP.

99. Anderson to Whiteford, May 10, 1964, series 4, box 6, folder 35, RTAP.

100. Anderson to Whiteford, May 10, 1964, series 4, box 6, folder 35, RTAP.

101. Whiteford to Anderson, June 2, 1964, series 4, box 6, folder 35, RTAP.

102. Whiteford to Anderson, June 2, 1964, series 4, box 6, folder 35, RTAP.

103. Retrieved from "Organ Index: Frankfurt am Main/Sachsenhausen, Dreikönigskirche," Organ Index, accessed July 4, 2022, https://organindex.de/index.php?title=Frankfurt_(Main)/Sachsenhausen,_Dreik%C3%B6nigskirche_(Hauptorgel).

104. Anderson to Whiteford, May 2, 1965, series 4, box 6, folder 35, RTAP.

105. Anderson to Tyrrell, May 2, 1965, ibid.

106. Klump, email with the author, April 11, 2017. Dr. Klump arrived at SMU during the summer of 1965 when the organ was in the midst of installation.

107. Klump, email with the author.

108. This description of the organ and controlled acoustical environment is found in the program materials printed for the Caruth Aeolian-Skinner's dedication program in 1965, series 4, box 6, folder 39, RTAP.

109. Dedication program, series 4, box 6, folder 39, RTAP.

110. "Dedication Slated for New Organ," Dallas Morning News, September 26, 1965, p. 8.

111. "Dedication Slated for New Organ."

112. "Remarks at Hamilton Dinner," series 1, box 22, folder 8, Willis M. Tate Papers, SMU Archives, DeGolyer, SMU.

113. Olin Chism, "Million-dollar chair honors SMU's Joel Estes Tate," Dallas Times Herald, December 2, 1984, p. C-9.

114. Dedication program, series 4, box 6, folder 39, RTAP.

115. Anderson to Whiteford, May 2, 1965, series 4, box 6, folder 35, RTAP.

116. Richard Jackson, "Dello Joio, Norman," Grove Music Online, accessed June 22, 2023, https://www-oxfordmusiconline-com.ezproxy.tcu.edu/grovemusic/view/10.1093/gmo/9781561592630.001.0001/omo-9781561592630-e-0000007496.

117. Norman Dello Joio, letter to Anderson, December 13, 1965, series 2, box 2, folder 26, RTAP.

118. William Payne, "Ovation Turns Salute to Organ," Dallas Morning News, October 18, 1965, p. 19.

119. Payne, "Ovation Turns Salute to Organ."

120. "Assistant Professor Receives Degree," *SMU Campus*, June 22, 1961, p. 1.

121. Peggy Bie, "Dora Poteet Barclay," blog, accessed April 18, 2017, http://www.oocities.org/~peggybie/Students.html. Dr. Carlton Young, former director of the MSM program, also recalled antipathy from some of Barclay's students.

122. *Southern Methodist University Annual Catalogue: Part V* (Dallas: SMU, 1961), 64.

123. *SMU Annual Catalogue: Part V*, 65.

124. "Season of 4 Events Dated by Organists," *Dallas Morning News*, October 24, 1965, p. 4.

125. "Noted Italian Organist Will Play at SMU," *Dallas Morning News*, December 21, 1965, p. 17.

126. "French Organist to Play at SMU Tuesday," *Dallas Morning News*, October 25, 1966, p. 7.

127. "SMU Orchestra Has Duruflé as Soloist for Wednesday," *Dallas Morning News*, October 26, 1966, p. 8.

128. Robert Anderson, typed remembrances, "Marie-Madeleine Duruflé," series 3, box 6, folder 5, RTAP.

129. Anderson, "Duruflé," RTAP.

130. Anderson, "Duruflé," RTAP.

131. Anderson, "Duruflé," RTAP.

132. "Lecture and Recital Set by Famed French Organist," *Dallas Morning News*, March 4, 1964, p. 6.

133. "Dallas Guild to Hear Blind Organist Play," *Dallas Morning News*, April 5, 1967, p. 15.

134. "SMU Schedules Lady Susi Jeans," *Dallas Morning News*, February 2, 1967, p. 3.

135. "Finn Viderø to Play Here Friday for Organist Guild," *Dallas Morning News*, April 17, 1968, p. 10.

136. The *Southern Methodist University Annual Catalogues* list all adjunct music faculty for those years.

137. This is a handwritten note found in series 1, box 1, folder 13, RTAP.

138. Klump, email with the author, April 9, 2017.

139. C. Michael Hawn, "Carlton R. Young," *Canterbury Dictionary of Hymnology*, accessed February 13, 2018, http://www.hymnology.co.uk.proxy.libraries.smu.edu/c/carlton-r-young.

140. Anderson, typewritten memo, "Southern Methodist University Owen Fine Arts Center Organs," series 4, box 6, folder 33, RTAP.

141. Sipe, email with the author, April 2017.

142. Lawrence Phelps, letter to Anderson, March 20, 1964, series 4, box 7, folder 5, RTAP.

143. Anderson, "SMU Owen Fine Arts Center Organs," series 4, box 6, folder 33, RTAP.

144. Sipe, email with the author, January 25, 2017.

145. Walter Holtkamp Jr., letter to Anderson, June 9, 1964, series 4, box 6, folder 34, RTAP.

146. Anderson to Holtkamp, July 27, 1968, series 4, box 6, folder 34, RTAP.

147. From the author.

148. Pfautsch to Anderson, c. late 1959, series 2, box 3, folder 13, RTAP.

149. Anderson, "Career Highlights," series 1, box 1, folder 1, RTAP.

150. "SMU Organist Joins Local Meet Recitalists," *Shreveport Times*, June 2, 1963, p. 84.

151. "Robert Anderson Plays for Guild," *Dallas Morning News*, July 11, 1964, p. 14.

152. "Organ Event Will Benefit Music Fund," *Dallas Morning News*, June 14, 1966, p. 13.

153. "Wesleyan Plans Organ Workshop," *Pantagraph* (Bloomington), May 19, 1968, p. 45.

154. "Dr. Anderson Will Present SMU Organ Concert Tuesday," *Dallas Morning News*, February 24, 1969, p. 10.

155. "SMU Will Hold Church Music Seminar," *Dallas Morning News*, December 26, 1967, p. 31.

156. "Church Gets Rare Organ," *Dallas Morning News*, September 16, 1963, p. 6.

157. "Convocation Address," August 30, 1990, series 1, box 1, folder 22, RTAP.

Chapter 6

1. "40 Teachers Added to Growing Faculty," *SMU Campus*, September 16, 1964, p. 1; "Kermit Hunter," *New York Times* obituaries, April 26, 2001, https://www.nytimes.com/2001/04/26/arts/kermit-hunter-historical-dramatist-90.html.

2. Kermit Hunter, letter to Willis Tate, June 14, 1966, Willis Tate Correspondence, 1965–1976, SMU Archives, DeGolyer, SMU (hereafter cited as WTC).

3. Hunter to Tate, August 24, 1966, WTC.

4. Hunter to Tate, June 29, 1967, WTC.

5. H. Neill McFarland, letter to Hunter, April 18, 1967, p. 3, WTC.

6. Hunter to Tate, May 25, 1967, WTC.

7. Hunter to Tate, January 16, 1967, p. 2, WTC.

8. Tate, letter to Robert Anderson, November 2, 1967, series 2, box 3, folder 22, RTAP.

9. Anderson, letter to John Tyrrell, December 9, 1965, series 4, box 6, folder 38, RTAP.

10. Anderson, letter to Donald Gillette and Roy Perry, December 20, 1965, series 4, box 6, folder 38, RTAP.

11. Anderson to Gillette and Perry, December 20, 1965, series 4, box 6, folder 38, RTAP.

12. M. A. Gariepy, letter to George Bushong, July 11, 1967, series 4, box 6, folder 38, RTAP.

13. Gariepy, letter to Anderson, June 14, 1968, series 4, box 6, folder 38, RTAP.

14. Gillette to Anderson, June, 27 1969, series 4, box 6, folder 38, RTAP.

15. George Klump, email to the author, April 8, 2017.

16. Klump, email.

17. An undated list of improvements Anderson specified for Aeolian-Skinner to address during this era is found in series 4, box 6, folder 38, RTAP.

18. John Tyrell, "Speech to the 1995 AIO Convention in San Jose, California," accessed June 22, 2023, https://organhistoricalsociety. org/aeolianskinner/john_tyrrell_transcript2.html.

19. Thomas V. Potter, letter to Anderson, January 16, 1969, series 4, box 6, folder 38, RTAP.

20. Hunter, letter to Mrs Harold Byrd, September 9, 1971, series 4, box 7, folder 1, RTAP.

21. Anderson to Hastings Harrison, undated, series 4, box 7, folder 1, RTAP.

22. "Organist Robert Anderson Named IWU Alumnus of the Year," *Pantagraph* (Normal, IL), April 16, 1972, p. A-7.

23. "James Tallis," obituary, *Diapason* 20, no. 12 (November 1969): 18.

24. Peter Planyavsky, *Anton Heiller: Organist, Conductor, Composer* (Rochester: University of Rochester Press, 2014), 78. See also *SMU Catalogue, 1969–1970* (Dallas: SMU Press), 154.

25. Advertisement in the *SMU Campus*, October 25, 1968, p. 9. The couple performed a concert of "Italian music for harpsichord and voice." The local media at the time advertised quite a number of their joint recitals.

26. Larry Palmer, *The Harpsichord in America* (Bloomington: Indiana University Press, 1989), 167.

27. Anderson, letter to Don Gillis, October 8, 1967, series 1, box 1, folder 13, RTAP.

28. "James Hathaway Tallis," Find a Grave, accessed January 9, 2018, https://www.findagrave.com/memorial/99309444/james-hathaway-tallis.

29. Recollections of Barbara Marquart, email to the author, April 8, 2017.

30. James Tallis, "Sonatina for Organ" (Chapel Hill: Hinshaw, 1976). There are several instances in the 1970s of SMU organ students playing this piece in their degree recitals.

31. "Trustee Board Ratifies New Appointments," *Daily Campus*, June 11, 1970, p. 1.

32. Larry Palmer, *Letters from Salzburg: A Music Student in Europe, 1958–1959* (Eau Claire, WI: Skyline, 2006), XV.

33. McFarland, letter to Anderson, May 14, 1971, series 2, box 3, folder 24, RTAP.

34. Paul C. Echols and Maria V. Coldwell, "Early-Music Revival," *Grove Music Online*, accessed March 18, 2018, https://doi-org.proxy.libraries.smu.edu/10.1093/gmo/9781561592630.article.A2235052.

35. *SMU Bulletin, 1973–74* (Dallas: SMU Press, 1973), 146.

36. *SMU Bulletin, 1974–75* (Dallas: SMU Press, 1974), 163.

37. *SMU Bulletin, 1976–77* (Dallas: SMU Press, 1976), 134.

38. "Inaugural Concert on the New Harpsichord," printed program of February 16, 1975, series 4, box 12, folder 6, Meadows Records.

39. "The Early Music Society of Southern Methodist University presents Songs of Spain in the Middle Ages and Renaissance," printed program of April 21, 1972, series 4, box 12, folder 5, Meadows Records.

40. "George Baker, Organist," personal website, accessed February 17, 2018, http://www.drgeorgebaker.com/organist/.

41. "George Baker: Master of Improvisation," *Tampa Tribune*, October 17, 1975, p. 56.

42. Wolfgang Rübsam, "Biography," personal website, accessed February 9, 2018, https://www.wolfgangrubsam.com/biography.

43. "Robert Bates," *Gothic*, accessed June 22, 2023, https://www.gothic-catalog.com/Robert_Bates_s/574.htm.

44. Award Winning Organist to Perform, *Orlando Sentinel*, January 22, 1982, p. 31.

45. "June Music Bustin' Out," *Dallas Morning News*, June 18, 1972, p. 1.

46. "AGO National Convention 1972: Dallas TX, June 18–24," *Diapason* 63, no. 9 (August 1972): 3.

47. "AGO National Convention 1972," 3.

48. Anderson to Gillette and Perry, December 20, 1965, series 4, box 6, folder 38, RTAP.

49. Vincent Persichetti, letter to Anderson, July 6, 1972, series 2, box 3, folder 12, RTAP.

50. "AGO National Convention 1972," 2. The piece is about 12 minutes long.

51. Persichetti to Anderson, series 2, box 3, folder 12, RTAP.

52. "AGO National Convention 1972," 2.

53. "AGO National Convention 1972," 2. The concert was held at Palmer's church, St Luke's Episcopal. In addition to the Bach BWV 903, the musicians performed Lester Trimble's (1923–1986) *Four Fragments from the Canterbury Tales* and the "Concertino for Flute, Viola, Cello, Harp and Harpsichord" by Vittorio Rieti (1898–1994).

54. "SMU Music Department Plans Summer Seminar," *Dallas Morning News*, May 14, 1972, p. 4.

55. "Organ Recital and Convocation," November 2, 1976. Program in the possession of this author.

56. "Honorary Degrees: 1918–Present," SMU, accessed, March 21, 2020, https://sites.smu.edu/des/registrar/HonoraryDegrees/?a=name.

57. Anderson, "Revision and Up-Dating of the Organ Facilities at Southern Methodist University. A Proposal Submitted by Dr. Robert Anderson, Professor of Organ," October 19, 1974, series 4, box 6, folder 32, RTAP.

58. Details on each of these organs are available at the OHS: www. pipeorgandatabase.com.
59. Lawrence Phelps, "A Short History of the Organ Revival," *Church Music*, no. 67 (1967): 27.
60. For a history of this organ, see the church website, "Our Story: The Organ," MMPC Albany, accessed June 22, 2023, https://mmpcalbany.org/history.
61. "European Organ Study Tour, 1971," mimeographed booklet, series 3, box 6, folder 20, RTAP.
62. Anderson to Charles Fisk, June 10, 1974, series 4, box 6, folder 32, RTAP.
63. "October 19, 1974 organ stoplist and proposal of Robert Anderson," series 4, box 6, folder 32, RTAP.
64. Bob Sipe, letter to Karl Schuke, July 27, 1974, series 4, box 6, folder 32, RTAP.
65. Alfred Kern, letter to Sipe, July 19, 1974, series 4, box 6, folder 32, RTAP.
66. Schuke to Sipe, July 10, 1974, series 4, box 6, folder 32, RTAP.
67. J. (?) Metzler, letter to Sipe, June 27, 1974, series 4, box 6, folder 32, RTAP: "Da wir gegenwärtig grosse Personalschwierigkeiten . . . bei gleichzeitig hohm Auftragsbestand, ist es uns leider night noch in nächster zeit grössere Arbeiten zu übernehmen."
68. Donald V. Corbett, letter to Sipe, July 9, 1974. Ibid. Brunzema had been appointed tonal director of Casavant in the spring of 1972.
69. Josef von Glatter-Götz, letter to Anderson, July 24, 1974, series 4, box 6, folder 32, RTAP.
70. Glatter-Götz to Anderson, July 24, 1974.
71. Glatter-Götz to Anderson, July 24, 1974.
72. Paul Gunzelmann, letter to Anderson, November 19, 1974, series 4, box 6, folder 32, RTAP.
73. Anderson to Fisk, November 17, 1974, series 4, box 6, folder 32, RTAP.
74. Anderson, letter to Perkins dean Joseph Quillian Jr., November 21, 1961, series 3, box 4, folder 11, RTAP. Anderson prefaces his letter saying, "Due to the . . . fact that I have only recently felt that I know the organ intimately and completely, I present these suggestions at this time." He proposed mechanical work "brought on by deterioration of minor parts" and "minor tonal alterations." In a letter from January 20, 1962, Roy Perry

responds that "we regret that it [the Perkins Chapel organ] has been somewhat neglected in its first ten years"; series 3, box 4, folder 11, RTAP.

75. Anderson, letter to O. G. Folsomo, March 28, 1972, series 4, box 6, folder 32, RTAP.

76. Anderson to Folsomo, March 28, 1972.

77. Anderson to Fisk, June 10, 1974, series 4, box 6, folder 32, RTAP.

78. Memo "Repairs or Improvements to the Organ." The memo is undated, but is within the context of correspondence from 1965, series 4, box 6, folder 32, RTAP.

79. The smaller specification is handwritten, the larger is typed. Although undated, the surrounding material is from the 1970s. In his letter to Charles Fisk of June 10, 1974, Anderson acknowledged that an "RP is a problem in regard to the space available, and the traditional BW placement of the second division will be almost mandatory." The use of the same nomenclature suggests this stoplist had been sent to Fisk for comment; series 4, box 6, folder 32, RTAP.

80. Laukhuff contract, May 13, 1977, series 4, box 6, folder 32, RTAP.

81. Terry, *From High on the Hilltop*, 51.

82. "Spiraling Energy Cost Boosting Utility Fee," *Daily Campus*, November 16, 1976, p. 1.

83. Hunter, letter to Charles and Kitty Trigg, December 4, 1975, p. 1, WTC.

84. Hunter to Triggs, December 4, 1975, p. 2.

85. Hunter to Triggs, December 4, 1975, p. 2

86. The couple would end up donating $10 million to build the SMU student center, which was hence accordingly named after them; Ross McSwain, "Mertzon Couple Funds SMU Facility," *San Angelo Standard-Times*, November 1, 1987, p. 2.

87. "Meadows School of the Arts Master Plan, October, 1973," Exhibit A, 1 of 3, Hillerbrand Subj. Files, #4–5, "Arts General," Southern Methodist University Provost's Operational Records, 1972–1986, SMU Archives, DeGolyer, SMU (hereafter cited as Provost's Records).

88. "Meadows School of the Arts Master Plan," Exhibit A, 2 of 3.

89. Hunter, memo to James Brooks, c. 1973, Hillerbrand Subj. Files, #4–5, "Meadows Budget, 1973–1985," Provost's Records.

90. Hunter, memo to Brooks, January 30, 1975, Brooks Subj. Files, #26, "Arts General, 1972–1973," Provost's Records.

91. "Final Report of the Music Task Force, November 5, 1980," p. 9, Hillerbrand Subj. Files, #4–5, "Music Division," Provost's Records.

92. Anderson, letter to William Hipp, March 26, 1976, series 1, box 1, folder 13, RTAP.

93. Anderson to Hipp, March 26, 1976, pp. 2, 6, 7

94. Anderson to Hipp, March 26, 1976, p. 1

95. Anderson to Hipp, March 26, 1976, p. 9

96. "Confidential Memo" from Eugene Bonelli, dean, January 13, 1981, Hillerbrand Subj. Files, #4–5, "Music Division," Provost's Records.

97. Michael Fleming, "Expert Help Re-Establishes Power of the Harpsichord," *Fort Worth Star-Telegram*, May 18, 1983, p. 19.

Chapter 7

1. Eugene Bonelli, memo, June 17, 1983, series 4, box 6, folder 40, RTAP.

2. Leroy Howe, memo, "Reflection Prior to Our Fall Meeting," July 24, 1991, series 1, box 1, folder 20, RTAP.

3. Robert Anderson, letter to Eugene Bonelli, June 2, 1986, series 1, box 1, folder 20, RTAP.

4. Anderson, letter to Hans Hillerbrand, September 12, 1983, series 1, box 1, folder 20, RTAP.

5. See folder of "Concert Tours, 1967–1995," series 1, box 1, folder 14, RTAP.

6. Anderson, "Career Highlights," series 1, box 1, folder 19, RTAP.

7. Becky Shockley, "Meadows Gets $1 Million Chair," *Daily Campus*, November 21, 1984, p. 1.

8. Camille Johnson, "Pianist Joselson Becomes First Tate Chair Holder," *Daily Campus*, October 7, 1986, p. 4.

9. See "About Joaquín Achúcarro," Joaquín Achúcarro Foundation, accessed December 29, 2019, https://www.achucarrofoundation. org/about,.

10. Jani Leuschel, "Meadows Adds Baroque Organ," *Daily Campus*, December 6, 1984, p. 5.

11. Anderson, letter to Susan Tattershall, March 15, 1975, series 4, box 7, folder 7, RTAP.

12. Anderson to Tattershall, March 15, 1975.

13. Anderson to Tattershall, March 15, 1975.

14. Guy Bovet, emails with the author, December 2019.

15. Jani Leuschel, "Meadows Adds Baroque Organ," *Daily Campus*, December 6, 1984, p. 5.

16. Maarten Vente, letter to Anderson, June 22, 1983, series 4, box 7, folder 7, RTAP. Although the letter is addressed to "Dear Sir," subsequent correspondence suggests Anderson knew of this opportunity before Bonelli did, and that the letter was to Anderson.

17. J. A. Steketee, director for Flentrop Orgelbau, letter to Anderson, April 11, 1984, series 4, box 7, folder 7, RTAP.

18. Vente to Anderson, June 22, 1983.

19. Susan Tattershall, emails with the author, February 2020.

20. Leuschel, "Meadows Adds Baroque Organ."

21. Larry Palmer, "The Portugese Baroque Organ in the Meadows Museum," typewritten manuscript, series 4, box 7, folder 7, RTAP.

22. "Caetano Organ Inaugural Concert," December 2, 1984, program booklet, series 4, box 7, folder 7, RTAP.

23. See "Alfred Kern et Fils (1979)," *OHS Pipe Organ Database*, accessed June 22, 2023, https://pipeorgandatabase.org/Organ-Details.php?OrganID=3148, for details on this sixty-nine-rank, three-manual instrument.

24. Leuschel, "Meadows Adds Baroque Organ."

25. Leuschel, "Meadows Adds Baroque Organ."

26. "Arts News," press release from Meadows School of the Arts, January 3, 1984, series 4, box 7, folder 7, RTAP.

27. Leuschel, "Meadows Adds Baroque Organ."

28. Leuschel, "Meadows Adds Baroque Organ."

29. Shazia Azra Aslam, "Dallas Turns Out for Opening of New Meadows Museum," *Daily Campus*, March 27, 2001, p. 10.

30. Palmer, "Fall Organ Festival."

31. The only central location to search for dates and an itemized list of organs in Dallas via time period is the *OHS Pipe Organ Database*, https://pipeorgandatabase.org/.

32. Anderson, "Robert Anderson Organ Students as of January 1985," typewritten manuscript, series 1, box 1, folder 13, RTAP.

33. David H. Fox, *A Guide to North American Organbuilders: Compiled from Historical Sources and the Work of Various Researchers* (Richmond, VA: Organ Historical Society, 1991), 213.

34. Grimes, *History of the Perkins School of Theology*, 96ff.

35. "Organs," Schudi Organ Company, accessed February 21, 2020, http://www.schudi.com/organs.

36. "The Schudi Pipe Organ," St. Thomas Aquinas Catholic Church, accessed January 1, 2020 https://www.stthomasaquinas.org/music/schudi-pipe-organ.

37. Lawson Taitte, "Master of the Meyerson Organ Paul Riedo Brings Impressive Credentials to New Post with DSO," *Dallas Morning News*, July 5, 1992, p. 1C.

38. Taitte, "After a Long Recital, SMU's New Organ Pipes Up Today," *Dallas Morning News*, September 19, 1993, p. 6C.

39. Guy Bovet, emails with the author, December 2019.

40. "Architect IM Pei to Design Dallas Symphony Concert Hall," *Los Angeles Times*, January 18, 1981, p. 173.

41. Andrea Weisgerber, "Dallas Concert Hall Comes with World-Class Price Tag," *Houston Chronicle*, September 3, 1989, p. 11.

42. Notes of organ subcommittee meeting of April 13, 1982, issued by the Dallas Symphony Association, series 4, box 7, folder 12, RTAP.

43. Organ subcommittee meeting, April 13, 1982.

44. Organ subcommittee meeting, April 13, 1982.

45. Olin Chism, "Organist Is a Major Key to Dallas Competition," *Dallas Morning News*, April 10, 1997, p. 1C.

46. For example, see "Minutes" of the meeting at the IM Pei office, NYC, on September 10, 1986, series 4, box 7, folder 16, RTAP.

47. Wayne Lee Gay, "Pulling Out All the Stops: The Magnificent New Organ at the Meyerson Symphony Center Is Ready at Last," *Fort Worth Star-Telegram*, August 30, 1992, p. 1.

48. Edwin L. Cox School of Business Faculty listing, SMU, accessed March 21, 2020, https://catalog.smu.edu/content.php?catoid=14&navoid=524.

49. "Opus 100," C. B. Fisk, accessed March 1, 2020, http://cbfisk.com/opus/opus-100/.

50. Anderson, letter to Virginia Fisk, December 20, 1984, series 4, box 7, folder 1, RTAP.

51. Bonelli, letter to V. Fisk, June 23, 1985, with an enclosed check for $92,000, series 4, box 7, folder 1, RTAP. The initial contract specified an overall price of $618,000, subject to inflation.

52. Anderson, letter to "Carol," September 21, 1986, series 4, box 7, folder 1, RTAP.

53. Anderson to Bonelli, April 28, 1985, series 4, box 7, folder 1, RTAP.

54. Anderson, letter to Steve Dieck, March 10, 1992, series 4, box 7, folder 3, RTAP.

55. This writer learned of Anderson's surgery from Frau Virginia Abdo, his first-period German teacher, who happened to be a friend of Robert Anderson.

56. Susan Ferré, "Fisk Dedication at SMU: A Review," *Diapason* 85, no. 4 (March 1994): 10.

57. John Ardoin, "SMU Organ Makes an Impressive Debut: Inaugural Concert Transcends Absence of Key Performer," *Dallas Morning News*, September 20, 1993, p. 23A.

58. Ferré, "Fisk Dedication at SMU."

59. Taitte, "New Organ's Heart, Sole: High-Heeled Alain Brings out Beauty in SMU's New Pipes," *Dallas Morning News*, September 25, 1993, p. 38A.

60. Ferré, "Fisk Dedication at SMU."

61. From the author.

62. *Why KSPL?*, C. B. Fisk, accessed February 15, 2020, http://cbfisk.com/wp-content/uploads/2019/06/cb-fisk-why-KSPL.pdf.

63. Printed program, "Joint Recital/Joint Dedication Recital: Robert Anderson/Larry Palmer," September 19, 1993, author's copy.

64. "Specification 2: Caruth Auditorium," series 3, box 7, folder 1, RTAP.

65. The wind stabilizer as originally installed was activated when the draw-knob was pulled, the organ's default position being unstable wind. In subsequent years this was reversed, and pulling the draw-knob now *activates* the unstable wind.

66. All subsequent programs for that autumn were printed in the dedication program book.

67. "Michael Farris," Eastman School of Music, accessed February 22, 2020, https://www.esm.rochester.edu/about/portraits/farris/.

68. Taitte, "Organ Springs to Life under Bovet's Touch," *Dallas Morning News*, November 20, 1993, p. 35A.

69. Inside, front cover of September 19 dedication program.

70. Charles Brenton Fisk, letter to Anderson, May 14, 1974, series 4, box 7, folder 13, RTAP.

71. Taitte, "No More Pipe Dreams: Dallas Day as an Organ Mecca Has Come," *Dallas Morning News*, September 19, 1993, p. 1C.

72. Taitte, "Pulling Out All the Stops: Convention Goers Will Hear an Aray of Organs and Artists in the Dallas Area," *Dallas Morning News*, July 10, 1994, p. 1C.

73. Taitte, "Pulling Out All the Stops."

74. Taitte, "Pulling Out All the Stops."

75. John Ardoin, "Susa Brings Church Opera to Convention," *Dallas Morning News*, July 10, 1994, p. 8C.

76. Wayne Lee Gay, "Organ Gets New Respect in Dallas Competition," *Fort Worth Star-Telegram*, April 7, 1997, p. 1.

77. John Ardoin, "Pipes Dream: First Notes Sound in Long-Awaited Organ Competition," *Dallas Morning News*, April 4, 1997, p. 30. Jury member Ludger Lohman had to resign from the jury for health reasons.

78. Ardoin, "Pipes Dream."

79. Gay, "Dallas Takes to Organs Like Fort Worth Takes to Pianos," *Fort Worth Star-Telegram*, January 26, 1996, p. 20. Ward Lay expressed hopes this event would become the "Super Bowl" of organ competitions!

80. Ardoin, "Pipes Dream."

81. Gay, "Organ Gets New Respect in Dallas Competition," *Fort Worth Star-Telegram*, April 7, 1997, p. 1. The Cliburn, of course, still offered the prestige that only an established competition could impart. The additional benefits offered to Cliburn laureates, such as performances and recording contracts, still easily eclipsed those of the Dallas competition.

82. Gay, "Organ Gets New Respect."

83. Scott Cantrell, "Local Hero Triumphs: Organist Welch Takes Top Prize with Bold Playing," *Dallas Morning News*, March 19, 2003, p. 31A.

84. Cantrell, "Served Piping Hot: Organist Sees Churchly Instrument Gathering Mainstream Steam," *Dallas Morning News*, April 7, 2002, p. 1C.

85. Jerome Weeks, "Fresh Air in the Meadows: New Dean Carole Brandt Brings Verve and Vision to the Challenges Facing the SMU Arts School," *Dallas Morning News*, August 28, 1994, p. 1C.

86. "Speech For Heart Patient of the Year Award," series 1, box 1, folder 29, RTAP.

87. "Heart Patient of the Year Award."

88. William Babcock, provost, letter to Anderson, May 21, 1996, Series 1, Box 1, Folder 28, RTAP.

89. Anderson, letter to Phillip Truckenbrod, June 3, 1996, series 1, box 1, folder 28, RTAP.

90. Contract for adjunct teaching issued August 15, 1996, series 1, box 1, folder 28, RTAP.

91. Cantrell, "Robert T. Anderson Led Organ Music Education at SMU," *Dallas Morning News*, June 2, 2009, p. 5B.

92. Cantrell, " Anderson Led Organ Music Education."

93. "Remembrances," series 1, box 1, folder 37, RTAP. This is a collection of emails and notes collected in a seven-page typed document.

94. Carlton Young, "Remembrances Given by Carlton R. Young in the Memorial Service for Robert Theodore Anderson, 1934–2009," Tuesday, September 22, 2009, Perkins Chapel, SMU, Dallas, TX. Typed document sent to the author from Young. A copy is also kept in series 1, box 1, folder 37, RTAP.

95. Young, "Remembrances."

96. "Remembrances."

97. Cantrell, "Vital Organs: Meyerson Instrument Has Set Standard for Other Concert Halls," *Dallas Morning News*, March 12, 2000, p. 1C.

98. "Opus 114," C. B. Fisk, accessed February 22, 2020, http://cbfisk.com/opus/opus-114/.

99. Cantrell, "Vital Organs."

Chapter 8

1. Larry Palmer, "Giving Thanks from A to Z, Part 2: Moving to Dallas (1970)," *Diapason* 110, no. 12 (November 2019): 21.

2. Palmer, "Giving Thanks."

3. "Harpsichord Recital Set," *Daily Campus*, November 5, 1970, p. 3.

4. Palmer, "Giving Thanks."

5. "Arts Center Plays On," *Daily Campus*, May 8, 1979, p. 5.

6. Palmer, "Giving Thanks."

7. Allan Kozinn, "Gustav Leonhardt, Master Harpsichordist Dies at 83," *New York Times*, January 18, 2012, p. A22.

8. Edward Gillilam, "Harpsichord Professor Leads Varied Life," *Daily Campus*, September 27, 1985, p. 7.

9. James Darling, "Professor Traces Resurgence of Harpsichord in America," *Daily Press* (Newport News, VA), July 16, 1989, p. 113.

10. Elizabeth Sheen, "Harpsichordists Play Bach," *Daily Campus*, February 19, 1985, p. 6.

11. Larry Palmer, "Program Planning," *Diapason*, August 28, 2019, https://www.thediapason.com/content/harpsichord-notes-18.

12. Mirabella Anca Minut, "Style and Compositional Techniques in Vincent Persichetti's Ten Sonatas for Harpsichord," (DMA diss., Ball State University, 2009), 70, accessed March 20, 2020, https://cardinalscholar.bsu.edu/bitstream/handle/123456789/193434/Mminut_2009-1_BODY.pdf;sequence=1; Palmer, "Giving Thanks."

13. Palmer, "Giving Thanks from A to Z, Part 2: Moving to Dallas (1970)," November 25, 2019, https://www.thediapason.com/content/harpsichord-notes-21.

14. Palmer, "Three-Score and Ten: Celebrating Richard Kingston," *Diapason* (May 2017): 12.

15. Michael Hawn and Carlton Young, "Perkins School of Theology, Southern Methodist University," *Canterbury Dictionary of Hymnology*, Canterbury Press, accessed March 5, 2020, http://www.hymnology.co.uk/p/perkins-school-of-theology,-southern-methodist-university.

16. Young, "Jane Manton Marshall," *Canterbury Dictionary of Hymnology*, Canterbury Press, accessed March 5, 2020, http://www.hymnology.co.uk/j/jane-manton-marshall.

17. Sam Hodges, "Jane Marshall, Revered Composer, Dies," United Methodist News Service, May 30, 2019, https://www.umnews.org/en/news/jane-marshall-revered-composer-dies-at-94.

18. Young, "Natalie Sleeth," *Canterbury Dictionary of Hymnology*, Canterbury Press, accessed March 5, 2020, http://www.hymnology.co.uk/n/natalie-sleeth.

19. Young, "Roger N. Deschner," *Canterbury Dictionary of Hymnology*, Canterbury Press, accessed March 5, 2020, http://www.hymnology.co.uk/r/roger-n-deschner.

20. CV provided to the author by Kenneth Hart.

21. "Christopher Anderson," SMU faculty profile, accessed March 18, 2020, https://www.smu.edu/Meadows/AreasOfStudy/Music/Faculty/AndersonChristopher.

22. Robert Miller, "Perots' Gift Endows SMU Chair," *Dallas Morning News*, May 5, 2011, p. D02.

23. "Stefan Engels," SMU faculty profile, accessed March 18, 2020, https://www.smu.edu/Meadows/AreasOfStudy/Music/Faculty/EngelsStefan.

24. "Stunning Organ by German Master Builder Rudolf Janke Donated to Meadows by Wolfgang Rübsam," Meadows School of the Arts press release, November 21, 2014,https://www.smu.edu/Meadows/NewsAndEvents/News/2014/141121-StunningOrganDonatedToMeadows.

25. From the author.

26. "Recommendations of the Chapel Renovation Committee, Perkins School of Theology," undated but probably ca. 1996, series 3, box 4, folder 11, RTAP.

27. "Dedication to Honor City Couple: Courtyard at SMU to Honor Prothros," *Wichita Falls Times Record News*, September 5, 1999, p. A4.

28. "George Baker, Biography," personal website, accessed March 9, 2020, http://drgeorgebaker.com/biography/.

29. Robert Miller, "Physician Adding MBA to Disciplines of Medicine, Music," *Dallas Morning News*, June 29, 1997, p. 2H.

30. "Bach to Joplin: Organist's Varied New CD to Benefit Perkins Instrument," *Dallas Morning News*, December 27, 1997, p. 6G.

31. From the author.

32. "The Rice Memorial Organ–Specification (2000)," accessed March 15, 2020, http://organweb.com/specs/All-Saints-Aeolian-Skinner-May2010.pdf

33. "The Inaugural Recital Celebrating the Renovation of the Aeolian-Skinner Pipe Organ in Perkins Chapel," program booklet, courtesy of George Baker.

34. Scott Cantrell, "Organist Turns Up Ooh La La: Lefebvre's Chapel Visit Is Delightfully French," *Dallas Morning News*, May 3, 2000, p. 29A.

35. From the author.

36. Stefan Engels and Jason Alden, "SMU A Ownership of Significant Historic 1927, E. M. Skinner No. 563 Organ," Meadows School of the Arts press release, accessed March 22, 2020, https://www.smu.edu/Meadows/NewsAndEvents/News/2019/SMU-gains-ownership-of-historic-organ.

37. "Skinner Organ Co. (Opus 563, 1927), *OHS Pipe Organ Database*, accessed June 22, 2023, https://pipeorgandatabase.org/organ/8292.

38. Stoplists and locations for all Skinner organs are available at https://organhistoricalsociety.org/aeolianskinner/ (accessed June 22, 2023).

39. Haig Mardirosian, *The Organ on Campus* (New York: American Guild of Organists, 2018), 8.

40. Mardirosian, *Organ on Campus*, 9.

41. "Pulling Out All the Stops for Organ Program," *Chicago Tribune*, February 29, 2004, https://www.chicagotribune.com/news/ct-xpm-2004-02-29-0402290477-story.html.

42. Mardirosian, *Organ on Campus*, 6.

43. Susan R. Masters, "Luther Seminary Indefinitely Suspends Its Sacred Music Master's Program," Minneapolis/St. Paul: Metro Lutheran, December 31, 2012, https://metrolutheran.org/2012/12/luther-seminary-indefinitely-suspends-its-sacred-music-masters-program/.

44. Ray Hardman, "Hartt School Winds Down Organ Program, Sells Pipe Organ," *Connecticut Public Radio*, April 30, 2015, https://www.ctpublic.org/arts-and-culture/2015-04-30/hartt-school-winds-down-organ-program-sells-pipe-organ.

45. Scott Cantrell, "Sound Investments," *Dallas Morning News*, April 18, 2010, p. E01.

Bibliography

Archives

Aeolian-Skinner Archives at the Organ Historical Society, Villanova, PA.

American Guild of Organists Archives, New York, NY.

Brattleboro Historical Society, Brattleboro, VT.

Dorothy Amann Papers. Southern Methodist University Archives, DeGolyer Library, SMU, Dallas, TX.

Eugene B. Hawk Papers. Bridwell Library, Perkins School of Theology, SMU, Dallas, TX.

Franklin D. Roosevelt Library, Hyde Park, NY.

Fred D. Gealy Papers. Bridwell Library, Perkins School of Theology, SMU, Dallas, TX.

Meadows School of the Arts Records. Southern Methodist University Archives, DeGolyer Library, SMU, Dallas, TX.

Merrimon Cuninggim Papers. Bridwell Library, Perkins School of Theology, SMU, Dallas, TX.

Perkins School of Theology Records. Southern Methodist University Archives, DeGolyer Library, SMU, Dallas, TX.

Robert Theodore Anderson Papers. Southern Methodist University Archives, DeGolyer Library, SMU, Dallas, TX.

Rotunda Collection. Southern Methodist University Archives, DeGolyer Library, SMU, Dallas, TX.

Southern Methodist University Provost's Operational Records, 1972–1986. Southern Methodist University Archives, DeGolyer Library, SMU, Dallas, TX.

Willis Tate Correspondence, 1965–1976. SMU Archives, DeGolyer, SMU.

Willis M. Tate Papers. Southern Methodist University Archives, DeGolyer Library, SMU, Dallas, TX.

Audio Recordings and Scores

Anderson, Robert. "Rejoice, the Lord is King." Carol Stream, IL: Hope, 1983.

Barclay, Dora Poteet, organist. *Dora Poteet Barclay Memorial Organ Recital Issue*. Dallas/Fort Worth Chapters of the American Guild of Organists, 1962. LP record.

Barclay, Dora Poteet, organist. Johann Sebastian Bach's Prelude and Fugue in G major, BWV 541. Undated recording from the East Texas Pipe Organ Festival at Perkins Chapel. Courtesy of East Texas Pipe Organ Festival.

Barclay, Dora Poteet, organist. Recording at TCU on January 28, 1957. Courtesy of East Texas Pipe Organ Festival.

Tallis, James. "Sonatina for Organ." Chapel Hill: Hinshaw, 1976.

Books

Anderson, Ames, Bruce Backer, David Backus, and Charles Luedtke, eds. *Perspectives on Organ Playing and Musical Interpretation: Pedagogical, Historical, and Instrumental Studies; A Festschrift for Heinrich Fleischer at 90*. New Ulm, MN: Graphic Arts, Martin Luther College, 2003.

Barnes, Edward Shippen. *School of Organ Playing*. Opus 31. Boston: Boston Music Company, 1921.

Brown, Ray Hyer. *Robert Stewart Hyer: The Man I Knew*. Salado, TX: Anson Jones, 1957.

Buck, Dudley. *Eighteen Studies in Pedal Phrasing*. Opus 28. 2 vols. New York: G. Schirmer, 1868.

Bulletin of Southern Methodist University. Dallas: SMU, 1937.

Bulletin of Southern Methodist University: Annual Catalogue 1915–16 and Announcements 1916–1917. Dallas: SMU, 1915.

Bulletin of Southern Methodist University: Annual Catalogue 1916–17 and Announcements 1917–1918. Dallas: SMU, 1916.

Bulletin of Southern Methodist University: Annual Catalogue 1917–1918 with Announcements 1918–1919. Dallas: SMU, 1917.

Bulletin of Southern Methodist University: Annual Catalogue with Registration for 1918–1919. Dallas: SMU, 1919.

Bulletin of Southern Methodist University, 1945–1946. Dallas: SMU, 1945.

Coleman, Robert, ed. *Coleman's Male Choir*. Dallas: Robert H. Coleman, 1928.

Dickinson, Clarence. *The Technique and Art of Organ Playing*. New York: H. W. Gray, 1922.

Ellis, Francis Arnold, and Skipper Steely. *First Church of Paris*. Paris, TX: First Methodist Church, 1985.

Feldhausen, Scott D. "A History of the University of Kansas Organ Program." DMA thesis, University Of Kansas, 1999.

Fox, David H. *A Guide to North American Organbuilders: Compiled from Historical Sources and the Work of Various Researchers*. Richmond, VA: Organ Historical Society, 1991.

Grimes, Howard. *A History of the Perkins School of Theology*. Edited by Roger Loyd. Dallas: SMU Press, 1993.

Hart, Kenneth. *A Day for Dancing: The Life and Music of Lloyd Pfautsch*. Denton: University of North Texas Press, 2014.

Henning, A. H. *The Story of Southern Methodist University, 1910–1930*. Volume I. Unpublished manuscript. Undated (1930s?).

Hosford, Mary Martha Thomas. *Southern Methodist University: Founding and Early Years*. Dallas: SMU Press, 1974.

Jackson, Kenneth T. *Crabgrass Frontier: The Suburbanization of the United States*. New York: Oxford University Press, 1985.

Karg-Elert, Sigfrid. *Everyone Is Amazed: Sigfrid and Katharina Karg-Elert's Letters from North America January to March, 1932*. Translated and annotated by Harold Fabrikant. Caufield, Australia: Fabrikant, 2001.

Karg-Elert, Sigfrid. *Your Ever Grateful, Devoted Friend: Sigfrid Karg-Elert's Letters to Godfrey Sceats, 1922–1931*. Edited by Godfrey Sceats and Harold Fabrikant. Caufield, Australia: Fabrikant, 2000.

Mardirosian, Haig. *The Organ on Campus*. New York: American Guild of Organists, 2018.

Maycher, Lorenz. *Conversations with William Teague*. Kilgore, TX: East Texas Pipe Organ Festival, 2013.

Palmer, Larry. *The Harpsichord in America*. Bloomington: Indiana University Press, 1989.

Palmer, Larry. *Letters from Salzburg: A Music Student in Europe, 1958–1959*. Eau Claire, WI: Skyline, 2006.

Payne, Darwin. *One Hundred Years on the Hilltop: The Centennial History of Southern Methodist University*. Dallas: SMU Press, 2016.

Planyavsky, Peter. *Anton Heiller: Organist, Conductor, Composer*. Rochester: University of Rochester Press, 2014.

Read, William, and Jan L. Youtie. *Telecommunications Strategy for Economic Development.* Westport, CT: Praeger, 1996.

Rinck, Christian Heinrich. *Practical Organ School.* Edited by William Best. London: Novello, n.d.

Rosenstiel, Léonie. *Nadia Boulanger: A Life in Music.* New York: W. W. Norton, 1982.

The Rotunda. Dallas: SMU Press, 1916.

The Rotunda. Dallas: SMU Press, 1917.

The Rotunda. Dallas: SMU Press, 1919.

The Rotunda. Dallas: SMU Press, 1923.

The Rotunda. Dallas: SMU Press, 1924.

Selden, Jack. *Seven Score and Ten: One Hundred Fifty Years of the Presbyterian Church in Palestine, Tex.* (Palestine, TX: Clacton Press, 1999).

Skinner, Ellouise W. *Sacred Music at Union Theological Seminary, 1836–1953: An Informal History.* New York: privately printed, 1953.

SMU Bulletin, 1973–74. Dallas: SMU Press, 1973.

SMU Bulletin, 1974–75. Dallas: SMU Press, 1974.

SMU Bulletin, 1976–77. Dallas: SMU Press, 1976.

SMU Catalogue, 1969–1970. Dallas: SMU Press, 1969.

Southern Methodist University Annual Catalogue: Part V, Dallas: SMU, 1961.

Southern Methodist University: Annual Catalogue with Registration for 1925–1926. Dallas: SMU, 1926.

Southern Methodist University: Annual Catalogue with Registration for 1927–1928. Dallas: SMU, 1927.

Southern Methodist University Bulletin 1961–62. Dallas: Southern Methodist University, 1961.

Southern Methodist University Bulletin 1962–63. Dallas: Southern Methodist University, 1962.

Terry, Marshall. *From High on the Hilltop: Marshall Terry's History of SMU.* Dallas: Three Forks, 2008.

Thomas, Mary Martha. "Southern Methodist University: The First Twenty-Five Years, 1915–1940." PhD diss., University of Michigan, 1971.

Tocqueville, Alexis de. "In What Spirit the Americans Cultivate the Arts." Chap. 21 in *Democracy in America,* trans. and ed. by

Harvey C. Mansfield and Delba Winthrop. Chicago and London: University of Chicago Press, 2000.

Wesley, Charles. *Hymns for Children.* Bristol: Farley, 1763.

Whiting, George Elbridge. *First Studies for the Organ: 24 Pieces consisting of preludes, postludes, pastorals and chorals varied intended for beginners in pedal obligato playing and especially adapted for church use.* 2 vols. Boston: Arthur Schmidt, 1879.

Newspaper and Journal Articles

Brooklyn Daily Eagle
Cameron Herald
Campus
Chicago Daily Tribune
Chicago Sunday Tribune
Chicago Tribune
Cincinnati Enquirer
Clarion-Ledger (Jackson, MS)
Corpus Christi Times
Corsicana Daily Sun
Daily Campus
Daily Press (Newport News, VA)
Dallas Morning News
Dallas Times Herald
Democrat and Chronicle (Rochester, NY)
Fort Worth Star-Telegram
Fresno (CA) Bee
Galveston Daily News
Houston Chronicle
Houston Post
Jewish Monitor (Dallas)
Los Angeles Times
New York Times
Odessa (TX) American
Pantagraph (Bloomington, IL)
Pantagraph (Normal, IL)
Pittsburgh Post-Gazette
San Angelo Standard-Times
Semi-Weekly Campus

Shreveport (LA) Times
SMU Campus
SMU Times
Tampa Tribune
Waco News-Tribune
Wichita Falls Times Record News
"Activities of Guild Members." *New Music Review and Church Music Review* (May 1920): 198–200.
"AGO National Convention 1972: Dallas TX, June 18–24." *Diapason* 63, no. 9 (August 1972): 1–3.
Burnham, Thomas Scott. "News and Notes." *American Organist*, no. 5 (January 1922): 41–44.
Burnham, Thomas Scott. "Texas Section." *American Organist*, no. 2 (January 1919): 38–39.
Criswell, W. A. "In Appreciation for Mrs. J. H. Cassidy." *Baptist Reminder*, Dallas: First Baptist Church, June 17, 1945: 1.
"Cyril Bradley Rootham." *Musical Times* 79, no. 1142 (April 1938): 307–8.
Demarest, Clifford. "A Message from the Warden." *American Organist*, no. 1 (June 1918): 327.
Ferré, Susan. "Fisk Dedication at SMU: A Review." *Diapason* 85, no. 4 (March 1994): 10–11.
FWR. "Reviews and New Music." *Musical Courier*, no. 85 (July 6, 1922): 65.
Haworth, Pati. "A Legacy of Love: Four Generations of Organ Philanthropy." *American Organist*, no. 46 (July 2012): 28–30.
"James Tallis." Obituary. *Diapason* 20, no. 12 (November 1969): 18.
Palmer, Larry. "A Fall Organ Festival in Portugal." *Diapason* 92, no. 3 (February 2001): 16.
Palmer, Larry. "Giving Thanks from A to Z, Part 2: Moving to Dallas (1970)." *Diapason* 110, no. 12 (November 2019): 21.
Palmer, Larry. "Three-Score and Ten: Young." Canterbury Dictionary of *Diapason* 108, no. 6 (May 2017): 12–13.
Phelps, Lawrence. "A Short History of the Organ Revival." *Church Music*, no. 67 (1967): 13–30.
Smith, Rollin. "Hillgreen, Lane & Co." *Tracker* 16, no. 1 (Winter 2017): 30–37.

Online Resources

Association of Religion Data Archives. "Methodist Church, 1939–1968." Accessed July 4, 2022. http://www.thearda.com/ Denoms/D_1432.asp.

Echols, Paul C., and Maria V. Coldwell. "Early-Music Revival." *Grove Music Online*. Accessed March 18, 2018.

Hardman, Ray. "Hartt School Winds Down Organ Program, Sells Pipe Organ." *Connecticut Public Radio*, April 30, 2015. https://www.ctpublic.org/arts-and-culture/2015-04-30/hartt-school-winds-down-organ-program-sells-pipe-organ.

Hawn, C. Michael. "Carlton R. Young." *Canterbury Dictionary of Hymnology*. Canterbury Press. Accessed February 13, 2018. https://hymnology.hymnsam.co.uk/c/carlton-r-young.

Hawn, Michael, and Carlton Young. "Perkins School of Theology, Southern Methodist University." *Canterbury Dictionary of Hymnology*. Canterbury Press. Accessed March 5, 2020. http://www.hymnology.co.uk/p/perkins-school-of-theology,-southern-methodist-university.

Hodges, Sam. "Jane Marshall, Revered Composer, Dies." *United Methodist News Service*, May 30, 2019. https://www.umnews.org/en/news/jane-marshall-revered-composer-dies-at-94.

Long, Christopher. "Lemmon, Mark." *Handbook of Texas Online*. AccessedFebruary14,2017.http://www.tshaonline.org/handbook/online/articles/fle64.

Minut, Mirabella Anca. "Style and Compositional Techniques in Vincent Persichetti's Ten Sonatas for Harpsichord." DMA diss., Ball State University, 2009. Accessed March 20, 2020. https://cardinalscholar.bsu.edu/bitstream/handle/123456789/193434/Mminut_2009-1_BODY.pdf;sequence=1.

Organ Historical Society. *Pipe Organ Database*. https://pipeorgandatabase.org.

"Organ Index: Frankfurt am Main/Sachsenhausen, Dreikönigskirche." Accessed 4 July, 2022. https://organindex.de/index.php?title= Frankfurt_(Main)/Sachsenhausen,_Dreik%C3%B6nigskirche_ (Hauptorgel).

Palmer, Larry. "Giving Thanks from A to Z, Part 2: Moving to Dallas (1970)." *Diapason*, November 25, 2019. https://www.thediapason.com/content/harpsichord-notes-21.

Palmer, Larry. "Program Planning." *Diapason*, August 28, 2019. https://www.thediapason.com/content/harpsichord-notes-18.

Palmer, Larry. "Three-Score and Ten: Celebrating Richard Kingston." *Diapason*, May 30 2017. https://www.thediapason.com/content/harpsichord-news-28.

Powell, Paul R. "Robert H. Coleman." *Canterbury Dictionary of Hymnology*. Canterbury Press. Accessed February 1, 2017. http://www.hymnology.co.uk.proxy.libraries.smu.edu/r/robert-h-coleman.

Schaarwächter, Jürgen. "Rootham, Cyril." *Grove Music Online. Oxford Music Online*. Oxford University Press. Accessed December 27, 2016. http://www.oxfordmusiconline.com.proxy.libraries.smu.edu/subscriber/article/grove/music/23807.

Texas Almanac Online. *Texas Almanac: City Population History from 1850–2000*. Accessed December 13, 2016. http://texasalmanac.com/sites/default/files/images/CityPopHist%20web.pdf.

Texas State Historical Association Online. "Algur Hurtle Meadows." Accessed April 5, 2017. https://tshaonline.org/handbook/online/articles/fmezk.

Texas State Historical Association Online. "Dallas-Fort Worth International Airport." Accessed April 2, 2017. https://www.tshaonline.org/handbook/online/articles/epd01.

Texas State Historical Association Online. "La Réunion." Accessed December 13, 2016. https://www.tshaonline.org/handbook/online/articles/uel01.

Texas State Historical Association Online. "Seth Ward, TX." Accessed December 31, 2016. https://tshaonline.org/handbook/online/articles/kbs20.

Tyrrell, John. "Speech to the 1995 AIO Convention in San Jose, California." Accessed 16 February, 2018. http://aeolianskinner.organhistoricalsociety.net/john_tyrrell_transcript.html.

Young, Carlton. "Natalie Sleeth." *Canterbury Dictionary of Hymnology*. Canterbury Press. Accessed March 5, 2020. http://www.hymnology.co.uk/n/natalie-sleeth.

Young, Carlton. "Roger N. Deschner." *Canterbury Dictionary of Hymnology*. Canterbury Press. Accessed March 5, 2020. http://www.hymnology.co.uk/r/roger-n-deschner.

Young, Carlton. "Jane Manton Marshall." *Canterbury Dictionary of Hymnology*. Canterbury Press. Accessed March 5, 2020. http://www.hymnology.co.uk/j/jane-manton-marshall.

Index